The Virgin Mary
and
Theology of the Body

The Virgin Mary
and
Theology of the Body

Donald H. Calloway, M.I.C.
Editor

Marian Press
2005

Nihil Obstat:
Rev. Richard J. Drabik, M.I.C.
Provincial Censor
May 31, 2005
Rev. Joseph G. Roesch, M.I.C.
2nd General Councilor, Rome
May 31, 2005

Imprimi Potest:
Very Rev. Walter M. Dziordz, M.I.C., D. Min.
Provincial Superior
May 31, 2005

Library of Congress Catalog Number: 2005928691

ISBN: 1–59614–136–0

Editor: *Donald H. Calloway, M.I.C.*
Proofreader: *David Came*
Typesetting: *Marina Batiuk*
Cover Design: *William Sosa*

Special thanks: *Adey & Aurora Milo, Russel & Donna Bodin, Jane Finn,
Brandt Dufrene, Jr.*
Cover art: *Madonna and Child* (c. 1475)
Giovanni Bellini (1430-1516)
© Board of Trustees, National Gallery of Art, Washington, D.C.
Samuel H. Kress Collection
Used with permission

Published by: *Marian Press*

Marians of the Immaculate Conception
Stockbridge, Massachusetts 01262

My son, from thy youth up, receive instruction:
and even to thy grey hairs thou shalt find wisdom.

Come to her as one that plougheth and soweth:
and wait for her good fruits.

For in working about her thou shalt labour a little
and shalt quickly eat of her fruits.

How very unpleasant is wisdom to the unlearned!
And the unwise will not continue with her.

She shall be to them as a mighty stone of trial:
and they will cast her from them before it be long.

For the wisdom of doctrine is according to her name:
and she is not manifest unto many.
But with them to whom she is known, she continueth
even to the sight of God.

Give ear, my son, and take wise counsel:
and cast not away my advice.

Put thy feet into her fetters,
and thy neck into her chains.

Bow down thy shoulder, and bear her:
and be not grieved with her bands.

Come to her with all thy mind:
and keep her ways with all thy power.

Search for her, and she shall be made known to thee:
and when thou hast gotten her, let her not go.

For in the latter end thou shalt find rest in her:
and she shall be turned to thy joy.

Then shall her fetters be a strong defence for thee,
and a firm foundation, and her chain a robe of glory.

For in her is the beauty of life:
and her bands are a healthful binding.

Thou shalt put her on as a robe of glory: and thou shalt
set her upon thee as a crown of joy.

Ecclesiasticus 6: 18-32

TABLE OF CONTENTS

PREFACE

One of the greatest gifts God and Our Lady gave to the Church in the post–Vatican II era was the papacy of John Paul II. In the long list of those who were called to serve the Mystical Body of Christ through the office of Peter, John Paul II, in my opinion, stands out as one of the greatest. The brilliance of his theological mind and the steadfastness of his unwavering fidelity to the Gospel were a blessing beyond comprehension in the deluge of ideologies that plagued the post–Vatican II period. As the Vicar of Christ John Paul II fought bravely as an indefatigable spiritual warrior, opposing all who sought to mar the beauty of the Bride of Christ, the One, Holy, Catholic and Apostolic Church. Seemingly fulfilling the prophecy of St. Don Bosco, John Paul II strove to lead God's people to safe harbor through the immovable *bodily* pillars of the Eucharist and Mary.

From the very beginning of his pontificate, and even before it, John Paul II was a Theologian of the Body. What he articulated during the Wednesday Audiences from September 5, 1979 to November 28, 1984, which have come to be known as the *Theology of the Body*, he, in some fashion or another, either implicitly or explicitly, incorporated into the vast majority of his teachings as the Vicar of Christ. In the annals of history, the Theology of the Body will inevitably be seen as part of the genius and legacy of John Paul II.

Another essential aspect of the theological genius that distinguished the papacy of John Paul II was the thoroughly Marian character of his thought and spirituality. As a priest who lived out his service to Jesus Christ through total consecration to Mary, John Paul II has left a Marian legacy that will bear fruit for years to come. There can be no doubt that his understanding of the importance of Mary in the life of the Church and the individual Christian, so wonderfully articulated in his encyclical *Redemptoris Mater*, was a hallmark of his pastoral service and apostolic zeal.

As John Paul II knew so well, Mariology—the area of theology through which Christians seek to know and love their spiritual mother—is both worthy of its own treatment and, at the same time, inseparably united to every other branch of theology. Contrary to many approaches in post-Vatican II Mariology, approaches in which studies on the Virgin Mary became completely subsumed under Ecclesiology (an approach never envisioned by the documents of Vatican Council II), the primary importance of approaching Marian studies from the dogmatic foundations of Divine Revelation, within a Christocentric context, was the methodology employed by John Paul II. Thus, in the most profound way, John Paul II was able to incorporate into his Marian writings the twentieth century "re–discovery" of the Mary–Church analogy and, at the same time, offer to God's people the dogmatic foundations of a Christo–typical Mariology.

There have been many books, commentaries, and theological studies written that have analyzed John Paul II's profound contributions and insights into both the Theology of the Body and Mariology. In a certain sense, the current book is no different; it is a book that never would have been possible without the life and thought of John Paul II. Yet, unlike many of the previous works, this book is a first of its kind in that it seeks to bring together in a very explicit way these two themes so very dear to the heart of John Paul II, namely, the Theology of the Body and the Virgin Mary. The ultimate purpose of this book is to incorporate Mary, *the masterpiece of embodied creaturely existence*, into the current studies being done on the Theology of the Body. From this perspective, this book is long overdue. It is quite surprising that a book of this nature has not been written already.

At first glance, the essays contained in this book might appear to deal with certain Marian topics from a purely anthropological perspective since the Theology of the Body deals directly with anthropology. As a perspective from which to grow in knowledge and love of the Virgin Mary, anthropology is a rather recent phenomenon in Mariology. As a hermeneutical tool it has the ability, according to the intention of the user, to either help or hinder a true understanding of Mary. Yet, and this must be understood, anthropology *per se* will never be able to fully convey the whole truth about the Virgin Mary unless it is led by Divine Revelation.

Having already noted that John Paul II always presented topics on the Virgin Mary within the framework of dogma, part of the genius of John Paul II's Theology of the Body was that he based his discussion on the body within the context of God's revelation, thus employing the hermeneutic of *theological anthropology*, that is, seeking to understand man and his destiny from God's perspective. Thus, when theological anthropology is combined with a Mariology rooted in Divine Revelation the result is a glimpse into how God sees the most beautiful and wonderful human person ever created.

It is for this reason that the essays in this book have as their underlying foundation for understanding anthropological issues dealing with the Virgin Mary what the Church teaches dogmatically to be true about the Virgin Mary. This was, indeed, the method John Paul II used; it is the method every theologian should use. Approaching anthropological issues in the field of Mariology from any foundation other than Divine Revelation (Scripture and Tradition interpreted through the Magisterium) will lead one into the errors witnessed by the vast majority of modern feminist studies done on the Virgin Mary.

With all the above in mind, this book does not claim to present an exhaustive treatment of the subject matter. On the contrary, the essays presented here, offering various insights and reflections on the place of Mary in John Paul II's Theology of the Body, are intended to serve as a catalyst for others to tap into this theological goldmine.

As a book that consists in a collection of essays, I have tried to collect contributions that reflect a wide variety of theological backgrounds. Each essay is written by a theologian deeply grounded in Catholic orthodoxy, using their skills for the glory of God, the good of the Church, and the salvation of souls. In addition, the international flavor of this collection of essays reflects a truly Catholic endeavor: Calkins, Haffner (Italy); Schumacher (Switzerland); Naumann (Australia); DeMarco (Canada); Calloway, Cole, Falcão Dodd, Gregoris, Howell (United States).

The essays themselves are varied, some offer studies on Marian themes that explicitly deal with the Theology of the Body as taught by John Paul II, while others present a Marian theme within a broader notion of a theology of the body, as, for example, the studies on St. Thomas Aquinas, John Henry Newman, Joseph Kentenich, and Adrienne von Speyr. As an added blessing, St. Joseph, a person often neglected in studies done both on the Theology of the Body and Mariology, finds a place of prominence in certain essays. Indeed, the spouse of the Virgin Mary, Guardian of the Redeemer, and universal patron of the Church has an important place in the topic at hand.

Lastly, in addition to the gratitude I owe to each of the contributors, this book would not have been possible without the support of my brothers in community, especially my Provincial Superior, and the many people who have helped me financially to see it to completion. I pray we all come to know in a deeper way the importance of incorporating the Virgin Mary into all that we do.

Totus Tuus, O Maria!

Fr. Donald H. Calloway, M.I.C.
Editor

THE VIRGINAL CONCEPTION AND BIRTH OF JESUS CHRIST AS RECEIVED AND HANDED ON BY THE CATHOLIC CHURCH

Msgr. Arthur B. Calkins, S.T.D.

The becoming flesh of the Son of God is a fundamental, irreducible article of the Catholic faith succinctly expressed in the Creed with the words "by the power of the Holy Spirit he was born of the Virgin Mary" (*Et incarnatus est de Spiritu Sancto ex Maria Virgine*). The words themselves appear, at times with slight variations, in some of the earliest forms of the Christian Creed[1] and were solemnly ratified by the First Council of Constantinople in 381 A.D. to express, within the limits of human language, the mystery which the Church received, believes, and transmits about the Incarnation of the Son of God.[2] It is the Catholic Church's perennial belief in two facets of this mystery that is the specific object of this study: the conception and birth of Jesus Christ by the Virgin Mary.

I. Foundational Principles

At the very beginning I would like to state my intentions and assumptions as clearly as possible and in doing so I would like to make my own the declaration of Professor John Saward in his excellent book, *Cradle of Redeeming Love*:

---

[1] Cf. Heinrich Denzinger, S.I., *Enchiridion Symbolorum Definitionem et Declarationum de Rebus Fidei et Morum.* Edizione Bilingue (XXXVII) a cura di Peter Hünermann (Bologna: Edizioni Dehoniane, 2000) #10–64. Hereafter cited as *D–H;* Jacques Dupuis, S.J. (ed.), *The Christian Faith in the Doctrinal Documents of the Catholic Church.* Originally prepared by Josef Neuner, S.J., & Jacques Dupuis: Sixth Revised and Enlarged Edition (New York: Alba House, 1998), #2–11. Hereafter cited as *TCF.*

[2] *D–H* #150; *TCF* #12.

I make no claim to originality. Self-consciously original theology tends always to be heretical theology. Orthodox theology has, by contrast, a blessed familiarity, for it does no more than assist the faithful in understanding what they already believe; its surprises are the outcome not of human ingenuity but of divine infinitude, the sign of a Truth that is ever ancient and ever new.[3]

To be even more explicit, I remain firmly convinced that the best approach to the Scripture texts which we will be considering is *via* the living Tradition of the Catholic Church and in this regard I would like to cite this fundamental text from *Dei Verbum*, the Second Vatican Council's Dogmatic Constitution on Divine Revelation:

The apostolic preaching, which is expressed in a special way in the inspired books, was to be preserved in a continuous line of succession until the end of time. Hence the apostles, in handing on what they themselves had received, warn the faithful to maintain the traditions which they had learned either by word of mouth or by letter (cf. 2 Th. 2:15); and they warn them to fight hard for the faith that had been handed on to them once and for all (cf. Jude 3). What was handed on by the apostles comprises everything that serves to make the People of God live their lives in holiness and increase their faith. In this way the Church, in her doctrine, life and worship, perpetuates and transmits to every generation all that she herself is, all that she believes.

The Tradition that comes from the apostles makes progress in the Church, with the help of the Holy Spirit. There is a growth in insight into the realities and words that are being passed on. This comes about in various ways. It comes through the contemplation and study of believers who ponder these things in their hearts (cf. Lk. 2:19 and 51). It comes from the intimate sense of spiritual realities which they experience. And it comes from the preaching of those who have received, along with their right of succession in the episcopate, the sure charism of truth. Thus as the centuries go by, the Church is always advancing towards the plenitude of divine truth, until eventually the words of God are fulfilled in her.[4]

In these paragraphs we have two very important assertions: (1) what we have received from the apostolic preaching must be handed on in its integrity, and (2) by the assistance of the Holy Spi-

---

[3] John Saward, *Cradle of Redeeming Love: The Theology of the Christmas Mystery.* (San Francisco: Ignatius Press, 2002), 14.

[4] *Dei Verbum* #8.

rit "there is a growth in insight into the realities and words that are being passed on." On this matter the *Catechism of the Catholic Church* offers a helpful clarification:

> Yet even if Revelation is already complete, it has not been made completely explicit; it remains for Christian faith gradually to grasp its full significance over the course of the centuries.[5]

In the course of this study we will see that there have been many intuitions regarding the virginal conception and birth of Christ in the course of the centuries, but not all of them have been genuine developments of the faith once delivered to the apostles. Some of these intuitions have proven to be aberrations, heresies which have distorted and misrepresented the faith. For this reason the Church has constant need of authoritative guidance in order to distinguish genuine developments from false ones. Hence

> the task of giving an authentic interpretation of the Word of God, whether in its written form or in the form of Tradition, has been entrusted to the living teaching office [Magisterium] of the Church alone. Its authority in this matter is exercised in the name of Jesus Christ. Yet this Magisterium is not superior to the Word of God, but is its servant. It teaches only what has been handed on to it. At the divine command and with the help of the Holy Spirit, it listens to this [Word of God] devotedly, guards it with dedication and expounds it faithfully. All that it proposes for belief as being divinely revealed is drawn from this single deposit of faith.

> It is clear, therefore, that, in the supremely wise arrangement of God, sacred Tradition, sacred Scripture and the Magisterium of the Church are so connected and associated that one of them cannot stand without the others. Working together, each in its own way under the action of the one Holy Spirit, they all contribute effectively to the salvation of souls.[6]

The magisterial teaching of the Catholic Church as exercised by Popes and Councils, then, will provide the fundamental framework for this study and in this regard we are fortunate to have recent authoritative statements of the papal magisterium on the virginal

---

[5] *Catechism of the Catholic Church* #66.
[6] *Dei Verbum* #10.

conception and birth of Christ. Among these I assign a very important place to the discourse given by Pope John Paul II at Capua (near Naples) on 24 May 1992 to commemorate the 16th centenary of the Plenary Council of Capua, a discourse which recapitulates the tradition and offers us at the same time valuable orientations for our investigation. Among the literally thousands of other papal documents, addresses and homilies devoted primarily or partially to Our Lady by John Paul II, I would also signal for special attention the seventy Marian catecheses which he delivered at general audiences from 6 September 1995 to 12 November 1997. These constitute a veritable compendium of Mariology, touching upon all of the major questions and providing a remarkable summary of his own teaching and a further consolidation of that of his predecessors and that of the Second Vatican Council. These catecheses may be justly regarded as an important exercise of the ordinary magisterium of the Roman Pontiff and thus should be received by the faithful "with religious submission of mind and will" (cf. Dogmatic Constitution on the Church *Lumen Gentium* #25).[7]

I further wish to emphasize that in treating of the Incarnation, we are dealing with a mystery of faith, a truth which admits of rational explanation, but which is so profound that we can never fully exhaust it. John Saward puts it beautifully:

> The human birth of the Son of God is a mystery in the strict theological sense: a divinely revealed reality that little ones can understand but not even learned ones can comprehend. Theological mysteries are truth and therefore light for the mind, but the truth is so vast, the light of such intensity, that the mind is dazzled and amazed. When a man meets a mystery of the faith, he finds not a deficiency but an excess of intelligibility: there is just too much to understand. Reverence for supernaturally revealed mysteries is therefore not reason's abdication, but reason's recognition, through faith, of a grandeur transcending its powers.[8]

---

[7] These seventy discourses are available in English as *Theotókos—Woman, Mother, Disciple: A Catechesis on Mary, Mother of God* with a Foreword by Eamon R. Carroll, O.Carm, S.T.D. (Boston: Pauline Books and Media, 2000). The translation varies in only minor details from the texts previously published in *L'Osservatore Romano*.

[8] Saward, *Cradle of Redeeming Love*, 47–48.

Happily, the interested reader who would like to pursue the theological concept of mystery in greater depth may refer to the first chapter of *Cradle of Redeeming Love* where the author develops it in a masterly fashion and with particular reference to the mystery of the Incarnation.[9] It will be noted that the above quote is in full harmony with what Pope John Paul II said in his discourse at Capua on 24 May 1992:

> The theologian must approach the mystery of Mary's fruitful virginity *with a deep sense of veneration for God's free, holy and sovereign action.* Reading through the writings of the holy Fathers and the liturgical texts we notice that few of the saving mysteries have caused so much amazement, admiration or praise as the incarnation of God's Son in Mary's virginal womb ...

> The theologian, however, who approaches the mystery of Mary's virginity with a heart full of faith and adoring respect, does not thereby forego the duty of studying the data of Revelation and showing their harmony and interrelationship; rather, following the Spirit, ... he puts himself in the great and fruitful theological tradition of *fides quærens intellectum.*

> When theological reflection becomes a moment of doxology and latria, the mystery of Mary's virginity is disclosed, allowing one to catch a glimpse of other aspects and other depths.[10]

One who is not willing to recognize that in attempting to scrutinize the mystery of the Incarnation he is treading on sacred ground (cf. Ex. 3:5) and, therefore, must approach with reverence and awe is doomed to remain in the darkness of agnosticism or worse. In fact, the concept of sacred ground brings us remarkably close to an allied notion very dear to the Fathers of the Church, viz. that Mary is *terra virgo*, the virgin earth from which emerged the Son of God.[11] Her fruitful virginity cannot be separated from the blessed fruit of which it is the sign.

---

[9] Cf. Saward, *Cradle of Redeeming Love,* 47–120.

[10] *Acta Apostolicae Sedis* 85 (1993), 664 ; *ORE* 1244:13 = (*L'Osservatore Romano,* weekly edition in English. First number = cumulative edition number; second number = page).

[11] Cf. Emmanuele Testa, O.F.M., *Maria Terra Vergine,* Vol. I: *I rapporti della Madre di Dio con la SS. Trinità (Sec. I–IX)* (Jerusalem: Franciscan Printing Press, 1984), 416–432. On St. Irenaeus' treatment of Mary as the virgin earth for the new Adam, cf. François–Marie Léthel, O.C.D., *Connaître l'amour du Christ qui surpasse toute connaissance: La Théologie des Saints* (Venasque: Éditions du Carmel, 1989), 77–88.

The Catholic tradition always witnesses to an indissoluble link between Mary's virginity and the Incarnate Word. This is clearly attested to by John Paul II in his discourse at Capua:

> For a fruitful theological reflection on Mary's virginity it is first of all essential to have *a correct point of departure*. Actually, in its interwoven aspects the question of Mary's virginity cannot be adequately treated by beginning with her person alone, her people's culture or the social conditions of her time. The Fathers of the Church had already clearly seen that Mary's virginity was a "Christological theme" before being a "Mariological question". They observed that *the virginity of the Mother is a requirement flowing from the divine nature of the Son*; it is the concrete condition in which, according to a free and wise divine plan, the incarnation of the eternal Son took place ... As a consequence, for Christian tradition Mary's virginal womb, made fruitful by the divine *Pneuma* without human intervention (cf. Lk. 1:34–35), became, like the wood of the cross (cf. Mk. 15:39) or the wrappings in the tomb (cf. Jn. 20:5–8), a reason and sign for recognizing in Jesus of Nazareth the Son of God.[12]

The fact that in studying the virginal conception and birth of Jesus Christ we are dealing first of all with a Christological theme is cogently brought home by John Henry Newman in one of his first Catholic sermons entitled "The Glories of Mary for the Sake of Her Son":

> They [the prerogatives with which the Church invests the Blessed Mother of God] are startling and difficult to those whose imagination is not accustomed to them, and whose reason has not reflected on them; but the more carefully and religiously they are dwelt on, the more, I am sure, will they be found essential to the Catholic faith, and integral to the worship of Christ. This simply is the point which I shall insist on—disputable indeed by aliens from the Church, but most clear to her children—that the glories of Mary are for the sake of Jesus; and that we praise and bless her as the first of creatures, that we may duly confess Him as our sole Creator.[13]

---

[12] *AAS* 85 (1993) 663; *ORE* 1244:13.

[13] Philip Boyce, O.C.D. (ed.), *Mary: The Virgin Mary in the Life and Writings of John Henry Newman* (Leominster, Herefordshire: Gracewing Publishing; Grand Rapids, MI: William B. Eerdmans Publishing Company, 2001), 131–132.

The link is indeed indissoluble and further on in the same sermon Newman did not hesitate to draw a very specific conclusion from it which is far more readily verifiable today than when he uttered it: "Catholics who have honoured the Mother, still worship the Son, while Protestants, who now have ceased to confess the Son, began then by scoffing at the Mother."[14]

II. The Mystery of the Virginal Conception

In his Marian catechesis of 10 July 1996, in which he dealt with the virginal conception as a biological fact, Pope John Paul II made this very straightforward declaration:

> The Church has constantly held that Mary's virginity is a truth of faith, as the Church has received and reflected on the witness of the Gospels of Luke, of Matthew and probably also of John. In the episode of the annunciation, the evangelist Luke calls Mary a "virgin," referring both to her intention to persevere in virginity, as well as to the divine plan which reconciled this intention with her miraculous motherhood. The affirmation of the virginal conception, due to the action of the Holy Spirit, excludes every hypothesis of natural parthenogenesis and rejects the attempts to explain Luke's account as the development of a Jewish theme or as the derivation of a pagan mythological legend.
>
> The structure of the Lucan text resists any reductive interpretation (cf. Lk. 1:26–38; 2:19, 51). Its coherence does not validly support any mutilation of the terms or expressions which affirm the virginal conception brought about by the Holy Spirit.[15]

The Pope's language is unmistakably clear. He discounts any attempt to explain the virginal conception of Jesus in terms of (1) parthenogenesis,[16] (2) midrash (development of a Jewish

---

[14] *Ibid.*, 37. Cf. the strikingly similar comment made by Matthias Joseph Scheeben quoted in Saward, *Cradle of Redeeming Love*, 175.

[15] *Insegnamenti di Giovanni Paolo II*, XIX/2 (1996), 75; *ORE* 1450:11; John Paul II, *Theotókos*, 112.

[16] Cf. Salvatore M. Perrella, O.S.M., *Maria Vergine e Madre. La verginità feconda di Maria tra fede, storia e teologia.* (Cinisello Balsamo : Edizioni San Paolo, 2003), 111–116. As Father Perrella points out on p. 12, even though no cases of parthenogenesis can be adduced within the human species, if such were to be the case the sex·of the one generated would have to be female. Dr. Catherine Brown Tkacz comes to the same conclusion in her article, "Reproductive Science and the Incarnation," *Fellowship of Catholic Scholars Quarterly* 25 (Fall 2002), 17–19.

theme)[17] or (3) derivation of a pagan mythological legend.[18] Further on in the same discourse he explicitly rejects a further and lethal hypothesis which undermines belief in the virginal conception of Jesus as the Church has always understood it:

> the opinion—that the account of the virginal conception would instead be a theologoumenon, that is, a way of expressing a theological doctrine, that of Jesus' divine sonship, or would be a mythological portrayal of him.[19]

A. Questionable Assumptions

Referring to the Gospel references to the miraculous conception of Jesus as a theologoumenon is the result of the program of radical demythologizing of the Gospels championed by Lutheran Scripture scholars Martin Dibelius (1883–1947), Rudolf Bultmann (1884–1976), and their followers. According to them, the belief that Jesus had no human father was a theological fabrication of the early Christian community in order to heighten Jesus' importance, in other words to "mythologize" him. Having established such assumptions, these scholars set about to de–mythologize the New Testament. Dibelius specifically maintained that the virginal conception is an entirely Christian legend resulting from a theologoumenon of Judeo–Hellenistic provenance. Bultmann went on to insist that it was a late excrescence which is in contradiction to the internal evidence of the Gospels.[20]

While I have no desire to judge the intentions of these men, neither, following the lead of John Paul II, do I have any intention of giving them serious attention: a theory which flies in the face of the New Testament evidence and the unbroken testimony of the great tradition may be readily dismissed. In fact, much subsequent biblical scholarship since Dibelius and Bultmann first advanced their positions demonstrates precisely why the Pope deemed it necessary in that same catechesis to affirm that:

---

[17] Cf. Raymond E. Brown, S.S., *The Birth of the Messiah: A Commentary on the Infancy Narratives in the Gospels of Matthew and Luke.* New Updated Edition (New York: Doubleday, 1993), 557–563.

[18] Cf. Perrella, *Maria Vergine e Madre*, 108–110.

[19] *Inseg* XIX/2 (1996), 77; *ORE* 1450:11; John Paul II, *Theotókos*, 114.

[20] Cf. Stefano De Fiores' preface to Perrella, *Maria Vergine e Madre*, 6–9.

The uniform Gospel witness testifies how faith in the virginal conception of Jesus was firmly rooted in various milieus of the early Church. This deprives of any foundation several recent interpretations which understand the virginal conception not in a physical or biological sense, but only as symbolic or metaphorical.[21]

Unfortunately, once the de-mythologizing currents were in the air, it was only a matter of time before they were passed off as compatible with Catholic belief in the so-called *Dutch Catechism* of 1966 and in the writings of Hans Küng, Piet Schoonenberg, Edward Schillebeeckx and numerous other Catholic theologians.[22]

Even more complex was the approach to the virginal conception of Jesus taken by the late noted American Sulpician exegete, Raymond E. Brown, S.S. (+1998). In a major essay on this topic he concluded thus:

> My judgment, in conclusion, is that the totality of the *scientifically controllable* evidence leaves an unresolved problem—a conclusion that should not disappoint since I used the word "problem" in my title—and that is why I want to induce an honest, ecumenical discussion of it. Part of the difficulty is that past discussions have often been conducted by people who were interpreting ambiguous evidence to favor positions already taken.[23]

He quoted that conclusion again in the appendix to his second edition of *The Birth of the Messiah*[24] in the course of a further treatment of the "Historicity of the Virginal Conception"[25]. I must humbly confess that that treatment baffles me as much as this statement in his earlier essay:

> Please understand: I am not saying that there is no longer impressive evidence for the virginal conception—personally I think that it is far more impressive than many who deny the virginal conception will admit. Nor am I saying that the Catholic position is dependent

---

[21] *Inseg* XIX/2 (1996), 76–77; *ORE* 1450:11; John Paul II, *Theotókos*, 114.

[22] Cf. De Fiores in Perrella, *Maria Vergine e Madre*, 9–12; Brunero Gherardini, *La Madre . Maria in una sintesi storico-teologica.* (Frigento (AV): Casa Mariana Editrice, 1989), 93–95.

[23] Raymond E. Brown, S.S., *The Virginal Conception and Bodily Resurrection of Jesus* (New York: Paulist Press, 1973), 66–67.

[24] Brown, *The Birth of the Messiah*, 698.

[25] *Ibid*, 698–708.

on the impressiveness of the scientifically controllable evidence, for I have just mentioned the Catholic belief that the Holy Spirit can give to the Church a deeper perception than would be warranted by the evidence alone. I am simply asking whether for Catholics a modern evaluation of the evidence is irrelevant because the answer is already decided through past Church teaching. The very fact that theologians are discussing the limits of infallibility and how well the criteria for judging infallibility have been applied suggests that further investigation is not necessarily foreclosed.[26]

In effect, Father Brown's work in this area seems to have been based on a number of working principles which I find it necessary to question: (1) the assumption that what he considered the "scientifically controllable" study of the Scriptures, largely following the canons of the Bultmannian school, may be separate from and independent of the content of Catholic faith; (2) the employment of a reductionistic and minimizing approach to Catholic dogma similar to that of Francis A. Sullivan, S.J. who, while not directly denying Catholic dogma, was prepared to challenge its weight on the basis of his evaluation of how it was defined;[27] and following from these (3) an ecumenical methodology which might be described as consensus based on the "lowest common denominator".

While I appreciate the vast apparatus of Father Brown's critical scholarship and the enormous accumulation of data which his publications have made available to the scholarly world, of which his monumental volume *The Birth of the Messiah* is an outstanding example, I cannot pass over his fundamental assumptions in silence precisely because of his towering influence in the world of biblical scholarship and his membership on the Pontifical Biblical Commission.[28] His name, more than any other, is identified with the acclaimed collaborative assessment by Protestant and Roman Catholic scholars entitled *Mary in the New Testament*. While he was not its sole author, he was a principal participant, coordinator, discussion leader and editor and, since the conclusions were always arrived at by the consensus of the participants, we may assume that he was in accord with the working hypotheses adopted. Here are some of them:

---

[26] Brown, *The Virginal Conception,* 37–38.
[27] On Father Sullivan's work, cf. Perrella, *Maria Vergine e Madre*, 52–55, 172, 217.
[28] Cf. John F. McCarthy, "The Pontifical Biblical Commission—Yesterday and

While we do not exclude the possibility and even the likelihood that some items of historical information about Jesus' birth have come to Luke, we are not working with the hypothesis that he is giving us substantially the memoirs of Mary. Rather, the possibility that he constructed his narrative in the light of OT themes and stories will be stressed. ...

Our contention, then, is that the Lucan annunciation message is a reflection of the christological language and formulas of the post–resurrectional church. To put it in another way, the angel's words to Mary dramatize vividly what the church has said about Jesus after the resurrection and about Jesus during His ministry after the baptism. Now this christology has been carried back to Jesus at the very moment of conception in His mother's womb. ...

All of this means that [Lk.] 1:32.33, 35 are scarcely the explicit words of a divine revelation to Mary prior to Jesus' birth; and hence one ought not to assume that Mary had explicit knowledge of Jesus as "the Son of God" during His lifetime. ... We do not deny the possibility of a revelation to Mary at the conception of her Son, but in the Lucan annunciation we are hearing a revelation phrased in post-resurrectional language. ...

Finally, in interpreting the virginal conception of Jesus as the begetting of God's Son, we recognize that Luke is not talking about the incarnation of a pre-existent divine being.[29]

Where do such assumptions leave one? The answer, I'm afraid, is "nowhere". This or that datum of the tradition may or may not be true. About what is true we can have no real certitude. This is the *reductio ad absurdum* which so much post-Bultmannian exegesis leaves us with. This de-stabilizing approach to the Word of God provides no satisfactory basis for either the study of Scripture or the practice of genuine ecumenism.[30] With regard to this state of affairs Professor Saward offers some very astute remarks:

Today," *Homiletic & Pastoral Review* (January, 2003): 8–13.

[29] Raymond E. Brown, Karl P. Donfried, Joseph A. Fitzmyer, John Reumann (eds.), *Mary in the New Testament.* (Philadelphia: Fortress Press; New York: Paulist Press, 1978), 111, 118–119, 122.

[30] For a critique of much of what has passed for ecumenism among Catholics in recent years cf. Brunero Gherardini, "Sulla Lettera Enciclica *Ut Unum Sint* di Papa Giovanni Paolo II," *Divinitas* 40 (1997): 3–12; *Una sola Fede—una sola Chiesa. La Chiesa Cattolica dinanzi all'ecumenismo* (Castelpetroso (IS): Casa Editrice Mariana, 2000).

Sadly, Liberal Protestant and Modernist Biblical scholars have seemed, for a large part of the last two centuries, to be determined to separate the evangelists as far as possible, in space and time as well as in direct contact, from the Jesus whose life and teaching they set forth. First, the critics 'prescind' from the dogmatic faith and Tradition of the Church, in order, so they allege, to attain a scientific reading of the texts. Secondly, they give prominence to what they take to be contradictions of fact or opinion between the sacred authors, or between the Bible and natural science. Thirdly, they destroy the historical identity of the evangelists. The Gospels—so they claim—were written, not by recognized disciples of Truth but by unknown and unknowable devisers of myth. The evangelists composed their narratives not in order to tell the honest truth about the Lord but to promote the religious interests (or 'theologies', as the critics like to say) of particular communities in the early Church. The Higher Critics are embarrassed by every physical marvel in the life of Jesus—His miracles, His bodily Resurrection, and the virginity of His Blessed Mother; like the Gnostics of old, they seem repelled by the Word's deep descent into the world of matter.[31]

These "Higher Critics" as John Saward justly concludes, "cannot teach us how to read the Holy Gospels."[32] They have not placed themselves, as the Pope exhorted theologians in Capua, "in the great and fruitful theological tradition of *fides quærens intellectum*" precisely because they do not approach the mystery "with a heart full of faith and adoring respect."[33] Happily, however, there are exegetes who have acquired the necessary technical skills and who also stand "in the great and fruitful theological tradition." From them we can learn as we shall see.

B. The Biblical Witness

Let us turn once again to the Pope's discourse of 24 May 1992 in Capua.

In our day the Church has deemed it necessary to recall the reality of Christ's virginal conception, pointing out that the texts of Lk.

---

[31] Saward, *Cradle of Redeeming Love*, 110.
[32] *Ibid*, 113.
[33] *AAS* 85 (1993), 664; *ORE* 1244:13. For further reflection on the mystery of the virginal conception in terms of objections and reasons of fittingness, cf. Saward, *Cradle of Redeeming Love*, 184–206.

1:26–38 and Mt. 1:18–25 cannot be reduced to simple etiological accounts meant to make it easier for the faithful to believe in Christ's divinity. More than the literary genre used by Matthew and Luke, they are instead the expression of a biblical tradition of apostolic origin.

To affirm the reality of Christ's virginal conception does not mean that an apodictic proof of the rational sort can be provided for it. In fact, the virginal conception of Christ is a truth revealed by God, which the human person accepts through the obedience of faith (cf. Rom. 16:26). Only the person who is willing to believe that God acts within the reality of this world and that with Him "nothing is impossible" (Lk. 1:37) can, with devout gratitude, accept the truths of the *kenosis* of God's eternal Son, of His virginal conception–birth, of the universal salvific value of His death on the cross and of the true resurrection in His own body of Him who was hung and died on the wood of the cross.[34]

In this illuminating statement the Pope makes several important points among which are the following: (1) the fundamental biblical texts regarding the virginal conception are Lk. 1:26–38 and Mt. 1:18–25; (2) they constitute "a biblical tradition of apostolic origin" ; (3) these texts do not provide "an apodictic proof of the rational sort", rather they require faith in the God who reveals. This third point is very appropriately made in the light of the presuppositions of the kind of biblical studies represented by the Catholic–Protestant collaborative volume *Mary in the New Testament*. This foundational assertion was already made with great clarity in the Profession of Faith of the Eleventh Council of Toledo of 675 which declares that the virginal conception is neither proved by reason nor demonstrated from precedent. Were it proved by reason, it would not be miraculous; were it demonstrated from precedent, it would not be unique.[35]

Now let us consider some of the principal biblical evidence for the virginal conception of Jesus insofar as space permits, recognizing that in particular as we explore the infancy narratives in Matthew and Luke we are dealing with Scripture texts which are extremely dense, whose fundamental sense has been understood from the earliest days of the Church's life, but which continue to

---

[34] *AAS* 85 (1993), 666–667; *ORE* 1244:14.
[35] *D–H* #533 [translation in Saward, *Cradle of Redeeming Love*, 187].

reveal their hidden treasures to those who approach with reverence and faith (cf. Mt. 13:52). I believe that what Canon René Laurentin says in the following statement about the infancy narrative of Luke applies to all of the Old and New Testament Scriptures which have reference to the virginal conception and birth of Christ:

> Luke 1–2 is a surprisingly rich Gospel. The more one delves into it, the more one is overwhelmed and surprised at the liberty with which criticism has attempted to pull it to pieces. Fortunately, unlike a monument or an organism, a text survives the violence to which it is subjected. It survives the autopsies and ends up intact after dissection. Interpretations come and go but the Gospel remains, bearer of a witness which goes beyond it.[36]

I begin with a recent insight by Father Ignace de la Potterie, S.J. into Luke 1:31, arguably the first explicit reference to the virginal conception in the Lucan infancy narrative. The angel says to Mary "you will conceive in your womb," but the words "in your womb" are omitted in many modern translations as being redundant.[37] Where else does a woman conceive, except in her womb, many would ask, but Father de la Potterie argues that Saint Luke was very particular about his vocabulary:

> "To conceive in your womb" is a paradoxical and new formula which is only found here in the entire Bible. For what reason did Luke introduce this strange, totally new and seemingly redundant expression? The reason is evident enough. To speak of the ordinary conception of a woman the Old Testament habitually employed two formulas: "to receive in her womb", e.g. Gen. 25:22, Is. 8:3 etc. in reference to the man from whom the woman receives the seed into her womb (the name of the man is sometimes indicated); or else "to have in her womb", after the woman's sexual relationship with the man, but here also, after having "received" the seed from the man; in this way it was indicated that a woman was now *pregnant*, e.g. Gen. 38:25, Am. 1:3 etc.[38]

---

[36] René Laurentin, *The Truth of Christmas Beyond the Myths: The Gospels of the Infancy of Christ* trans. by Michael J. Wrenn and associates. (Petersham, MA: St. Bede's Publications, 1986), 2.

[37] Ignace de la Potterie, S.J., "'Et voici que tu concevras en ton sein' (Lc 1, 31): l'ange annonce à Marie sa conception virginale," *Marianum* 61 (1999), 100.

[38] de la Potterie, "Et voici," 101–102 (my trans.).

He points out that the expression "conceive in your womb" has an indirect reference to the Greek text of Isaiah 7:14 and Matthew 1:23[39] and he goes on to draw out the implications:

> For Mary, by contrast [with Elizabeth] Luke employs twice the verb "to conceive", but here *with* the addition of "in your womb"; the first text is precisely the one under consideration: "*you will conceive in your womb*" (1:31); further on, we read again: "... He was called Jesus, the name given by the angel before He was conceived *in the womb* [of Mary]" (2:21). This formula "in your womb", seemingly useless and pleonastic, is unique in the entire Bible; it is the sign of a particular meaning, a sign which becomes still more clear when we note that it is found uniquely in these two adjacent texts (1:31; 2:21) both of which concern Mary: they announce precisely her virginal conception.

> From the perspective of salvation history and theology, these two "linguistic facts" (retaining the verb "to conceive", but *with* the specification "in your womb") must have a double signification in the case of Mary: on the one hand, the use of the traditional verb "to conceive" commonly used for many other women, indicated for Mary also, the physical realism of a real *bodily* conception, not a mythical one as some would maintain (we are not dealing here with a theologoumenon!). On the other hand, the expression "in your womb", added *for her alone*, reveals that this physical conception had to be entirely *within* ("in your womb"), without the previous penetration of any "masculine semen" coming from without. Such a totally interior conception would have to be accomplished by a real power, certainly, but a non-physical one; it obviously required a fecundating action, but a *spiritual* one. Moreover, our text thus prepared and anticipated verse 1:35 where it would be explained that the Holy Spirit would descend on Mary, to activate *in her*, that is to say "in the womb" of Mary, a real, but purely *interior* conception. Such a conception, without sexual contact, due to the "power of the Most High", must necessarily be a virginal conception.[40]

Of course, those who want to scrutinize Fr. de la Potterie's argument in detail should read the entire article,[41] but I trust that I have supplied the gist of it here and would now like to present his final word:

---

[39] de la Potterie, "Et voici," 101. Interestingly, Raymond Brown duly notes this terminology in *Birth of the Messiah*, 145 (footnote 34) and 300 (footnote 11), but draws no conclusion.

[40] de la Potterie, "Et voici," 102 (my trans.).

[41] *Marianum* 61 (1999): 99–111.

The conclusion of all of this is that the evangelist, in verse 1:31, is rigorously inspired by the formulas of the biblical tradition, but by way of some truly *radical* modifications he succeeds already here in stating the Christian newness: the *virginal conception* of Mary and the imposition on her Son of the *name of Jesus* will henceforth allow the world to understand the mystery of the Incarnation of the Son of God. And this woman who subsequently brings forth her son *Jesus* virginally into the world thus becomes the Mother of God.[42]

Now let us consider Luke 1:34, a text most crucial to our argument, in which Mary asks her question: "How shall this be since I do not know man?" Here is how the Holy Father outlined the matter in his catechesis of 24 July 1996:

Such a query seems surprising, to say the least, if we call to mind the biblical accounts that relate the announcement of an extraordinary birth to a childless woman. Those cases concerned married women who were naturally sterile, to whom God gave the gift of a child through their normal conjugal life (1 Sm. 1:19–20), in response to their anguished prayers (cf. Gen. 15:2; 30:22–23; 1 Sm. 1:10; Lk. 1:13).

Mary received the angel's message in a different situation. She was not a married woman with problems of sterility; by a voluntary choice she intended to remain a virgin. Therefore, her intention of virginity, the fruit of her love for the Lord, appeared to be an obstacle to the motherhood announced to her.

At first sight, Mary's words would seem merely to express only her present state of virginity ... Nevertheless, the context in which the question was asked: "How can this be?" and the affirmation that follows: "since I do not know man," emphasize both Mary's present virginity and her intention to remain a virgin. The expression she used, with the verb in the present tense, reveals the permanence and continuity of her state. ...

To some, Mary's words and intentions appear improbable since in the Jewish world virginity was considered neither a value nor an ideal to be pursued. The same Old Testament writings confirm this in several well-known episodes and expressions.[43]

---

[42] de la Potterie, "Et voici," 110 (my trans.).
[43] *Inseg* XIX/2 (1996), 103, 104; *ORE* 1452:7; John Paul II, *Theotókos*, 116, 117.

This entire catechesis is strikingly incisive in its transmission of the Church's tradition as well as in its grasp of the state of much modern scholarship on this question.[44] Interestingly, the Holy Father's brief analysis of Our Lady's declaration follows what I believe is still the classic and most complete analysis of the matter, that written by Father Geoffrey Graystone, S.M.[45]

The Pope continues with an explanation of Mary's resolve which indicates how the understanding of "full of grace" [*kecharitoméne*][46] has continued to develop under the guidance of the Holy Spirit in the Catholic Church:

> However, the extraordinary case of the Virgin of Nazareth must not lead us into the error of tying her inner dispositions completely to the mentality of her surroundings, thereby eliminating the uniqueness of the mystery that came to pass in her. In particular, we must not forget that, from the very beginning of her life, Mary received a wondrous grace, recognized by the angel at the moment of the annunciation. "Full of grace" (Lk. 1:28), Mary was enriched with a perfection of holiness that, according to the Church's interpretation, goes back to the very first moment of her existence. The unique privilege of the immaculate conception influences the whole development of the young woman of Nazareth's spiritual life.

> Thus, it should be maintained that Mary was guided to the ideal of virginity by an exceptional inspiration of [the] Holy Spirit.[47]

Appropriately, in speaking of Mary's intention of virginity the Pope points to "the uniqueness of the mystery that came to pass" in Mary and this as a direct consequence of her immaculate conception.

---

[44] Cf. Brown, *Birth of the Messiah*, 298–309; Brown et al, *Mary in the New Testament*, 114–126.

[45] *Virgin of All Virgins: The Interpretation of Luke 1:34* (Rome: Doctoral Dissertation presented to the Pontifical Biblical Commission, 1968).

[46] Cf. Ignace de la Potterie, S.J., *Mary in the Mystery of the Covenant.* Trans. Bertrand Buby, S.M. (New York : Alba House, 1992), 17–20; In addition, see the following articles by Ignace de la Potterie, S.J., "Kecharitoméne en Lc 1,28: Étude philologique," *Biblica* 68 (1987): 357–382; "Kecharitoméne en Lc 1,28: Étude exégétique et théologique," *Biblica* 68 (1987): 480–508; Ernesto della Corte, "Kecharitoméne (Lc 1, 28) Crux interpretum," *Marianum* 52 (1990): 101–148.

[47] *Inseg* XIX/2 (1996), 105; *ORE* 1452:7; John Paul II, *Theotókos*, 118.

Obviously it took time, under the guidance of the Holy Spirit, for the Church as listener to the Word of God and Teacher (*Ecclesia discens et docens*) to penetrate ever more deeply into the understanding of Mary's determination to remain a virgin and of her virginal marriage to Joseph. Once again the Holy Father summarizes the development of this tradition beautifully in his catechesis of 21 August 1996:

> In presenting Mary as a "virgin", the Gospel of Luke adds that she was "betrothed to a man whose name was Joseph, of the house of David" (Lk. 1:27). These two pieces of information at first sight seem contradictory. The Greek word used in this passage does not indicate the situation of a woman who has contracted marriage and therefore lives in the marital state, but that of betrothal. Unlike what occurs in modern cultures, however, the ancient Jewish custom of betrothal provided for a contract and normally had definitive value. It actually introduced the betrothed to the marital state, even if the marriage was brought to full completion only when the young man took the girl to his home.
>
> At the time of the Annunciation, Mary thus had the status of one betrothed. We can wonder why she would accept betrothal, since she had the intention of remaining a virgin forever. Luke is aware of this difficulty, but merely notes the situation without offering any explanation. The fact that the Evangelist, while stressing Mary's intention of virginity, also presents her as Joseph's spouse, is a sign of the historical reliability of the two pieces of information.
>
> It may be presumed that at the time of their betrothal there was an understanding between Joseph and Mary about the plan to live as a virgin. Moreover, the Holy Spirit, who had inspired Mary to choose virginity in view of the mystery of the Incarnation and who wanted the latter to come about in a family setting suited to the Child's growth, was quite able to instill in Joseph the ideal of virginity as well.[48]

The seeming contradiction between Mary's disposition to remain a virgin and her betrothal to Joseph may cause endless difficulties for the "Higher Critics" and lead to bizarre hypotheses,[49] but it can also lead faithful Christians to an ever more profound

---

[48] *Inseg* XIX/2 (1996), 214–215; *ORE* 1455:7; John Paul II, *Theotókos*, 127–128.

[49] Cf. Brown, *Birth of the Messiah*, 303–309; Brown et al, *Mary in the New*

appreciation of the multi-faceted mystery of the Incarnation, as the Pope indicated. Indeed, as he subsequently affirmed:

> This type of marriage to which the Holy Spirit led Mary and Joseph can only be understood in the context of the saving plan and of a lofty spirituality. The concrete realization of the mystery of the Incarnation called for a virgin birth which would highlight the divine sonship and, at the same time, for a family that could provide for the normal development of the child's personality.[50]

III. The Mystery of the Virginal Birth

The words of the Holy Father cited above lead us appropriately to the mystery of the virgin birth which is described in this way in the *Catechism of the Catholic Church*:

> The deepening of faith in the virginal motherhood led the Church to confess Mary's real and perpetual virginity even in the act of giving birth to the Son of God made man. In fact, Christ's birth 'did not diminish His mother's virginal integrity but sanctified it.'[51]

Tertullian put it succinctly: "It was necessary for the author of a new birth to be born in a new way."[52] Literally hundreds of similar illuminating statements such as this can be found throughout the entire tradition.[53] Effectively this new birth "without corruption" has always been understood to refer to the "birth of the Child without bodily lesion of the Mother, and absence of all pain and afterbirth."[54] In summarizing the Patristic, scholastic, and more recent tradition on this matter John Saward states:

Testament, 114–115. Manuel Miguens, O.F.M. considers the biblical evidence in responding to Raymond Brown's provocative essay on "The Virginal Conception" in his *The Virgin Birth: An Evaluation of Scriptural Evidence* second edition (Boston: St. Paul Editions, 1981). It is only to be regretted that in the final section of the book he shows himself ready to accept a very "low" Christology.

[50] *Inseg* XIX/2 (1996), 215; *ORE* 1455:7; John Paul II, *Theotókos*, 128.

[51] *CCC* #499. Cf. *Lumen Gentium* #57 which likewise speaks of "the birth of Our Lord, who did not diminish his mother's virginal integrity but sanctified it."

[52] *Nove nasci debebat novæ nativitatis dedicator. De Carne Christi* 17 [*Corpus Christianorum Latinorum* 2, 903].

[53] Cf. Saward, *Cradle of Redeeming Love*, 206–217.

[54] Peter Damian Fehlner, *Virgin Mother, The Great Sign.* (Washington, NJ: AMI Press, 1993), 1–2.

According to the Church's Doctors, this freedom from corruption means that the God-Man leaves His Mother's womb without opening it (*utero clauso vel obsignato*), without inflecting any injury to her bodily virginity (*sine violatione claustri virginalis*), and therefore without causing her any pain.[55]

Evidently the same questionable assumptions which undermine belief in the virginal conception are at work in this area as well[56] with the addition of a major challenge which emerged with the publication of Dr. Albert Mitterer's 1952 study *Dogma und Biologie* which questioned Our Lady's physical integrity and the absence of pain.[57] Mitterer's work and the discussion which it provoked resulted in a *monitum* issued by the Holy Office (now Congregation for the Doctrine of the Faith) stating that

> theological works are being published in which the delicate question of Mary's virginity *in partu* is treated with a deplorable crudeness of expression and, what is more serious, in flagrant contradiction to the doctrinal tradition of the Church and to the sense of respect the faithful have

and thus prohibiting the publication of such dissertations in the future.[58] Unfortunately, in the light of the general confusion which has afflicted the Church for the past forty years this prohibition has been effectively ignored by many well known theologians[59] including the late Karl Rahner, S.J.[60] whose authority is readily invoked by many others.

A. The Magisterium

The Church's Magisterium has been entirely consistent and unflagging in upholding belief in Mary's virginity in childbirth.[61]

---

[55] Saward, *Cradle of Redeeming Love*, 206.

[56] Cf. Cardinal Leo Scheffczyk, *Maria, Crocevia della Fede Cattolica* trans. from German by Manfred Hauke (Lugano: Eupress, 2002), 88–90.

[57] Cf. Perrella, *Maria Vergine e Madre*, 9, 204–205, 215–216; Fehlner, *Virgin Mother*, 1–4.

[58] Cf. *Ephemerides Mariologicæ* 11 (1961), 137–138; René Laurentin, *A Short Treatise on the Virgin Mary.* Trans. Charles Neumann, S.M., (Washington, NJ: AMI Press, 1991), 328–329. In addition, see the commentary in Fehlner, *Virgin Mother*, 19–21.

[59] Cf. Fehlner, *Virgin Mother*, 2–4; Perrella, *Maria Vergine e Madre*, 204–218.

[60] "Virginitas in Partu," *Theological Investigations* Vol. 4 (Baltimore: Helicon, 1966): 134–162.

[61] Cf. Fehlner, *Virgin Mother*, 6–20.

In commenting on the re-statement of this article of faith made in *Lumen Gentium* #57 and subsequently quoted in the *Catechism of the Catholic Church* #499, Father Fehlner states:

> After the phrase "sanctified it" the Council appended references to indicate the precise sense in which virginal integrity at the time of Christ's birth is to be understood. Three references are given by the Council in note 10: to canon 3 of the Lateran Synod of 649, to the Dogmatic Tome of Saint Leo the Great to Flavian, and to the passage of Saint Ambrose in his work on the education of virgins. ...
>
> From all the references which Vatican II might have chosen to illustrate the faith of the Church in Our Lady's virginal integrity at childbirth these three, utterly unequivocal, are found in the definitive text. No clearer indication could have been given that this mystery, inseparable from the Nativity of the Savior, is of crucial importance to faith as such. Even the slightest question or doubt about the reality of meaning of that mystery, whether it concerns the Mother or the Child, cannot be tolerated.[62]

In his discourse in Capua on 24 May 1992 Pope John Paul II noted a highly significant correlation with regard to Patristic teaching on the *virginitas in partu* and the Resurrection, thus linking his magisterium with the teaching of the Fathers:

> It is a well-known fact that some Church Fathers set up a significant parallel between the begetting of Christ *ex intacta Virgine* [from the untouched Virgin] and His resurrection *ex intacto sepulcro* [from the intact sepulchre]. In the parallelism relative to the begetting of Christ, some Fathers put the emphasis on the virginal conception, others on the virgin birth, others on the subsequent perpetual virginity of the Mother, but they all testify to the conviction that between the two saving events—the generation—birth of Christ and His resurrection from the dead—there exists an intrinsic connection which corresponds to a precise plan of God: a connection which the Church, led by the Spirit, has discovered, not created.[63]

How important it is to grasp in this case—as well as with regard to all that I have tried to convey thus far—that, under the guidance of the Spirit, the Church receives and discovers, but does not create.

---

[62] Fehlner, *Virgin Mother*, 21–22.
[63] *AAS* 85 (1993), 665; *ORE* 1244:13.

In that same discourse the Holy Father points out precisely how the insight into this correlation comes about:

> In adoring reflection on the mystery of the incarnation of the Word, one discerns *a particularly important relationship between the beginning and the end of Christ's earthly life*, that is, between His virginal conception and His resurrection from the dead, two truths which are closely connected with faith in Jesus' divinity.

> They belong to the deposit of faith; they are professed by the whole Church and they have been expressly stated in the creeds. History shows that doubts or uncertainty about one has inevitable repercussions on the other, just as, on the contrary, humble and strong assent to one of them fosters the warm acceptance of the other.[64]

In reflecting on this converging evidence[65] I cannot help but be struck by the juxtaposition of these same themes in the late Raymond E. Brown's controversial essays published together under the title of *The Virginal Conception & Bodily Resurrection of Jesus*. Quite evidently there is a profound link between these complementary mysteries which touch the beginning and end of Christ's earthly life. Those who treat them without "adoring reflection" and as expendable assumptions should not be surprised to arrive at "shipwreck of the faith" (cf. 1 Tim. 2:19) or to lead others to it. Without any *anathema*, this is, nonetheless, the solemn warning of the magisterium.

B. The Biblical Witness

Two very prominent Old Testament messianic texts point to the mystery of the virginal birth of Christ. The first occurs immediately after Genesis 3:15, known in the tradition as the *protoevangelium*, which speaks of the "woman," the "New Eve" through whom redemption will come.[66] In the following verse the Lord God addresses Eve stating "I will greatly multiply your pain in childbearing; in pain you shall bring forth children, yet your desire shall

---

[64] *AAS* 85 (1993), 664–665; *ORE* 1244:13.
[65] Cf. Perrella, *Maria Vergine e Madre*, 222–226; Saward, *Cradle of Redeeming Love*, 237, 239–240.
[66] Cf. the Pope's catechesis of 24 January 1966, *Inseg* XIX/1 (1996), 115–117; *ORE* 1426:11; John Paul II, *Theotókos*, 61–63.

be for your husband, and he shall rule over you." Father Stefano
Manelli's comment on these two verses is very insightful:

> The two verses of Genesis 3:15 and 16, so sharply contrasting one
> another, make it psychologically impossible for them to refer to
> one and the same person. Immediately after having spoken so
> solemnly of how the "woman" with her "seed" is to triumph over
> the serpent, God speaks of how Eve must endure suffering and
> humiliation for the rest of her life. On what grounds is it possible
> to understand in each the same "woman"? Nor, similarly, can one,
> with any kind of consistency, suppose in the same person, Eve, a
> plan of life to unfold simultaneously under the sign of victory
> (Gen. 3:15) and the sign of subjection to suffering and man (Gen.
> 3:16).
>
> Rather, the point of departure for the logical development of this
> powerful and fruitful *antithesis* between Eve and Mary, noted by
> the earliest Fathers, such as St. Justin and St. Irenaeus, and com-
> mented upon down the centuries since, is the reality of that con-
> trast between Eve and the "woman" of Genesis 3:15.[67]

The Roman Catechism (also known as *The Catechism of the
Council of Trent)* draws out the Marian implications of verse 16:

> To Eve it was said: "In pain you shall bring forth children" (Gen.
> 3:16). Mary was exempt from this law, for preserving her virginal
> integrity inviolate, she brought forth Jesus the Son of God, with-
> out experiencing, as we have already said, any sense of pain.[68]

With a genial intuition which can serve as a way of summarizing what we have just presented, Haymo of Halberstadt (†853)
stated: "Just as she conceived without pleasure, so she gave birth
without pain."[69]

---

[67] Stefano M. Manelli, F.I., *All Generations Shall Call Me Blessed: Biblical
Mariology.* trans. Peter Damian Fehlner, F.I. (New Bedford, MA: Academy of the
Immaculate, 1995), 26–27.

[68] Robert I. Bradley, S.J. and Eugene Kevane (eds.), *The Roman Catechism*
(Boston, MA: St. Paul Editions, 1985), 50. Cf. also Laurentin, *Treatise*, 64, 333,
338.

[69] *Expositio in Apocalypsim* 3, 12; *PL* 117:1081D–1082A [quoted in John Saward,
The Way of the Lamb: The Spirit of Childhood and the End of the Age. (Edinburgh:
T&T Clark, 1999), 153, n. 9.

The other major Old Testament prediction which sheds light on the mystery of the virgin birth is that of Isaiah 7:14.[70] I believe that John Saward is right in stating that

> Isaiah prophesied that the Mother of Emmanuel would be a virgin not only in conceiving Him in the womb (*Ecce virgo concipiet*) but also in bringing Him forth from the womb (*et virgo pariet*, cf. Is. 7:14).[71]

With regard to the Gospel witness, one should not be surprised that the Holy Spirit might continue to bring to light treasures once known to the saints, but overlooked by the "Higher Critics" as well as those which can be acquired by pondering in one's heart after the manner of the Virgin herself (cf. Lk. 2:19, 51). With regard to the exegesis of the Fathers, I find the reasoning of Ignace de la Potterie on the best translation of Luke 1:35b very cogent:

> We discover, however, since the time of the Fathers up to the present, four different versions. One either makes "*hagion*" ("holy") the subject and translates as Legrand does: "that is why *the holy* (child) who is to be born will be called Son of God"; or one makes of "*hagios*" an attribute of "will be," as in the Jerusalem Bible and the lectionary: "And so the child *will be holy* and will be called Son of God"; or one also reads "holy" an attribute of "called"; this latter is the translation recently proposed by A. Médebielle in his article "Annunciation" in the *Supplément au dictionnaire de la Bible*: "This is why the one to be born *will be called* holy, Son of God." These are the usual three translations. At the same time there is a fourth possibility which modern authors no longer think of, but which was very popular among the Fathers of the Church and during the Middle Ages. This reading, we think, is philologically the only one that is satisfactory; we then consider "holy," not as a complement of "will be" (this word is not found in the Greek text), nor of "will be called"; "holy" is rather to be taken as the complement of "will be born."
>
> The word "holy," in this instance, informs us about the *manner* in which the child will be born, that is to say in a "holy" manner. We therefore translate it so: "This is why *the one who will be born holy* will be called Son of God." Here it is not a question of the

---

future holiness of Jesus: that is totally outside of the perspective of the Annunciation and of the birth of the child. The child of Mary "will be born holy" in the levitical meaning: it is the birth of Jesus that will be "holy", without blemish, intact, that is "pure" in the ritual sense. If we read the text in this way, we set up here a biblical argument favoring that which the theologians call "*virginitas in partu*," the virginity of Mary while giving birth. The message of the angel to Mary contains then not only the announcement of the virginal *conception*, but also of the virginal *birth* of Jesus.[72]

Father de la Potterie's years of patient study have yielded other fruit in this area as well, especially his extensive analysis of John 1:13. Here I can only hope to indicate some of the major components of his argument, referring the interested reader to de la Potterie's own exposition.[73] In effect, what he proposes is that this controverted verse of the prologue to Saint John's Gospel should be translated thus:

> *He is* not born of blood(s),
> nor of the will of the flesh
> nor of the will of man,
> but *He was begotten of* God.[74]

In defending this translation as a reference to the virginal conception and birth of Christ, the first major objection to be overcome is that the Greek manuscripts of Saint John's Gospel all give this text in the plural as a reference to the children of God referred to in Jn. 1.12: they "who were born, not of blood nor of the will of the flesh, nor of the will of man, but of God". Here is de la Potterie's response:

Since the Greek manuscripts are fifty or one hundred years more recent, it is really too simple to want to relate to them, and ignore a period that precedes them. The reality is that *all* the texts from the second century witnessing to our passage have the singular.

---

[72] de la Potterie, *Mary in the Mystery of the Covenant*, 31; cf. his entire treatment of this text in pages 30–33; also Saward, *Cradle of Redeeming Love*, 208.

[73] Cf. "Il parto verginale del Verbo incarnato: 'Non ex sanguinibus ... sed ex Deo natus est' (Gv 1,13)," *Marianum* 45 (1983): 127–174; *Mary in the Mystery of the Covenant*, 96–122.

[74] de la Potterie, *Mary in the Mystery of the Covenant*, 96, 98.

And in addition, it is interesting to notice that all these witnesses, when they are localized geographically, are not concentrated in one area, but are diffused all over the Mediterranean basin: in Asia Minor, most likely also in Palestine (Justin), at Rome (Hippolytus), in Gaul (Irenaeus), in Northern Africa (Tertullian), and at Alexandria in Egypt. That is a very important fact because it demonstrates that in the second century, during a time in which rapid means of communication did not yet exist, this text was universally read only in the singular. And this within one century of the composition of the Fourth Gospel.

We find that, for the first time, the plural form occurs only at the end of the second century; and these two or three witnesses are *all* concentrated at Alexandria in Egypt. One could conclude that the plural form took birth in this milieu, where the polemic battles with the Gnostics were in full force. ...

Tertullian maintains then that the Valentinians have falsified the text of John 1:13 in order to be able, after the fact, to base their Gnostic doctrine of the rebirth of the "Spirituals" or "Perfect" on it.

But then, obviously the question arises: how did it happen that the singular original form was lost? This is not easy to answer because there are very few traces available. However, we believe—and this remains partially a hypothesis—that the reason for the change is above all to be looked for in the fact that the earliest Church Fathers, who were still reading the text in the singular, did not know how to explain the first of three negatives in verse 13: "non ex sanguinibus."[75]

In explaining the original sense of "non ex sanguinibus" de la Potterie has recourse to the doctoral thesis of Peter Hofrichter[76] who points out that

in several texts of the Old Testament, and later in the Jewish tradition, the word "blood" is also used in the plural for the loss of blood which is linked with a women's period; that is with menstruation and childbirth, hence of a *birth*. The basic text for this is found in Leviticus 12:4–7.[77]

---

[75] *Ibid*, 99–101.

[76] *Nicht aus Blut sondern monogen aus Gott geboren. Textkritische, dogmengeschichtliche und exegetische Untersuchung zu Joh 1, 13–14* (Würzburg: "Forschung zur Bible," 31, 1978).

[77] de la Potterie, *Mary in the Mystery of the Covenant,* 111.

What conclusion can we make from this text for the interpretation of the first negation in verse 13 of the prologue: "not born of blood(s)"? In the context for the laws of purification it signifies that Jesus, in being born, did not cause an *effusion of blood* in His mother; in other words, at the birth of Jesus there would not have been any ritual impurity in His mother because in her there would not have taken place any shedding of blood. There would then be here a scriptural indication for what the theologians have in mind when they speak of the "*virginitas in partu*," the virginity of the birthing of Jesus.[78]

The author then goes on to cite the testimonies of Hippolytus, Ambrose, Jerome, John Damascene and Thomas Aquinas in support of his argumentation.[79] Quite evidently it is this thesis of Ignace de la Potterie which Pope John Paul II had in mind in his Marian catechesis of 10 July 1996:

This truth [of the virginal conception], according to a recent exegetical discovery, would be explicitly contained in verse 13 of the Prologue of John's Gospel, which some ancient authoritative authors (for example, Irenaeus and Tertullian) present, not in the usual plural form, but in the singular: "He, who was born not of blood nor of the will of the flesh nor of the will of man, but of God." This version in the singular would make the Johannine Prologue one of the major attestations of Jesus' virginal conception, placed in the context of the mystery of the Incarnation.[80]

It should simply be pointed out that Father de la Potterie's "exegetical discovery" bears as much on the virginal birth as on the virginal conception, whereas the subject of the Pope's catechesis of 10 July 1996 was the conception.

C. The Allegorical Sense of Scripture

Constraint of space does not allow me to present an exposition of the Fathers on this subject. Here I wish simply to underscore that much of the Patristic treatment of the virginal conception and birth of Christ is based on what the *Catechism of the*

---

[78] *Ibid*, 112.

[79] *Ibid*, 112–113. He cites even more authorities in his article "Il parto verginale del Verbo incarnato: 'Non ex sanguinibus ... sed ex Deo natus est' (Gv 1,13)," *Marianum* 45 (1983), 153–158.

[80] *Inseg* XIX/2 (1996), 76; *ORE* 1450:11; John Paul II, *Theotókos*, 113.

Catholic Church, following the tradition, calls the allegorical sense of Scripture.[81] It is precisely the allegorical sense of Scripture which the *Roman Catechism* proposes with regard to our subject:

> Since the mysteries of this admirable conception and nativity are so great and so numerous, it accorded with Divine Providence to signify them by many types and prophecies. Hence the Fathers of the Church understood many things which we meet in the Sacred Scriptures to relate to them, particularly that gate of the Sanctuary which Ezekiel saw closed (see Ezk. 44:2) ... Likewise the bush which Moses saw burn without being consumed (see Ex. 3.2).[82]

It is by means of this allegorical sense, as John Saward tells us, that The Fathers find types of the virginity *in partu* in Ezekiel's prophecy of the closed gate of the Temple (cf. Ezek. 44:2) and in the 'garden enclosed' and 'fountain sealed up' of Solomon's canticle (cf. Song 4:12).[83]

IV. Conclusion

By way of conclusion, I would like to quote again from the magisterium of Pope John Paul II. In referring to the parallel between the begetting of Christ *ex intacta Virgine* [from the untouched Virgin] and his resurrection *ex intacto sepulcro* [from the intact sepulchre], he stated that there is "an intrinsic connection which corresponds to a precise plan of God: a connection which the Church, led by the Spirit, has discovered, not created".[84] I believe that this statement may also be predicated of the two facets of the mystery of the Incarnation which we have been studying. The Church has received the revelation of this mystery as handed on by the Apostles and their successors; it is the recipient and custodian of the mysteries, but not their fabricator.

---

[81] *CCC* #115–118.
[82] *Roman Catechism* 50.
[83] Saward, *Cradle of Redeeming Love*, 208. Cf. Saward passim, 208–217. On Ezek. 44:2, cf. Manelli, *All Generations*, 75–78.
[84] *AAS* 85 (1993), 665; *ORE* 1244:13.

THEOLOGY OF THE BODY
AND MARIAN DOGMAS

Fr. Donald H. Calloway, M.I.C.

Introduction

The Theology of the Body as taught by Pope John Paul II during the Wednesday audiences from September 5, 1979 to November 28, 1984 is becoming more and more acclaimed as a revolutionary approach to understanding the embodiedness of human persons.[1] In offering to the Church and the world a catechesis of the body, a theology of the body, John Paul II has shown himself a true shepherd by responding to the twentieth century *scandalum carnis*. There can be no doubt that the body was perceived as an enigma by much of twentieth century thought. For example, Caryll Houselander, fully aware of the twentieth century infatuation with the body, wrote in 1944: "There has surely never been an age in which so many people were so particularly preoccupied with their bodies as this age, and yet to so little profit."[2] For this reason, the Theology of the Body as taught by John Paul II is a theological response, in the form of a theological anthropology based in Divine Revelation, to the modern quest to understand the origin, meaning, and destiny of the human body.[3]

---

[1] Perhaps the most well known English collection/edition of these audiences can be found in *The Theology of the Body: Human Love in the Divine Plan*, (Boston: Daughters of St. Paul, 1997). These texts, when quoted, will henceforth be cited as *TOTB*, with proper page number and date.

[2] Caryll Houselander, *The Reed of God*, (Westminster, MD: Christian Classics, Inc., 1990), 56. [Originally published in 1944].

[3] It should be noted that even before John Paul II began his catecheses on the human body, there were many people who noted that a theology of the body was needed. For example, in a sermon titled "The Cult of Mary in the Age of the Cult

Part of the reason for why this aspect of revelation—God's knowledge shared with us concerning the human body—lay dormant for so many centuries is because the twentieth century, perhaps unlike any century in human history, with all of its technological advances, came to view the human body as a mere instrument to be used in the never ending quest for self-gratification and pleasure. For example, one has only to think of the various types of sins—all bodily sins—that became commonplace, many even becoming legal, during the twentieth century: abortion, euthanasia, pornography, prostitution, drugs, wars, suicide, terrorism, homosexual acts, adultery, contraception, concentration camps, genocide, sex changes, cloning, and the list goes on and on. Some philosophers have even ventured to label the current era in history the 'post-human' era. Thus, a theology of the body could not have come at a more apropos epoch in history. God has saved a great treasure for our times.

Anyone who has read John Paul II's Theology of the Body knows that what he has essentially done is offer to the world a revolutionary way of understanding all created things, most especially, human bodiliness. The various applications of John Paul II's thought are only now beginning to take firm root in various branches of theology (e.g., Moral Theology, Eschatology, Sacramental Theology). What is often overlooked, however, is the fact that *the* very real and concrete *creaturely* embodiment of the content of John Paul II's Theology of the Body is rarely brought out and explored, namely, the Blessed Virgin Mary. Surprisingly, when

of the Flesh," preached in Italian at the Basilica of Our Lady of Pompeii, Naples, Italy on December 8, 1969, Cardinal John Wright suggested a "need for a Christian *theology concerning the flesh*, so that our culture may be refined by it, our civilization may be cured of excess and purified of decadence, our lives made sane and *holy* by it." See *Mary: Our Hope: A Selection from the Sermons, Addresses, and Papers of Cardinal John J. Wright*. ed. R. Stephen Almagno, O.F.M., (San Francisco: Ignatius Press, 1984), 117. Also, during the years when John Paul II was giving his catecheses on the body, the Jesuit Robert Brungs, in an article dealing with the influences of biotechnology on the human body, noted that in light of the rapid advancements in biotechnology "the times demand a much fuller doctrinal explication of the meaning of our bodied existence." See "Biotechnology and Bodiliness," *Communio: International Catholic Review* 8 (Spring, 1981), 159. Lastly, Cipriano Vagaggini even wrote a book dealing with a theology of the body, *The Flesh: Instrument of Salvation, A Theology of the Human Body*, (Staten Island, NY: Alba House, 1969).

one reads through the various commentaries on the Theology of the Body, the reader becomes aware of a lack of reference to the most perfect human person that ever lived, or ever will live, the Mother of Jesus Christ, the Immaculate Conception. How can this be since Mary is the apex of what it means to be a complete and fully redeemed human person? Does not the *created* exemplar of all *human* persons have something to teach us concerning that fundamental dimension of human personhood that we call the body? The answer is "Yes."

In a certain sense, the theology of the body remains incomplete without the full incorporation of the Marian dimension; Mary makes the Theology of the Body concrete and real, taking it away from the mere realm of theory and abstract principles. As a Pontiff completely consecrated to the Virgin Mary, John Paul II fully recognized the central place of Mary in salvation history.[4] Yet, it seems that when it comes to his Theology of the Body, John Paul II has left it to us to discover and explore the intimate connection between what he teaches in his catecheses on the body and what the Church teaches about Mary; in particular, what the Marian dogmas teach us about the human body. This is, indeed, virtually unexplored theological territory.[5]

The purpose of this essay is not to present a comprehensive comparative study of John Paul II's theology of the body and the Church's dogmatic teachings on Mary. Rather, the purpose of this essay is to extract from the theology of the body four basic points

---

[4] John Paul II's pontificate was undoubtedly very Marian, both in doctrinal teachings and in the example of devotion. He has a "theological method" that interweaves rigorous intellectual precision with heartfelt filial reverence for the mystery of Mary. This is why he deliberately chose to end almost everything he did with a reference to Mary. Mary, for John Paul II, is the embodiment of his doctrinal teaching. Concerning this, David L. Schindler rightly and insightfully notes the following: "The pope's appeals to Mary at the end of nearly every encyclical are not matters of window–dressing or mere "piety." See "Christology and the *Imago Dei*: Interpreting *Gaudium et Spes*," *Communio: International Catholic Review* 23 (Spring, 1996), 175.

[5] While certain notable theologians and Mariologists have explored various anthropological issues dealing with the human body from a Mariological perspective, their studies, as most of them note, remain incomplete. See, for example, the following works: René Laurentin, "Mary and Womanhood in the Renewal of Christian Anthropology," *Marian Library Studies* 1 (1969) [New Series]:

and compare them with what the Church teaches dogmatically about the Virgin Mary, noting the ways in which what John Paul II taught about the human body is affirmed and exemplified in what the Church teaches about Our Lady. As a matter of course, a brief presentation of John Paul II's Theology of the Body, with the four selected points, will appear first, followed by the application of the four Marian dogmas, examining how each dogma about Mary reveals a concrete embodiment of John Paul II's teaching. What John Paul II did implicitly all throughout his pontificate, this essay seeks to do explicitly, namely, interweave and ground what the Church teaches us about the body with what the Church teaches and holds to be true about the Virgin Mary.[6]

The Theology of the Body

Currently there are many books that deal with John Paul II's Theology of the Body, some of these even offer insightful and explanatory commentaries on the topic.[7] Many Catholic colleges, universities and seminaries recognize the importance of offering to a younger generation a sound theological understanding of the body, and are now offering classes that focus on the Theology of the Body;

77–95; Frederick M. Jelly, O.P., "Mariology and Christian Anthropology," *Catholic Theological Society of America Proceedings of the Thirty–Fourth Annual Convention, Atlanta, Georgia, June 13–16, 1979.* Volume 34: 211–219; Frederick M. Jelly, O.P., "Towards a Theology of the Body through Mariology," *Marian Studies* 34 (1983): 66–84; Germain Grisez, "Mary and Christian Moral Principles," *Marian Studies* 36 (1985): 40–59; Benedict M. Ashley, O.P., "Moral Theology and Mariology," *Anthropotes* 7 (1991): 137–153.

[6] For the person desiring to learn more about the Mariological thought and writings of John Paul II, the following selections offer excellent introductions: Edward D. O'Connor, C.S.C., "The Roots of Pope John Paul II's Devotion to Mary," *Marian Studies* 39 (1988): 78–114; Frederick L. Miller, "The Marian Orientation of Spirituality in the Thought of Pope John Paul II," *Communio: International Catholic Review* 17 (Winter, 1990): 566–579; Antoine Nachef, *Mary's Pope: John Paul II, Mary, and the Church since Vatican II.* (Franklin, WI: Sheed & Ward, 2000).

[7] See, for example, Mary Shivanandan, *Crossing the Threshold of Love: A New Vision of Marriage*, (Washington, D.C.: Boston, 1999); Christopher West, *Theology of the Body Explained: A Commentary of John Paul II's "Gospel of the Body,"* (Boston: Pauline Books & Media, 2003); Walter J. Schu, L.C., *The Splendor of Love: John Paul II's Vision for Marriage and Family*, (New Hope Publications, 2003); Sam Torode, *Body and Gift: Reflections on Creation* [2003], *Purity of Heart: Reflections on Love and Lust* [2004], *Heaven and Earth: Reflections on Resurrection* [2005] (South Wayne, WI: Philokalia Books).

there have even emerged Theology of the Body study groups. The need for such an understanding of the human body cannot be underestimated, and many people are finding renewal in their faith through discovering the teachings of John Paul II. George Weigel, the acclaimed biographer of John Paul II, has even asserted that the Theology of the Body represents "a kind of theological time bomb set to go off, with dramatic consequences, sometime in the third millennium of the Church."[8] In my humble opinion, I believe Weigel is absolutely correct.

The purpose of this section of the essay is to extract from John Paul II's overall catechesis four particular points that are fundamental to his presentation of the human body. These four points encapsulate what John Paul II is trying to teach modern society about the body. They are: 1) The Body Is A Gift, 2) The Body Is Nuptial, 3) The Body Is Fruitful, 4) The Body Is Essential To The Human Person.

I. The Body is a Gift

During the twentieth century, the body, with its gender, unique features and finite limitations, began to be seen by many people as a burden, something to be overcome and manipulated—all of this so that one could feel "at home" in one's body. Thus began such procedures as sex changes, plastic surgery and genetic manipulation. In a certain sense, it can be said that the twentieth century preoccupation with the body has led to a schizophrenic approach to what to do with the body: either worship it as divine, or seek to manipulate it (or even kill it) through technological means. What the world has fundamentally overlooked, however, is that the body is a precious gift from God, even with all its limitations, vulnerabilities and imperfections.

John Paul II, as a shepherd of souls, sought to enter into the discussion on the human body from the perspective of theological anthropology, that is, what God has revealed about the human body. He reminded us of the fact that in the beginning—original creation, and all human conception—God made all things good (Gen.1:31), including the human body. Almost from the very beginning of his

---

[8] George Weigel, *Witness To Hope: The Biography of Pope John Paul II*, (New York: HarperCollins, 1999), 343.

Wednesday catecheses John Paul II placed the created human body within the context of a "fundamental and original gift."[9] More specifically, he emphatically stated: "The first chapters of Genesis introduce us to the mystery of creation, this is, the beginning of the world by the will of God, who is omnipotence and love. Consequently, every creature bears within it the sign of the original and fundamental gift."[10] What is important to remember here is that for human persons, unlike angelic persons, the body is part of the 'original and fundamental gift'.

Furthermore, according to John Paul II's thought, man cannot fully understand himself without a full acceptance of the gift of human embodiedness. The body is not something extrinsic to what it means to be a human person—a theme we will cover later in the essay. The "adequate anthropology" of John Paul II is built upon this necessary fact: the body is a gift from God, and this includes its sex, male or female. In short, man will not be able to be nuptial or fruitful—live within interpersonal communion—unless he sees his body as a gift freely given and, in turn, a gift to be freely given away.

Concerning the issue of the sex of the human body (masculinity and femininity), and its being a fundamental-given from God—a very apropos theological issue in light of the twentieth century quest for androgyny—John Paul II emphatically stated the following: "Masculinity and femininity—namely, sex—is the original sign of a creative donation and an awareness on the part of man, male—female, of a gift lived in an original way. Such is the meaning with which sex enters the theology of the body."[11] Thus, a human person's embodied sex must be understood as part of the original and fundamental gift of creation—in the beginning of time, and in the beginning of every human conception.

Likewise, acceptance on the part of men and women of their particular sex is what allows for self-transcendence and real communion with others. Concerning this, John Paul II stated: "There is a deep connection between the mystery of creation, as a gift springing from love, and that beatifying "beginning" of the existence of man as

---

[9] See *TOTB*, 57 [January 2, 1980].
[10] *Ibid*, 59.
[11] *TOTB*, 62 [January 9, 1980].

male and female, in the whole truth of their body and their sex, which is the pure and simple truth of communion of persons."[12] What John Paul II is essentially saying is that the sex of each person is a gift that leads to self-transcendent communion. On the other hand, when a person does not view his body as an original and fundamental gift his relations with other persons (divine, angelic or human) will lack the quality of self-sacrificing, self-transcendent (trinitarian) love. Why? For no other reason than that man must first view his embodiedness as a gift in order to fully and freely give his bodiliness away to an other; this giving away must always be life-giving, either physical or spiritual. In this sense, the body is a sacrament revealing and express-ing the deeper *communio personarum*.[13]

To view one's sex as the consequence of purely cultural con-ditioning, or a fortuitous cosmic process, is to become, at least in thought, homosexual, a condition that can neither bear fruit nor be revelatory of a true *theological* (Trinitarian) communion with oth-ers. This anti-trinitarian approach to the body eliminates all differ-ence, and thus all fruitfulness; it views the body not as a fundamen-tal-given from a God who has made us in His image, but, rather, as a burden that we can manipulate and alter until *we* achieve our own definition of what it means to be embodied human persons. Contra-ry to this line of thought, John Paul II grounds the mystery of our body—gift (masculinity and femininity) in the gratuity of God revealed at the beginning of creation: "Right from the beginning, the theology of the body is bound up with the creation of man in the image of God. It becomes, in a way, also the theology of sex or rather the theology of masculinity and femininity, which has its starting point here in Genesis."[14]

II. The Body Is Nuptial

The body as nuptial is also a key element in John Paul II's Theology of the Body.[15] He highlights the nuptial element of the body in his insightful exegesis of the two creation accounts. Accord-ing to the first creation account, man was created in 'original soli-

---

[12] *Ibid*, 61.

[13] See *TOTB*, 75–77 [February 20, 1980].

[14] *TOTB*, 47 [November 14, 1979].

[15] Nuptiality is essentially understood to mean the giving of oneself in freedom to

tude', that is, man is a being created for his own sake. Yet, what John Paul II sought to emphasize was the fact that man's original solitude is a preparation for a communion of persons, *communio personarum*—and this communion of persons is nuptial.[16] This brings about John Paul II's concept of an 'adequate anthropology',[17] an approach to understanding man from a trinitarian perspective, that is, man made in the image of the God who is a communion of persons.

The Conciliar document *Gaudium et Spes*, a document which Cardinal Karol Wojtyla had a hand in shaping, gave to the world a profound statement when it declared that: "Man cannot find himself without a complete gift of himself" (*GS*, 24). What this essentially means is that man was made for communion, and since all human persons have a body, the body becomes the 'sacrament' revealing the deeper communion of persons.[18] The body is a sign that conveys the love of the person, and thus every human person is to make of their body a gift to an other; through baptism all Christians make of their body a sacrifice to God (see Rom. 12:1), but each has a particular call as to how to consecrate his body to God, for example, consecrated life, sacramental marriage or consecrated virginity.

The metaphysical and ontological foundations of what John Paul II sought to convey in stating that the body is made for nuptiality, that is, to be given away to an other in self-possessing love, is the Trinitarian God. God, in His essence, is a nuptial God, a divine *communio personarum*. Since there are three divine persons, each of these persons communicates His all to the other two. Thus, according to John Paul II, the second creation account is a "preparation for understanding the Trinitarian concept of the «image of God»."[19]

III. The Body is Fruitful

Nuptial love brings forth life. Where there is true love, trinitarian love, there is always fruit. Man, in his concrete embodiedness, was not created to remain in solitude. On the contrary, due to the

an other, receiving the other as gift, and bearing fruit through interpersonal love. Cf. *TOTB*, 60–72.

[16] See *TOTB*, 60–63 [January 9, 1980].

[17] See *TOTB*, 57–60 [January 2, 1980].

[18] See *TOTB*, 75–77 [February 20, 1980].

[19] *TOTB*, 46 [November 14, 1979].

trinitarian imaging, man is called to fecundity through inter-personal communion, thus the divine injunction: "Be fruitful and multiply" (Gen.1:28). Nuptiality reaches its climax through the mutual exchange of love that ultimately results in a third, that is, the fruit of love between two concrete persons.

On the opposite end, where there is no self-donation in love, there is sterility. For man, since he is an embodied being, his nuptial person is expressed through the body, and thus the body becomes, in some fashion (physically and/or spiritually) fecund. This is why all human persons, no matter what their particular vocation in life, are called to bear fruit. For example, the married couple is called to bear fruit, physical fruit (children), if possible, but spiritual fruit necessarily. Those in consecrated life, often called *mother* or *father*, surrender their bodies to God in order to bear abundant spiritual fruit. Even those who remain in the single state must bear spiritual fruit. Fecundity is a mandate of both original creation and the new–creation.

According to John Paul II, man, both as masculine and as feminine, finds the fulfillment of embodied love in paternity and maternity.[20] He stated: "On this threshold [the beginning of man and woman] man, as male and female, stands with the awareness of the generative meaning of his body. Masculinity conceals within it the meaning of fatherhood, and femininity that of motherhood."[21] What this means is that written into the very ontological, God–given, structure of what it means to be an embodied human person is the notion of fruitfulness and vocation. Each individual's vocation is a fundamental call to fruitfulness, and each human person does this through their body. Once again, John Paul II will bring out the trinitarian foundation of embodied human love: "With that knowledge [knowledge of the generative power of the body], man goes beyond the solitude of his own being, and decides again to affirm this being in an "other." Both of them, man and woman, affirm it in the new person generated."[22]

---

[20] See *TOTB*, 80–83 [March 12, 1980].
[21] *TOTB*, 85 [March 26, 1980].
[22] *Ibid*, 86 [April 2, 1980].

IV. The Body is Essential

Contrary to many of the technological and new-age philosophies at work today, which posit that the human body is nothing more than a sensory mechanism for self-gratification, John Paul II emphatically reasserts the Christian teaching that the body is an essential part of the human person and not simply an exterior shell that will be shed once this temporal existence is ended. In our modern world, where escapism and anti-materialistic conceptions of nirvana reign, the need for understanding the body as a gift that both blesses time and eternity is of paramount importance. This is precisely where John Paul II's Theology of the Body manifests the wisdom of the Judeo–Christian understanding of the body by emphasizing that the body is from God. As a matter of fact, Christianity not only teaches that the body is a fundamental-given from God, it also teaches that because of the incarnation and resurrection of Jesus Christ, the human body is raised to a new dignity, and will exist for all eternity as the living temple of God.[23] For this reason, the Christological statement in *Gaudium et Spes* chapter 22 is the "key" to unlocking the mystery of man (anthropology): "In reality it is only in the mystery of the Word made flesh that the mystery of man truly becomes clear. For Adam, the first man, was a type of Him who was to come, Christ the Lord, Christ the new Adam, in the very revelation of the mystery of the Father and of His love, fully reveals man to himself and brings to light his most high calling."[24]

Continuing with this thought, John Paul II offered in his catecheses a certain theological anthropology based on the Resurrection of Jesus Christ, an historical event which makes of everything a new–creation.[25] The Resurrection, due to its being the perfection of the human person, means that the human body will be perfected and brought to a state that reveals the full glory of the human body.[26] Thus, the human body contains within itself an eschatological dimension—and this eschatological dimension is grounded within the very ontological structure of the human person. Once a human per-

---

[23] See *TOTB*, 205–208 [February 11, 1981].

[24] *Gaudium et Spes,* 22.

[25] See *TOTB*, 238–257 [December 2, 9, 16, 1981; January 13, 27, 1982; February 3, 10, 1982].

[26] See *TOTB*, 240–245 [December 9, 16, 1981].

son is born, body and all, that person will be with his body forever, either in heaven or in hell.

Included in this theological anthropology is the fact that the body, every human body, is a gendered body. What this implies is that even the sex of the human body is more than just temporal; sex, too, is eternal. This has wide implications for the eschatological dimensions of the Theology of the Body.[27] The important thing to remember here is that John Paul II understood the human body, in its entirety, as being grounded in ontological reality.

The Role of Mariology and Marian Dogmas

Mariology is the study of the Blessed Virgin Mary. As a field of study it seeks to understand her role in salvation history through examining her privileges and titles. Yet, that is not all it is. From the very beginning of reflections on the Virgin Mary, especially in the Fathers of the Church, there has been an understanding, a theological tool, called the Mary-Church analogy. What this theological tool seeks to emphasize is the notion that whatever statements we make concerning the Virgin Mary have some bearing and significance for the Church, the Church understood as both a collective whole and the individual Christian. In short, as Adrienne von Speyr noted: "Whatever the Lord did to His Mother He did with His Church in mind."[28] Thus, the study of Mariology has always taught something about man and his relationship with God through faith, as *Lumen Gentium* states: "Having entered deeply into the history of salvation, Mary, in a way, unites in her person and re-echoes the most important doctrines of the faith."[29]

In a rather lengthy quote, Fr. Donald Keefe gets to the core of why Mariology needs to be an essential dimension in all theological fields of study:

> The Marian doctrines are . . . not only not negotiable, not dispensable to the Christian faith: their exploration is an essential task of

---

[27] Cf. Benedict Ashley, O.P., *Theologies of the Body: Humanist and Christian.* (Braintree, MA: Pope John XXIII Center, 1985), especially pp. 579–605.
[28] Adrienne von Speyr, *Handmaid of the Lord*, E.A. Nelson. (San Francisco: Ignatius Press, 1985), 139.
[29] *Lumen Gentium*, 65.

theology, and any systematic theology which would ignore these doctrines, or fail to integrate them . . . is doomed to lapse into that kind of "identity system" which von Balthasar properly condemned in Barth's dogmatics, which is latent in Tillich's systematic theology, and which is all too easy to extrapolate from any theology which would prefer, for its principle of exploration, some immanent dynamism, human or cosmic, whose relation to the grace of the New Creation is at best and finally uninteresting. The Marian doctrines enter theology at the level of method, for the conversion process which the Christian faith demands of any prior anthropology, cosmology, sociology, politics or other humane discipline in order that it become a theology is that by which such a discipline loses its immanent necessity, to become Christocentric.[30]

What this profound statement basically posits is that in order to fully understand the world from God's perspective, the masterpiece of God, the Virgin Mary, must be incorporated into the study. Even more specifically, since we are here dealing with the field of theological anthropology (especially human embodiedness), the late Orthodox theologian, Alexander Schmemann was absolutely correct when he laconically noted: "Mariology is . . . the "locus theologicus" *par excellence* of Christian anthropology."[31] In other words, the study of man must not have abnormality as its starting point—a common error among many of the modern methods used in the social and psychological sciences—but, rather, start with normality, the blueprint for what it means to be an embodied human person. This is why in order to move beyond what modern ideological thinkers state about the human body, John Paul II began his study of man from a protological perspective, that is, "in the beginning". The implications for what this means for a relationship between Mariology and the study of anthropology is that we have to look to what divine revelation

[30] Donald J. Keefe, S.J., "Mary as Created Wisdom, the Splendor of the New Creation," *The Thomist* 47 (1983), 419.

[31] Alexander Schmemann, "Mary: The Archetype of Mankind," *The University of Dayton Review* 11 (Spring, 1975), 83. In a different article, Schmemann made the following profound statement regarding the place of Mary in understanding creation: "She—Mary—is the ultimate "doxa" of creation, its response to God. She is the climax, the personification, the affirmation of the ultimate destiny of all creation: that God may be finally all in all, may fill all things with Himself. The world is the "receptacle" of His glory, and in this it is "feminine." And in the present "era," Mary is the sign, the guarantee that this is so, that in its mystical depth the world is already achieving this destiny." See "On Mariology in Orthodoxy," *Marian Library Studies* [New Series] 2 (1970), 31.

(God's knowledge) tells us about Mary, the model and prototype of all human embodiedness.[32]

To further illustrate the necessary place of Marian studies in Christianity, one of the greatest theologians of the twentieth century, Hans Urs von Balthasar, noted: "Without Mariology Christianity threatens imperceptibly to become inhuman."[33] Without Mariology the age-old tendency to construct a dualistic cosmology and anthropology is never far away. However, as the late John Cardinal Wright aptly noted: "By the teachings of the faith on the Madonna, the flesh is made the twin of the spirit—no longer its rival."[34] In Mary all the glories of Christ's saving work are made clear and perfectly evident, they are made real and concrete. Even Karl Barth, though somewhat erroneous in his classification of terminology, noted the importance of Marian dogmas for *all* Catholic theology when he stated: "Marian dogma is neither more nor less than the critical, central dogma of the Roman Catholic Church, the dogma from the standpoint of which all their important positions are to be regarded and by which they stand or fall."[35] Regardless of the fact that he is mistaken in stating that Marian dogma(s) are the *central* dogma of Catholicism, he is absolutely right to note that the Church's teaching on Mary makes *all* Catholic teaching stand or fall!

The Virgin Mary is the greatest among creatures because she responded to God with her pure *fiat*, a total cooperation that intimately involved all of her being. Everything that Mary did she did with her body. For this reason, Sr. Mary Timothy Prokes is correct to point out that "the privileges celebrated in Mary are grounded in her body."[36]

---

[32] It must be remembered that Jesus Christ, the incarnate Son of God, is ultimately the one who provides meaning for the human body. Yet, since God has seen fit to create an immaculate representative from humanity, a non–divine creature, means that that same immaculate creature serves as the model of what it means to be human, and respond perfectly to God, in the strictly creaturely state, body and soul.

[33] Hans Urs von Balthasar, *Elucidations*. Trans. John Riches (San Francisco: Ignatius Press, 1975), 112.

[34] Cardinal John J. Wright, *Mary, Our Hope: A Selection from the Sermons, Addresses, and Papers of Cardinal John J. Wright*. (ed.) R. Stephen Almagno, O.F.M. (San Francisco: Ignatius Press, 1984), 127.

[35] Karl Barth, *Church Dogmatics, Volume 1.2: The Doctrine of the Word of God*, Trans. G.T. Thomson & Harold Knight. (Edinburgh: T&T Clark, 1980), 143.

[36] Mary Timothy Prokes, F.S.E., *Toward a Theology of the Body*. (Grand Rapids, MI: Eerdmans, 1996), 172.

Without Mary the teaching of the Church on the human body remains abstract and theoretical. Interestingly, during the 13th International Marian Congress at Zagreb on August 13, 1971, Cardinal Suenens asked Karl Rahner what he thought was the reason for the decline in Marian devotion. The answer Rahner gave is a theological affirmation that the Virgin Mary, especially her divine maternity, makes Christianity real and concrete: "Too many Christians, whatever their religious obedience may be, tend to make Christianity an ideology, an abstraction. And abstractions do not need a mother."[37] Without Mary, Christianity is easily reduced to the realm of philosophical theory. For this reason, the statement made by Cardinal Christopher Schönborn could not be more accurate: "Mary is the guarantor of Christian realism."[38]

In light of all the above quotes on the essential part that Mariology needs to play in theology as a whole, it is surprising that so few (hardly any) theologians have explored the interconnectedness between what John Paul II taught in his Theology of the Body and what the Church teaches about the Virgin Mary.[39] Without a doubt, this is an area of theology that stands in need of serious investigation.[40] Therefore, while in no way positing that the following section of the essay offers a comprehensive treatment of the subject, it will seek to highlight the intimate connection that can be made between the four selected key points of John Paul II's theology of the body and the four Marian dogmas of the Catholic Church.[41]

---

[37] Cardinal Leo Jozef Suenens, "Mary and the World of Today," *L'Osservatore Romano* [English Edition] June 15, 1972. p.4. The original article by Suenens appeared as "Marie et le monde d'aujourd'hui," in *La Documentation Catholique* (3 Octobre 1971), 878–880.

[38] Christopher Schönborn, O.P., "Mary—Heart of Theology—Theology of the Heart," in *The Alliance of the Hearts of Jesus and Mary*, (ed.) Mary Alexis Montelibano–Salinas (Philippines: Salesiano Publishers, Inc., 1988), 271.

[39] The only systematic treatment I have been able to find that deals explicitly with this topic is a Masters thesis done by Marianne Lorraine Trouvé, F.S.P., *The Gift of the Woman—Virgin, Mother, Spouse: The Marian Teaching of John Paul II in Light of the Theology of the Body* (M.T.S. thesis: University of Dayton, 2000).

[40] Approaching Mariology from an anthropological perspective was stressed by both Paul VI in the Apostolic Exhortation *Marialis Cultus* (1974) and by the Congregation for Catholic Education's Letter *The Virgin Mary in Intellectual and Spiritual Formation* (1988). Unfortunately, many of the anthropological studies in Mariology undertaken in recent years have neglected the doctrinal and dogmatic underpinnings of the Church's teachings on the Virgin Mary.

[41] Another very important element in seeking to understand the many facets of

I. The Immaculate Conception: The Body is a Gift

The dogma of Mary's Immaculate Conception was proclaimed in 1854 by Bl. Pius IX in the Bull *Ineffabilis Deus*. The mystery of the Immaculate Conception, that is, Mary's having been created free from the stain of original sin in all the dimensions of her being, is a free gift of God's superabundant mercy; Mary did not earn or merit the unique privilege of being immaculately conceived. What is often overlooked regarding the teaching of the Church on the Immaculate Conception, however, is the fact that Mary was preserved from original sin in both soul *and* body. The gift of the Immaculate Conception is an embodied gift. Thus, Mary's femininity, her God-given gift of being a woman, is also part of the goodness of God's creation in the Immaculate Conception.

This fundamental act of mercy, The Immaculate Conception, serves as *sign* and *hope* indicating the superabundant goodness of God's love for creation. For as John Paul II stated: "The Immaculate Conception is . . . the promising dawn of the radiant day of Christ."[42]

Mary's body, due to the theological truth that it serves as the "promising dawn" of the new creation in which all things are made new, represents the prototypical model of each individual human being in their creaturely embodiedness. What Mary has at the beginning, namely, sinlessness, all will have at the end of life if they cooperate with the gift of their embodiedness. Mary shows us how to accept the gift of our embodiedness, and this includes the God-given sex of the body. In this it is important to note that Mary's exemplarity of what it means to accept the gift of one's body, means that the

human bodiliness would be through the theological truth of Mary's participation in redemption as Co–Redemptrix. This doctrine of the Church emphasizes that mankind, as seen in a unique way through the Virgin Mary, can indeed participate in redemption through the uniting of one's suffering with that of the God–man. Currently there are many studies being done on Mary's unique participation in redemption and on her role as Co–Redemptrix. In a very profound way, a dogmatic definition of Mary as Co–Redemptrix would offer to mankind a concrete example of how bodily suffering, when done in union with Christ and for the love of God and neighbor, can be redemptive.

[42] John Paul II, "For the 12th World Day of the Sick, 11 February 2004—Message to Cardinal Javier Lozano Barragán, President of the Pontifical Council for Health Pastoral Care," December 1, 2003. *L'Osservatore Romano*, English Edition, January 21, 2004.

body is not an obstacle to be overcome but, rather, a gift to be lived. Mary delights in her body, especially in its God-given sex: femininity. It is precisely in her gift of being a woman, that Mary was fashioned and called by God to be the *Theotokos*. The gift of her body is exactly what helps her to become the *Theotokos*. Just think of what would have happened if Mary had rebelled against the gift of her feminine body! *We* would be in a very different situation today.

Mary's gift of the Immaculate Conception, in contrast to much of the feminist thought of today, does not separate her from us. On the contrary, the gift of the Immaculate Conception serves as our model of how to accept the free, gratuitous gift of our embodiedness and cooperate with God in our salvation and the salvation of others. Salvation, the new creation, is an embodied reality. In a certain sense, the Immaculate Conception serves as a blueprint for how humanity is to respond to God's love. For this reason, Benedict Ashley states that "the Catholic understanding of the role of Mary in the plan of salvation is, as it were, a summary of the theology of the body and its historic development in the Church shows how the guidance of the Holy Spirit has overcome the dualistic influences of Platonism on Christian thought."[43]

In short, what the Immaculate Conception teaches us concerning a theology of the body is that if a person accepts and cooperates with their God–given body and sex, they will bear fruit for eternal life. On the other hand, if they choose to rebel and reject the gift of their body, they are on the road to self-destruction and anthropological frustration, that is, hell.

II. Perpetual Virginity: The Body is Nuptial

The Church's teaching on Mary's perpetual virginity was defined in 649 at the Lateran Council by Pope St. Martin I. While this dogma declares that Mary was a virgin before the birth of Christ (*virginitas ante partu*), during the birth of Christ (*virginitas in partu*), and after the birth of Christ (*virginitas post partum*), it also teaches us something essential for understanding what it means to be a virgin, namely, virginity is essentially nuptial because it is the ser-

---

[43] *Theologies of the Body: Humanist and Christian*, 536.

vant of love. "The perpetual virginity of Mary," according to Jutta Burggraf, "signifies her bridal state as well as the overshadowing by the Holy Spirit."[44]

As was stated earlier, an essential dimension of John Paul II's Theology of the Body is that the human body is nuptial, that is, meant to be a sacrament of the person and an expression of the communion of persons existing between individuals. In essence, the body is meant to be given away to an other in spousal love, either through sacramental marriage or through the choice to respond to God's call of consecrating one's body to the Lord through the vow of chastity.[45] Yet, in order to be able to fully give oneself away, one must have, as Cardinal Angelo Scola calls it, "possession in detachment,"[46] that is, the mature self-possession needed to make a mutual exchange based upon the mystery of otherness as gift. For Mary, this self-possession is her acceptance and cooperation with the gift of both her Immaculate Conception and her call to be a perpetual virgin in her body as a response to God's gift of Himself to her. Having self-possession gives one the freedom to give oneself away; one cannot give what one does not possess (*nemo dat quod non habet*). This is why Mary's *embodied* virginity serves as the model of freedom for the Church. The Congregation for the Doctrine of the Faith summed this point up well:

> Mary is totally dependent upon God and completely directed towards Him, and, at the side of her Son, she is *the most perfect image of freedom and of the liberation* of humanity and of the universe. It

---

[44] Jutta Burggraf, "The Mother of the Church and the Woman in the Church: A Correction of Feminist Theology Gone Astray," trans. Maria Shrady in *The Church and Women: A Compendium*. (ed.) Helmut Moll (San Franciso: Ignatius Press, 1988), 253.

[45] Within the context of consecrated life, John Paul II develops this theme: "*One cannot correctly understand virginity*—a woman's consecration in virginity—*without referring to spousal love*. It is through this kind of love that a person becomes a gift for the other. Moreover, a man's consecration in priestly celibacy or in the religious state is to be understood analogously." See *Mulieris Dignitatem*, 20. Cf. Fidelis Stöckl, O.R.C., *Mary, Model and Mother of Consecrated Life: A Marian Synthesis of the Theology of Consecrated Life Based on the Teachings of John Paul II*. (Quezon City, Philippines: ICLA Publications, 2003); Thomas Philippe, O.P., *Mystical Rose: Mary, Paradigm of the Religious Life*. (ed.) Edward D. O'Connor, C.S.C. (Huntington, IN: Our Sunday Visitor, 1995).

[46] See Angelo Scola, "The Nuptial Mystery at the Heart of the Church," *Communio: International Catholic Review* 25 (Winter, 1998), 658.

is to her as Mother and Model that the Church must look in order to understand in its completeness the meaning of her own mission.[47]

John Paul II so emphasized the fact that the virginal body is nuptial that he dedicated seven audiences to this theme.[48] Contrary to what modern society believes about virginity, namely, that it is a sign of isolation and seclusion, John Paul II presented virginity within a context of deep nuptial love. This is why he affirmed that the *virgin* Mary is the bride/spouse of God.[49]

John Paul II also noted that part of what it means to be in the image of God is being able to be a gift to an other: "To say that man is created in the image and likeness of God means that man is called to exist "for" others, to become a gift."[50] This is simply a reiteration of the teaching of Vatican Council II in its document *Gaudium et Spes*, where it states that "man can fully discover his true self only in a sincere giving of himself."[51] This notion of giving oneself away in self-possession is exactly what the dogma of Mary's perpetual virginity teaches us about the human body. This is why Mary can be both espoused to God and espoused to St. Joseph. Her body is a sacrament through which she expresses her nuptial person to those whom she loves.

III. Theotokos: The Body is Fruitful

The dogmatic teaching of Mary's Divine Motherhood was the first dogma proclaimed by the Church about the Blessed Virgin Mary. It was declared in 431 at the Council of Ephesus. While the

[47] Congregation for the Doctrine of the Faith, *Instruction on Christian Freedom and Liberation* (22 March 1986), 97

[48] The dates of these general audiences were: July 3, 1996; July 10, 1996; July 24, 1996; July 31, 1996; August 7, 1996; August 21, 1996 and August 28, 1996. The texts for these audiences can be found in John Paul II, *Theotókos*, 108–132.

[49] See, e.g., John Paul II, "Mary, Eschatological Icon of the Church," General Audience, March 14, 2001, *L'Osservatore Romano*, English Edition, 12–21 March 2001, p.11; "Mary, Bride of Divine Love," Angelus Message, July 4, 1999, *L'Osservatore Romano*, English Edition, 7 July 1999, p.1; "Hail, Bride of the Holy Spirit!," Address of June 7, 1999 in Lichen, Poland, *L'Osservatore Romano*, English Edition, 16 June 1999, p.6; "To Women Religious in Jasna Gora (June 5, 1979)," in *John Paul II Speaks to Religious: Principal Allocutions from November 1978 to December 1980*, (Chicago: Little Sisters of the Poor, 1981), 72–75; "Mary Responds to God with Spousal Love," General Audience of May 1, 1996 in John Paul II, *Theotókos*, 83–86.

[50] John Paul II, *Mulieris Dignitatem*, 7.

[51] *Gaudium et Spes*, 24.

main theological focus of this particular dogma is to emphasize the dual nature of Jesus Christ, divine and human, it also teaches us something essential about what it means to be a person, namely, we are called to be fruitful, some physically, but all spiritually. In this sense Mary's fruitfulness serves as the model for both because she is not only the physical *Theotokos*, but, also, the universal spiritual mother of the redeemed.

Since the body is a "sacrament" meant to be given away to an other in nuptial love, a nuptial love that expresses an existing communion of persons, each human body has within it the capacity for bearing fruit. The vocation to bear fruit applies to all, those whose call is to sacramental marriage, consecrated life, and the single state. How can this be? Basically, since a constitutive element of what it means to be human is that we are to make of our bodies a gift to an other, whether this "other" be strictly God or another human being, all are called to fruitfulness. It should be mentioned that not everyone in a sacramental marriage may be able to bear fruit physically due to physiological impairments, but all are definitely called to bear spiritual fruit. For this reason, some of the early Church Fathers, in order to show that Mary's spiritual model of fruitfulness is a universal model, noted that she first heard and conceived in her ear (heart), then, afterwards, in her womb.[52]

It is the Church's teaching that for those who offer their bodies to their spouses in nuptial love, they must remain open to life, to bearing fruit through childbearing. Any sexual act that goes against openness to life is anti-Trinitarian, and against their God-given gift of embodiedness. The same principle also applies to those consecrated to a life of virginity; they too must offer up their bodies to their spouse (God) in order to allow Him to fructify their lives and make them fruitful—only the fruitfulness involved here occurs in the spiritual realm instead of the physical, though the body still remains an essential element in serving as the "sacrament" expressing the communion of persons between God and the creature. Thus, for the consecrated person, the body becomes a sacrifice unto God, allowing Him to dispose of as He wills for the good of others—that others might have life.

---

[52] See St. Augustine, *De sancta virginitate* 3: *PL* 40.

On the part of Mary, her divine motherhood shows us that she fully gives her body away in virginity in order to allow God to fructify her. Her complete nuptial surrender to God in her human person, body and soul, is what brings about the Incarnation. She is a woman deeply in love with God, so much so that certain Mariologists have posited her bridal-motherhood to be the fundamental Marian principle.[53] The late Dominican Mariologist Frederick Jelly summed up the core of the bridal element in the dogma of the divine motherhood, especially its universal nuptial significance for all body-persons:

> At the "nuptials" which transpired during her religious experience of the joyful mystery of the Annunciation, Mary was fully free to give her graced consent to the wedding between divinity and humanity through the Word made flesh in her virginal womb. The Holy Spirit, who unites the Persons within the bosom of the triune God from all eternity, in time transformed the body-person Mary by over-shadowing her in the unitive action of the Incarnation. The most intimate relationship between a divine Body-Person and a human body-person ensued between this mother and her Son who is also God's own Son. Such is what appears to be meant by those in our Christian Tradition who favor enriching Mary's concrete motherhood of Christ with bridal symbolism and imagery. Not to be interpreted literally in its sexual connotations, still it does emphasize the intimate union between the divine and the human which took place within Mary's body . . . And the unique gift of her calling to be the immaculate and virginal *Theotokos* would become the Archetype for the Trinitarian transformation of all redeemed body-persons who are called to receive Christ into their lives and to become "spiritual mothers" in helping bring Him forth in the lives of others.[54]

IV. Assumption: The Body is Essential

The dogma of Mary's bodily assumption into heaven was proclaimed in 1950 by Pius XII in the Encyclical *Providentissimus*

---

[53] Without a doubt, Matthias J. Scheeben is the theologian who most developed the bridal–motherhood principle. See Matthias J. Scheeben, *Mariology Vol. I & II*, Trans. T.L.M.J. Geukers, (St. Louis: Herder Book Co., 1946 & 1947). Adhering closely to the thought of Scheeben, the following works also bring out the bridal–maternal dimension within the Marian Tradition: Charles Feckes, *The Mystery of the Divine Motherhood*, (New York: Spiritual Book Associates, 1941); Donal Flanagan, "The Image of the Bride in the Earlier Marian Tradition," *Irish Theological Quarterly* 27 (1960): 111–124; "Mary, Bride of Christ," *Irish Theological Quarterly* 28 (1961): 233–237.

[54] Frederick M. Jelly, O.P., "Towards a Theology of the Body Through Mariology,"

Deus. Along with the fact that this dogma declares that Mary is with God in heaven in both her body and soul, it also essentially teaches that after *our* earthy life is over, we will continue to be body–persons, either in heaven or in hell, that is, we do not shed our bodies, as though they were a shell to be discarded. All of this has profound theological and eschatological significance for anthropology, especially in light of many of the dualistic tendencies of today.

What is interesting from an historical perspective, concerning the time in which the dogma of Mary's Assumption into heaven was proclaimed, is the fact that it was declared when the dignity of the human body was under serious attack.[55] Sr. Mary Prokes makes the following points concerning the timeliness of the dogma in human history:

> The definition of Mary's Assumption into glory as a total embodied human person came at a particularly apt moment. The first half of the twentieth century had opened the secrets of matter in a dramatic manner—but these secrets had been exploited through unparalleled devastation of bodies and the material universe.[56]

And

> The definition was promulgated nine years after atomic bombs devastated Japan. It followed close upon the exposé of pogroms, concentration camps and death by radiation, the legacy of World War II. Despite attempts at genocide and devastation of millions of bodies, the *dogma* affirmed that Mary was taken up into glory as a whole person.[57]

In essence, Mary's Assumption teaches us that no matter what ideological definitions of the body are at work in a particular era, God made the body good and desires it to be with Him in

Marian Studies 34 (1983), 81.

[55] See Fulton J. Sheen, "The Assumption and the Modern World," *The Thomist* 14 (January, 1951): 31–40.

[56] Mary Timothy Prokes, *Toward a Theology of the Body*, (Grand Rapids: Eerdmans, 1996), 168. Cf. Paul Haffner, *The Mystery of Mary,* (England: Gracewing, 2004), 227.

[57] Mary Timothy Prokes, "The Nuptial Meaning of Body in Light of Mary's Assumption," *Communio: International Catholic Review* 11 (Summer, 1984), 165.

heaven. Contrary to many of the modern ideological definitions concerning the body, and its treatment as a non–essential and "extrinsic" appendage to our "real" self, the Assumption of Mary into heaven teaches us something about the goodness of *our* body, breaking down the dualistic tendency in modern thought that pits the spiritual life over and against material existence. John Paul II made this point in the following way:

> . . . Mary's assumption reveals the nobility and dignity of the human body. In the face of the profanation and debasement to which modern society frequently subjects the female body, the mystery of the assumption proclaims the supernatural destiny and dignity of every human body, called by the Lord to become an instrument of holiness and to share in His glory.

> Mary entered into glory because she welcomed the Son of God in her virginal womb and in her heart. By looking at her, the Christian learns to discover the value of his own body and to guard it as a temple of God, in expectation of the resurrection. The assumption, a privilege granted to the Mother of God, thus has immense value for the life and destiny of humanity.[58]

Conclusion

The relationship between what John Paul II taught in the Theology of the Body and what the Church teaches about the body through her Marian dogmas should, at this point, be clear: namely, the dogmatic formulations about the Virgin Mary both affirm and complement what John Paul II taught about the human body. As a matter of fact, it can be stated with certainty that if these two areas— John Paul II's theology of the body and the Church's Marian dogmas—were in theological discord, there would exist a serious problem due to the fact that "to speak of Mary," as Cardinal Ratzinger states, "is to touch on the *nexus mysteriorum*—the inner interwovenness of the [Christian] mysteries, which are manifold, in relation, and yet one."[59] Mary is at the heart of all the teachings of the Church because she is at the heart of Christianity. Every teaching about Mary will affirm, must affirm, a teaching about Christ and His Church. Mary does not stand on her own. Rather, as image, model

---

[58] John Paul II, *Theotókos*, 208.
[59] Joseph Cardinal Ratzinger, "On the Position of Mariology and Marian

and prototype of the Church, her role is always to point to Christ and His saving mission being carried out in and through the Church. Thus, all of Mary's privileges are meant to be a hermeneutical tool, a theological method, teaching us something about what God has planned for us. In this sense, Fr. Paul Haffner is correct to note that Mariology serves as a "theological synthesis" and the "crossroads of theology, where all the various strands meet."[60] Archbishop Fulton Sheen, employing his uncanny ability to convey Catholic truths through simple analogies, once put it this way:

> She [Mary] holds all the great Truths of Christianity together, as a piece of wood holds a kite. Children wrap the string of a kite around a stick and release the string as the kite climbs to the heavens. Mary is like that piece of wood. Around her we wrap all the precious strings of the great Truths of our holy Faith—for example, the Incarnation, the Eucharist, the Church. No matter how far we get above the earth, as the kite may, we always have need of Mary to hold the doctrines of the Creed together. If we threw away the stick, we would no longer have the kite; if we threw away Mary, we would never have Our Lord. He would be lost in the Heavens, like our run-away kite, and that would be terrible, indeed, for us on earth.[61]

Christianity is an embodied religion, and without a proper understanding of the body, Christianity cannot be fully understood. This is precisely why John Paul II sought to give to the world a theological anthropology that presents to the world an objective teaching on the human body. The Virgin Mary, both in her ongoing maternal mediation and in what the Church teaches about her, plays a crucial role in theology in helping us to better understand that Christian teachings concerning the body are not abstract philosophical ideas, but real, concrete embodied realities. Adrienne von Speyr put it this way:

> Mary's flesh was absolutely necessary for the forming of the Son; and the Son, in order to become flesh and not just to be the prod-

Spirituality Within the Totality of Faith and Theology," in *The Church and Women: A Compendium.* (ed.) Helmut Moll. (San Francisco: Ignatius Press, 1988), 74.

[60] *The Mystery of Mary*, 20.

[61] Fulton J. Sheen, *The World's First Love.* (San Francisco: Ignatius Press, 1996), 75–76.

uct of an idea, allowed Himself to sink into flesh through the Spirit. This being so, it follows that having a body is, for the whole of Christianity, not merely something concrete, but rather something absolutely necessary for explaining, grasping, and apprehending Christianity.[62]

All in all, the purpose of this essay is to generate and stimulate thought on how John Paul II's revolutionary teaching on the human body can be further understood and exemplified in the Marian dogmas of the Catholic Church. While in no way claiming to be a comprehensive treatment of the subject, it is my hope that the richness of the Church's teaching on Mary will begin to be incorporated into the growing body of knowledge being written on the Theology of the Body. By way of conclusion, I present the closing remarks made by Archbishop John Myers in a pastoral letter to the people of his diocese concerning the Catholic teaching on the human body: "Let us ask Mary, who bore the deity in diapers, who was and is *Theotokos*, Mother of God, and who exemplified the meaning and dignity of the human body for her son, to be our model and patroness in the work that lies ahead."[63]

---

[62] Adrienne von Speyr, *Mary in the Redemption*, Trans. Helena M. Tomko. (San Francisco: Ignatius Press, 2003), 68.
[63] Archbishop Myers, "Catholic Teaching on the Human Body," [December 8, 2002] *Origins* (January 9, 2003), 503.

MARY'S VIRGINITY, THEOLOGY OF THE BODY, AND ST. THOMAS AQUINAS

Fr. Basil B. Cole, O.P., S.T.D.[*]

Introduction

One of the main purposes of John Paul II's discourses during 1982 was to give the Church an official Theology of the Body, not only in employing newer ways to describe the body's unity with the soul (a defined doctrine at the Fourth Lateran Council, reaffirmed at the First Vatican Council), but, also, to show its spousal meaning.[1] In doing so, John Paul II happily manifested to the world a revitalized teaching of the Catholic Church on the goodness of marriage and, at the same time, the even better state of virginity, yet in such a way, linguistically, so as not to degrade or think askance of the vocation to marriage. This approach would have ramifications on his later writings concerning Mary as virgin and mother.

Virginity and Marriage

On March 10, 1982, John Paul II spoke of virginity and celibacy in light of his ongoing catechesis of the Theology of the

[*] I wish to thank my confreres, Giles Dimock, O.P. and Paul Conner, O.P., and Dr. Peter Kwasniewski of Gaming, Austria for reviewing drafts of this essay and offering timely criticisms to clarify my thoughts.

[1] As a matter of faithfulness to the Italian original of John Paul II, the terminology often put forth as the "nuptial meaning" of the body, should be translated as the "spousal meaning" of the body. Cf. Michael Waldstein, "The Project of a New English Translation of John Paul II's Theology of the Body on its 20th and 25th Anniversary," *Communio: International Catholic Review* 31 (Summer, 2004): 345-351.

Body.[2] He called virginity a vocation to "an exclusive donation of self to God."[3] Renouncing a one-flesh union is not a negative opposition to marriage.[4] Nor does such a choice mean a devaluation of marriage itself.[5] Rather, it is a charismatic choice whereby someone begins to live the life of heaven on earth, a preparation for the kingdom of God, albeit without the beatific vision.[6] This choice also gives a person a "new and even fuller form of intersubjective communion with others."[7] Requiring the sacrifice of a human spouse and children, which necessitates the ability to live with a sense of loss, continence for the sake of the kingdom does find fulfillment in other ways than the natural vocation to marriage and family life. On one level, it is a renunciation of several natural goods but, on another level, it is an affirmation of higher (supernatural) goods.[8]

The individual who is drawn by grace to virginity or celibacy is not necessarily superior to those in the married state due to the fact that "perfection of the Christian life ... is measured with the rule of charity."[9] In other words, prayer and contemplation are not themselves the ultimate end of the consecrated life but, rather, divine love is the ultimate end. This does not deny the terminology used to describe the religious state of the three vows (poverty, chastity, obedience) as the *state of perfection* (*status perfectionis*)— perhaps more aptly put as *the canonical state of being perfected by divine love*. Perfection in this context means living a life that strives for perfection of charity with the many helps of the religious state itself, needed because members of all religious institutes are imperfect. One could rightly, from a certain point of view, call it the state of imperfection since all the members are imperfect. *De facto*, as John Paul II reminded all Catholics, anyone living in the state of marriage can surpass someone in perfection in the religious state

---

[2] See John Paul II, *Theology of the Body: Human Love in the Divine Plan,* (Boston: Daughters of St. Paul, 1997), 262 passim. Hereafter cited as *TOTB.*
[3] *Ibid.,* 262.
[4] See *TOTB,* 263.
[5] See *TOTB,* 273.
[6] See *TOTB,* 264, 270-271.
[7] *TOTB,* 273.
[8] See *TOTB,* 286.
[9] *TOTB,* 277.

simply by possessing more charity.[10] Nevertheless, both states, marriage and virginity, express the conjugal meaning of the body because they involve a "total gift of oneself," yet for different purposes, expressed in radically different ways.

St. Thomas' Contribution to Understanding the Purpose of Virginity

Aquinas used words similar to those used by John Paul II when he asked whether or not virginity is better than marriage.[11] He had already noted that the virtue of virginity must be strengthened by a vow (*ST* II-II, 152, 3 ad 4) since it implies that one is giving oneself exclusively and totally to God. Later on, he explains why this is so:

> As Gregory says, religious perfection requires that one offer his whole life to God. But a man cannot give his whole life to God here and now because it is not a simultaneous whole but is lived successively. Hence a man cannot give his whole life to God except by the obligation of a vow.[12]

In other words, a vow generously gives to God one's whole future, or as St. Thomas put it elsewhere, citing St. Anselm, it is one thing to give the fruits of a tree but another to give the whole tree itself.[13] With these reflections in mind, St. Thomas then clearly faces the question posed in the answer to the second objection on whether virginity is more excellent than marriage:

> Though virginity is better than conjugal continence, a married person can be better than a virgin on two counts. First from very chastity, as having a spirit more prepared to be ungrudging about virginity, were it called for, than some who in fact are virgins . . . Next, because one who is not a virgin may have more excellent virtue. Thus, Augustine (*De Virgin.* xliv), *Let a virgin recognize that her solicitude for the things of God may well go with an unconscious immaturity which is not ripe for martyrdom, whereas another woman she looks down on is already prepared to drink the chalice of the Lord's passion.*[14]

---

[10] See *TOTB*, 277.

[11] See *ST* II-II, 152, 4.

[12] *ST* II-II, 186, 6 ad 2.

[13] See *ST* II-II, 88, 6.

[14] *ST* II-II, 152, 4 ad 2.

Self-giving as the Key to Understanding the Way to Live as a Spouse

The theology of the body crafted by John Paul II, not only during his early audiences but, also, continued throughout his pontificate, has nothing substantially new to say from a Thomistic point of view in its analysis of the body/soul relationship; John Paul II did, however, express in new ways the body's spousal meaning, that is, that the human body is oriented toward self-giving either in marriage or virginity. This means that there is an in-built inclination toward married life and, for a very few, a potential for a deeper marriage or a friendship-intimacy with the Lord Jesus on a supernatural or spiritual plane, the other two persons of the Blessed Trinity being included, of course. Hence, the Second Vatican Council speaks of the gift of religious life as a special or exceptional gift.[15] Using the notion from *Gaudium et Spes* that we attain full identity "only in sincere self-giving,"[16] John Paul II described virtue in a very positive way. Put in a negative way, the meaning would be that self-centered people will never develop character or a sensitive conscience because they tend to equate their real needs with what they desire according to the criteria of the pleasure of the senses and other criteria, namely, the desire for created goods without reference to what is reasonable. To explain: Like the sin of Adam and Eve, some people can love themselves in a disorderly way, undermining their true vocation and sense of values due to their living by the pleasures of the senses (as in lust or gluttony) or even the spirit (as in avarice). St. Thomas shows throughout his writings that the foundations for undermining the moral life reduce themselves to false self-love flowing from either avarice and pride or unreasonably turning to created things and thereby, as a consequence, turning away from God.

By contrast, a true understanding of the moral life means that the human person is created to be social and in collaborative union with others, including God; following one's senses, on the other hand, looks to self as the exclusive or primary measure of happi-

---

[15] See *Lumen Gentium*, 12; *Perfectae Caritatis*, 12; *Optatam Totius*, 10.

[16] *Gaudium et Spes*, 24. This theme is further developed by John Paul II in his General Audience of February 6, 1980. Cf. *TOTB*, 71-72.

ness, allowing personal pleasure to over-ride the needs of others. A truer perspective means human persons must take into account not only their own legitimate needs but also relationships with other persons, including the Triune God.

Mary's Body

The physical body of the Blessed Mother is a linchpin in Catholic thought, most especially from the dogmatic teaching that she conceived Jesus by the power of the Holy Spirit and not through a conjugal act with her husband St. Joseph.[17] It is part of Catholic Tradition that Mary bore her Son without losing her bodily integrity (virginity), and this implies that Jesus' birth was in some ways natural and in other ways miraculous.[18]

In addition, the Church teaches that after the birth of Jesus Mary remained a virgin in her marriage to Joseph, after Joseph's death, and until she departed from this world. Mary's departure from this world was also a bodily event since her body was taken up together with her soul into heaven as a reward for her virginal life.

To appreciate the consequences of Mary's "fullness of grace," one needs only to turn to the *Catechism of the Catholic Church* and its presentation on original sin:

> The harmony in which they [Adam and Eve] had found themselves, thanks to original justice, is now destroyed: the control of the soul's spiritual faculties over the body is shattered; the union of man and woman becomes subject to tensions, their relations henceforth marked by lust and domination. Harmony with creation is broken: visible creation has become alien and hostile to man. Because of man, creation is now subject to its bondage to decay. Finally, the consequence explicitly foretold for this disobedience will come true: man will return to the ground, for out of it he was taken. Death makes its entrance into human history.[19]

> The doctrine of original sin, closely connected with that of redemption by Christ, provides lucid discernment of man's situa-

---

[17] Cf. *CCC*, 496-507, 510, 966.
[18] Cf. Arthur B. Calkins, "The Virginitas in Partu," *Fellowship of Catholic Scholars Quarterly* 27.1 (Spring, 2004): 9-13.
[19] *CCC*, 400.

tion and activity in the world. By our first parents' sin, the devil has acquired a certain domination over man, even though man remains free. Original sin entails captivity under the power of him who thenceforth had the power of death, that is, the devil. Ignorance of the fact that man has a wounded nature inclined to evil gives rise to serious errors in the areas of education, politics, social action and morals.[20]

Our Lady's Immaculate Conception freed her from the many outcomes of original sin. She was capacitated to receive not only the fullness of grace from the beginning of her existence but, also, its increase in intensity throughout her human life on earth through acts of virtue done under the inspirations of the Holy Spirit.

While St. Thomas Aquinas did not teach Mary's freedom from original sin, he explained beautifully a consequence of her fullness of grace, not possessed by anyone before or since, save her Son:

> Grace overflowed into her body. The Blessed Virgin was full of grace as regards the overflow of grace from her soul into her flesh, or body. For while it is a great thing in the saints to be endowed with grace so that their souls are holy, the soul of the Blessed Virgin was so full of grace that it overflowed into her flesh, fitting it for the conception of God's Son. Thus Hugh of St. Victor says, "the Holy Spirit had so kindled in her heart the fire of divine love that it worked wonders in her flesh, yea, even so that she gave birth to God made man." And St. Luke says, "For the Holy One that shall be born of thee shall be called the Son of God" (Lk.1:35).[21]

This is the only time in his writings where St. Thomas speaks about grace overflowing into the body of anyone, with the possible exception of Christ's body at the transfiguration. The purpose for Mary was to condition her body to receive the sacred body of Jesus Christ into her womb; she had already received the fullness of grace in her soul. Grace in this life is normally understood as a perfection of the soul, being a share in divine life itself that presupposes human nature, which grace elevates and purifies. St. Thomas teaches that grace somehow floods, or overflows, into the very

[20] *Ibid*, 407.
[21] St. Thomas Aquinas, "Commentary on the Hail Mary," in *The Aquinas Catechism*, (Manchester, NH: Sophia Institute Press, 2000), 165-166.

body of Mary because she will be like a tabernacle of the Incarnation, housing the Son of God for a period of months before His birth.

Furthermore, the dogma that Mary was conceived without original sin (*Ineffabilis Deus*) provides further consequences for her body, for example, Mary remained free from all experiences of concupiscence.[22] This means that neither her intellect nor her will were influenced by disordered appetites, that is, her passions themselves were always both reasonable and subservient to the theological virtue of charity. Or, put another way, unreasonable desires from an uncontrolled imagination for sensible goods, which normally pull the senses from what is reasonable, did not exist in her. As a result, her decision-making and choices would never be false about the meaning of human actions or life itself.[23] Likewise, her emotions, whether of love, tenderness, and the like, were always fully under the control of her reason and faith. The virtues of courage and temperance, inspired and formed by divinely infused love, both elevated and formed her emotions, never killing or repressing them.

St. Joseph as Husband of Mary and Virginal Father of Jesus

What about St. Joseph's relationship to the wounds of original sin? To understand this delicate question St. Thomas can be of great help. While he did teach that Mary was sanctified in the womb, this, and other ideas of his, cannot be applied to Mary since they have been rendered false by reason of the defined dogma of Blessed Pius IX (*Ineffabilis Deus*). Yet, what St. Thomas writes about Mary in the *Summa* (III, 27, 3) can more reasonably be applied to St. Joseph since, according to the Tradition, he was neither immaculately conceived, as was his wife, nor given the fullness of grace.

The Common Doctor's idea's on Mary's sanctification in the womb are not found in Sacred Scripture, which says nothing *explicitly* about the Immaculate Conception of Mary or the sanctification of St. Joseph. However, the very idea is suggested by the bib-

---

[22] Cf. *CCC*, 396-409.
[23] Cf. *CCC*, 37.

lical texts concerning Jeremiah and John the Baptist who, Aquinas holds, were given the privilege of being sanctified in their mother's wombs.[24] Given what the Church teaches about St. Joseph, and her devotion to him, it seems reasonable to deduce that St. Joseph was likewise sanctified in the womb as were Jeremiah and John the Baptist, even if not explicitly asserted in Scripture.

The problem investigated in article 3 of question 27, is whether or not Mary experienced first movements of sin, a consequence of original sin (*fomes peccati*, translated as "inflammation of sin" by Thomas Heath, O.P.).[25] Here is the quotation of the last paragraph of Aquinas' answer with my comments between brackets, which apply the ideas of St. Thomas to the person of St. Joseph:

> It would seem better to say that in the sanctification of the womb inflammation of sin was not removed in essence from the Virgin [this is not true according to the solemn definition of Bl. Pius IX] but that it was rendered harmless [all of this is probably true for St. Joseph by reason of fittingness]. Of course this was not achieved by an act of her reason [here St. Thomas means deliberate human acts], as in holy people, since she did not have the use of her reason from the first moment of her existence in her mother's womb [only Christ had that according to St. Thomas], but rather by the abundance of grace given to her in her sanctification [this is probably true of St. Joseph]. And still more perfectly by divine providence keeping her sensuality from all inordinate movements [again, this is probably true for St. Joseph]. But afterwards in the conception of Christ's flesh, where immunity of sin was to shine for the first time, we believe that complete freedom from the inflammation of sin passed over from the child to the mother [this seems to be true for St. Joseph as well].[26]

Another way of looking at St. Joseph's personal holiness and possession of grace is to read another article (art. 4) of that same question in the *Summa*. Here St. Thomas speaks exclusively of Mary using arguments of fittingness, but the theologian can also see the same reasons, though proportionately less, for St. Joseph's grace preserving him from committing sin as well:

[24] See *ST* III, 27, 1 & 6.
[25] See St. Thomas Aquinas, *Summa Theologiae*, Vol. 51, Our Lady, trans. Thomas Heath, O.P. (New York: McGraw-Hill, 1969).
[26] *ST* III, 27, 3.

When God chooses people for some special job He prepares them and endows them to be able to do it, as the Scripture notes, *He is the one who has given us the qualifications to be administrators of God* (2 Cor. 3:6). Now the Blessed Virgin [and I would add St. Joseph] was chosen by God to be His mother [and St. Joseph commanded by "the angel of the Lord" to serve as the father of Jesus]. There can be no doubt, therefore, that God by His grace made her [and St. Joseph] worthy of the office . . . But she [and St. Joseph] would not have been worthy to be the mother of God [and he would not have been worthy as the reputed father] if she [or he] had ever sinned. The first reason is that the parent's honour goes over to the child, as *Proverbs* states, *The children's glory is their father* [St. Joseph is not chosen to be the biological father but to supply all the psychological and personal input of a father]. The second reason is the marvelous intimacy she [and St. Joseph] had with Christ. He took flesh from her [but he also took protection and education from St. Joseph] . . . The third reason is the unique way Christ who is the *Wisdom of God* came to dwell in her. He was present not only in her soul but in her womb as well [He was also present in St. Joseph's arms and affections].[27]

In the next article (art. 5), St. Thomas speaks of Mary's sinlessness. He argues that this effect in her, sinlessness, was due to the closeness she possessed to Christ and, therefore, to the source of all grace. Likewise, by reasoning, the same arguments of fittingness can be applied to St. Joseph:

Now Christ in His Godhead is the authoritative principle of grace and in His humanity is the instrumental principle of grace. We read that *grace and truth have come through Jesus Christ* (Jn. 1:17). But the Blessed Virgin Mary was nearest to Christ in His humanity since He received His human nature from her [and secondarily St. Joseph was nearest to Him as guardian and spiritual father]. Hence it was her due to receive a fuller intensity of grace than others [and, likewise, it was St. Joseph's due to receive a fuller intensity of grace than others, save for Mary].[28]

These explicit thoughts on Mary in the text of Aquinas, and implicit ones that I have brought out and applied to St. Joseph, enable the theologian to see how important the marriage of Mary and Joseph really was. These ideas give a glimpse into how they were able to maintain virginity while, at the same time, be the best of friends.

[27] *ST* III, 27, 4.
[28] *ST* III, 27, 5.

Mary and Her Self-Giving

John Paul II's encyclical *Redemptoris Mater* also brings out a further nuance, offering a deeper understanding of Mary's annunciation. Developing certain thoughts from his Theology of the Body, he will offer very insightful reflections concerning Mary's consent to be the Mother of God at the annunciation:

> Mary consents to God's choice, in order to become through the power of the Holy Spirit the Mother of the Son of God. It can be said that this *consent to motherhood* is above all a *result of her total self-giving to God in virginity.* Mary accepted her election as Mother of the Son of God, guided by spousal love, the love which totally "consecrates" a human being to God. By virtue of this love, Mary wished to be always and in all things "given to God," living in virginity. The words "Behold, I am the handmaid of the Lord" express the fact that from the outset she accepted and understood her own motherhood as a total *gift of self,* a gift of her person to the service of the saving plans of the Most High. And to the very end she lived her entire maternal sharing in the life of Jesus Christ, her Son, in a way that matched her vocation to virginity.[29]

Giving Birth to Jesus and Breast Feeding Her Son as Self-Giving[30]

Birth is an act of the child and of the mother, an interpersonal event of welcoming the newborn in the way of love. In North America normal childbirth has suffered from the domineering of medicine, replacing nature with technology. Birth and reproduction are seen in terms of production. Life and babies are delivered during labor. Sometimes, physicians who are in a hurry administer hormones to speed up powerful contractions so that the baby is pushed along the birth canal faster than the cervix can dilate, a process which requires forceps to extract the baby. This routine intervention has led to the use of anesthesia and, afterwards, to postpartum distress.

In contrast, giving birth is a natural and normal act for a healthy mother and child. It is not an illness to be treated. Birth is an

---

[29] *Redemptoris Mater*, 39.

[30] See William Virtue, *Mother and Infant*, (Rome: University of St. Thomas Aquinas, 1995), especially chapters three and four, which covers these questions in greater depth; See, also, Joseph Cardinal Mindszenty, *The Mother*, trans. Benedict P. Lenz, C.Ss.R. (St. Paul: Radio Reply Press, 1949), especially chapter 14 "About Mother's Milk" pp.114-119.

act of the infant and the mother, assisted by the cooperative art of midwifery or obstetrics when needed. Birth has its own onset and duration. Thus, there is a great need for privacy so that the woman may feel unobserved and free to relax so that hormonal changes will proceed normally.

When the baby is born, he is in a quiet alert state; there is also usually a cry of joy from the mother. Through the first eye-to-eye encounter of mother and child, the expressive power of the human face provides welcoming affirmation which the child receives anew through breast feeding. Breastfeeding is the norm that ensures good mothering and optimum development of the child and hence a serious moral obligation of mothers. This goes against the thought of radical feminists who claim that it is demeaning to have a mother stay at home with child.

The dependency of infants, children, and men upon women is most evident: a basic human need for physical, emotional and interpersonal love. Feeding and loving always have been associated with mothers and women. Being nourished physically and emotionally always strengthens the human person. This communion of mother and child at the breast fosters a bond that forms the child's capacity for love and moral action. Again, this is the norm of nature, to ensure good mothering and optimum development of the child. Remembering that giving birth, with the subsequent act of breastfeeding, was both a supernatural and natural act requiring Mary's cooperation, it follows that Mary's fulfillment of this role brought her many graces because her vocation was to foster maternal-infant communication and communion.

Breastfeeding which nurtures the personality, as well as the body, is the natural, normative way of mothering the infant. Motherhood, like birth, is difficult, but with the help of natural inclinations, learned skills, and God's grace, a woman can give herself to her infants needs. The gift of nursing an infant is a maternal sign of the donative meaning of the body (phrase of John Paul II) in the communion of persons.

Mother's milk is superior milk, and nursing yields emotional and spiritual benefits which allow the newborn and mother to form an unbreakable bond. Unlike other mammals, a face-to-face relationship occurs during human nursing; the baby can see about nine inches, just enough to see his mother's face. Even after half an hour, mothers can identify their own infant by smell alone. And after two days, infants can distinguish the fragrance of their own mother's breast.[31] These experiences would have occurred between Mary and her Son.

The first suckling is a milk called colostrums, which has enormous immunological properties for developing the proper intestinal microbial flora, crucial for the baby's digestive adaptability. When this milk declines after a week, then a different kind of milking takes place, releasing two hormones in the mother called oxytocin (increasing maternal tenderness for the infant) and prolactin (regulating the "supply and demand" for the baby's daily differing needs). One property of foremilk is to quench the baby's thirst. There is also hindmilk which is richer. Different milks prevent excessive weight gain in the baby. These naturally regulated and different kinds of milk are necessary not only for the baby but also for an ovulation in the mother. A mother's milk tastes sweet and produces a chemical called casmorphin, a chemical resulting in the bliss seen in a suckling infant. Finally, mother's milk also has an anti-diarrhea benefit that prevents dehydration of infants when ill.[32] It is easy to understand why artists have portrayed Mary suckling her infant, and theologians have seen this as a metaphor for the Church feeding her members.

Spousal Meaning of the Body in Relationship to St. Joseph and Mary

To appreciate more fully John Paul II's insight into the spousal meaning of the body, there is need to turn to a little known doc-

---

[31] Cf. Desmond Morris, *Babywatching*, (New York: Crown Books, 1992); Also, Marshal Klaus and John Kennel, *Parent-Infant Bonding*, (St. Louis: Mosby Publ., 1982).

[32] St. Albert the Great made the point that a mother's milk matches the food the fetus received in the womb. See *Quaestiones Super De Animalibus*, Bk. XVIII, Q. 8.

ument written in 1989 on St. Joseph called *Redemptoris Custos*. After articulating his Theology of the Body earlier in his pontificate, several years later, John Paul II used the key concepts of virginity and marriage in discussing both Mary and St. Joseph. He shows how virginity and marriage in their lives produced the great works of God, specifically the incarnation and redemption.

The case of the relationship between Mary and St. Joseph is unique. As John Paul II teaches concerning St. Joseph's vocation:

> "Joseph did as the angel of the Lord commanded him; he took his wife" into his home (Mt. 1:24): what was conceived in Mary was "of the Holy Spirit." From expressions such as these are we not to suppose that his *love as a man was also given new birth by the Holy Spirit?* Are we not to think that the love of God which has been poured forth into the human heart through the Holy Spirit (cf. Rm. 5:5) molds every human love to perfection? This love of God also molds - in a completely unique way - the love of husband and wife, deepening within it everything of human worth and beauty, everything that bespeaks an exclusive gift of self, a covenant between persons, and an authentic communion according to the model of the Blessed Trinity.[33]

Here we see how clearly John Paul II incorporates into his thought the Thomistic concept that grace does not destroy nature but elevates it. The completely chaste human love of St. Joseph and Mary is taken up into a mutual gift of self. John Paul II continues:

> "Joseph . . . took his wife; *but he knew her not*, until she had borne a son" (Mt. 1:24-25). These words indicate *another kind of closeness in marriage.* The deep spiritual closeness arising from marital union and the interpersonal contact between man and woman have their definitive origin in the Spirit, the Giver of Life (cf. Jn. 6:63). *Joseph, in obedience to the Spirit, found in the Spirit the source of love,* the conjugal love which he experienced as as man. And this love proved to be greater than this "just man" could ever have expected within the limits of his human heart.[34]

---

[33] *Redemptoris Custos*, 19.
[34] *Ibid.*

Once again, John Paul II shows what spiritual love can do under the power of grace. Here conjugal love is not denied St. Joseph, even though he is called to renounce holy conjugal acts in order to preserve the most holy virginity of Mary. Due to the grace of the Holy Spirit, this commitment does not eviscerate his conjugal feelings for his wife but, rather, elevates and purifies them.

Spiritual Paternity, an Outcome of Celibate Love

The graces given to St. Joseph also shape the paternal love for "his" Son, which he was commanded to take by the angel of the Lord (cf. Mt. 1:22):

> Since it is inconceivable that such a sublime task would not be matched by the necessary qualities to adequately fulfill it, we must recognize that Joseph showed Jesus by a special gift from heaven, all the natural love, all the affectionate solicitude that a father's heart can know. Besides fatherly authority over Jesus, God also gave Joseph a share in the corresponding love, the love that has its origin in the Father "from whom every family in heaven and on earth is named" (Eph. 3:15).[35]

Likewise, what is true for St. Joseph by logical derivation is also true for Mary since she is both Virgin and Mother. Both Mary and St. Joseph's virginity was spousal and maternal/paternal, respectively.[36] This is the reason why the relationship between Mary and St. Joseph is so unique and why John Paul II says it transcends all states of life.[37] With this in mind, we are now in a position to understand John Paul II's thought in a deeper way:

> The grace of the hypostatic union is connected precisely with this absolute fullness of supernatural fruitfulness, fruitfulness in the Holy Spirit, participated by a human creature, Mary, in the order of continence for the kingdom of heaven. Mary's divine maternity is also, in a certain sense, a superabundant revelation of that fruitfulness in the Holy Spirit to which man submits his spirit, when he freely chooses continence in the body, namely, continence for the kingdom of heaven.[38]

---

[35] *Ibid.*, 8.
[36] See *TOTB*, 268-269.
[37] See *Redemptoris Custos*, 30. Actually, John Paul II states this of St. Joseph, but by inference, it can also be applied to the Blessed Virgin Mary.
[38] *TOTB*, 269.

St. Thomas and the Passions[39]

Another important dimension of John Paul II's teaching concerning the Theology of the Body is again supplied by St. Thomas Aquinas.[40] This concerns the theology of the passions (the emotions, which in human persons are bodily/spiritual phenomena). So, in order to understand the emotional dimension of Mary's virginity and her marriage to St. Joseph, and her role in the redemption of the world, it is necessary to briefly review the core of St. Thomas' thought on the passions and of the Church's official teaching. In short, without passion, Mary's virginity and marriage to St. Joseph would seem to make of her (and St. Joseph) marionettes of God instead of true and authentically free examples of human persons.

The Common Doctor is the first theologian to systematically organize a teaching about the human emotions. He teaches that they are disposed to be guided by reason.[41] Aristotle's *Rhetoric* is the main, if not the only, pre-Christian work to treat the emotions in a positive manner.[42] St. Thomas, following Aristotle, calls them "passions," which have many varying manifestations. In modern parlance, they are referred to as emotions, or moods, and they have many variations. St. Thomas gives us a more generic understanding of them, requiring a deeper reflection due to his being so subtle and detailed. In Catholic thought, the emotions are essential to human dignity, which is a composite of body and soul. They are bodily responses either without forethought (such as pain generating sorrow, experienced from physical infirmities) or as an overflow on the body of acts of deliberation based on reason and faith, or a lack thereof.[43]

---

[39] This section is based largely upon "The Passions," in Albert Plé, *Man and His Happiness*, (Chicago: Fides Publishers Association, 1957), 141-175. Cf. Peter A. Kwasniewski, "Are Passions Good?" *The Catholic Faith* 6.5 (September-October, 2000): 12-17.

[40] See *ST* I-II 22-48.

[41] See *ST* I-II, 17, 7.

[42] See Servais Pinckaers, "Les passions et la morale," *Revue des sciences philosophiques et theologiques* 74 (1990), 379; cf. Simo Knuuttila, *Emotions in Ancient and Medieval Philosophy* (Oxford : Oxford University Press, 2004), 239.

[43] For example, there is a spiritual delight for someone suffering when speaking with a consoling friend. This consolation arrives because the sufferer feels loved by a friend who visits him. It is for this reason, and so many other reasons, that

Since human nature is bodily, it necessarily shares in the reality of the animal kingdom, which is why the definition of man is "rational animal." St. Thomas goes on to teach that man has a sensible appetite composed of two links or different functions of reacting, as all animals do. The concupiscible function of the appetite reacts to sensible good, or suffers sensible evils in a general way. The irascible, or aggressive function, of the appetite tends to energetically pursue difficult goods or repel/endure difficult evils. The irascible appetite is the defender against perceived enemies to self, and the concupiscible appetite is the preserver of life.

Cicero, and especially the Stoics, taught that every passion was bad. The Thomistic conception of reason intervening in passion, far from killing all of the passions, gives them a human quality called virtue, specifically, the cardinal virtues of temperance and courage. These in turn are necessary for prudence and justice to become rooted in the intellect and will, otherwise unreasonable emotion rules to the detriment of respecting other's rights, fulfilling one's own responsibilities, and taking the time to think through decisions by reflecting upon circumstances.

To briefly summarize, sometimes in Scripture the passions are portrayed as evil, sometimes they are portrayed as good. For example, we find in the Book of James the following negative idea: "Everyone who is tempted is attracted and seduced by his own wrong desire. Then the desire conceives and give birth to sin, and when it is fully grown, it too has a child, and the child is death" (James 1: 14-15). Yet, we also read that Jesus himself sighs with sadness (Mk. 8:12), experiences anxiety (Lk. 19:41), groans in sorrow (Jn. 11:33), cries (Mk. 15:37), becomes angry (Mk. 3:5; Mt. 21:12-13), feels sadness over others' misfortunes (Mt. 7:36; Mk. 1:41; Lk. 7:13), feels tenderness (Mk. 10:16; Lk. 14:34), and experiences the desire for food (Lk. 4:2).

St. Thomas will say, oddly at first, that a human being in heaven without a body is not quite fully happy since he is not himself, simply existing as a separated soul, the soul being the form of the body. See *ST* I, 76. Furthermore, St. Thomas notes the following: "Now since the soul is part of the human body, it is not the entire human being, and my soul is not I. So, even if the soul reached salvation, in another life, neither I nor any human being would thereby do so." See *Super primam epistolam ad Corinthios*, lectura, commenting on 15:19, as quoted in Germain Grisez, *Living a Christian Life*, Chapter 8, Question 2, footnote 8.

The Church's Teaching on the Passions

It is clear that the *Catechism of the Catholic Church,* which in this matter can be thought of as a summary of St. Thomas' teaching, offers a correct understanding of the passions:

> In themselves passions are neither good nor evil. They are morally qualified only to the extent that they effectively engage reason and will. Passions are said to be voluntary, "either because they are commanded by the will or because the will does not place obstacles in their way" [*ST* I-II, 24, 1]. It belongs to the perfection of the moral or human good that the passions be governed by reason.[44]

> Strong feelings are not decisive for the morality or the holiness of persons; they are simply the inexhaustible reservoir of images and affections in which the moral life is expressed. Passions are morally good when they contribute to a good action, evil in the opposite case. The upright will orders the movements of the senses it appropriates to the good and to beatitude; an evil will succumbs to disordered passions and exacerbates them. Emotions and feelings can be taken up into the *virtues* or perverted by the *vices.*[45]

> In the Christian life, the Holy Spirit Himself accomplishes His work by mobilizing the whole being, with all its sorrows, fears and sadness, as is visible in the Lord's agony and passion. In Christ human feelings are able to reach their consummation in charity and divine beatitude.[46]

Since the fall, some emotional experiences tend to pull the human person away from moral norms, and when left unchecked, they become enslaving vices, even though, as St. Thomas observes, they are disposed to be led by reason. Unfortunately, we can also find a mistaken ascetical theology in some thinkers throughout history who have called for *apatheia,* or the complete suppression of desire.

Looking at Some Emotions of Mary through the Eyes of St. Thomas

Due to constraints of space, this section will try to show how the analysis of several particular emotions can help the thinker delve more deeply into the nature of Mary's relationships. The

---

[44] *CCC*, 1767.

[45] *Ibid.,* 1768.

[46] *Ibid.,* 1769.

first emotion to look at is love, the passion that inclines us to the good. Here Aquinas shows his readers how love for friends is distinct from love of things:

> The two kinds of love—love-of-desire and love-of-friendship—will therefore arise from two different ways of considering the unity between the lover and the object loved. When one has love-of-desire, for a thing, one sees it as contributing in some-way to one's well being. When one has love-of-friendship for a person, one wants good things for him as one does for one-self; one therefore looks on him as another self, wishing him well in the same way as one does oneself. That is why a friend is described as an other self (*Ethic. ix. 4*), and Augustine says (*Confess. iv. 6*), *Someone well called his friend, 'half of my soul'*.[47]

Since Mary was married to St. Joseph, their love for each other must have been very deep, wanting the best for one another. This love requires, necessitates, that when either would be in danger, the other would also feel the danger and even oppose it:

> Love of friendship seeks the friend's good: wherefore, when it is intense, it causes a man to be moved against everything that opposed the friend's good. In this respect, a man is said to be zealous on behalf of his friends when he makes a point of repelling whatever may be said or done against the friend's good. In this way, too, a man is said to be zealous on God's behalf, when he endeavors to the best of his means to repel whatever is contrary to the honor or will of God.[48]

Lest anyone thinks that being fully chaste means lacking in pleasure, St. Thomas, relying on both observation and common sense, shows that one outcome of doing good to others is delight and pleasure:

> Take the sources of altruistic action: this may be such as to make it pleasurable on three scores. First, there is the fact of being in a position to confer benefits: on this count doing good to another may give pleasure by making one more vividly aware of possessing so much oneself that one can share it with others. This is why a man takes pleasure in his children, or in the works he produces: it is his own fullness that they are sharing. A second cause may be

---

[47] *ST* I-II, 28, 1.
[48] *ST* I-II, 28, 4.

a habitual inclination: it can become second nature to do good to others: and this makes it a pleasure for the open-handed man to make gifts. A third source is one's motive: love on one person may move one to help another. It is a pleasure to suffer or do things for a friend, because love is the main cause of pleasure.[49]

So, all the acts of Mary done in her family would produce a very deep delight since she possesses such a deep love for both her Son and her husband. Furthermore, since Mary is full of grace, she possesses an acute ability to reason and ponder the truth of life and her own experiences as a woman/mother/wife in synthesis, grasping the unity of her life. This also produces great pleasure:

> Now, wondering means 'wanting to know something': it is aroused when a man sees an effect and does not know its cause, or when he does not know or cannot understand how this cause could have that effect. Wondering therefore can cause him pleasure when it carries with it a real prospect of finding out what he wants to know. This is why anything that rouses wonder can give pleasure; for instance, rare things, and all representations, (such as paintings or sculptures), even of things which themselves give no pleasure. For the mind takes pleasure in comparing the representation with the original. As Aristotle says, since comparing one thing with another is the distinctive and proper activity of reason. For this reason too, as Aristotle says (*Poet. iv.*), *Escaping great peril gives us the greater pleasure by arousing wonderment.*[50]

With all the above in mind, it would not be far afield to see in the daily life of the Holy Family a sense of friendliness, affability and politeness. As St. Thomas says of this small virtue:

> Because by nature man is a social being, in common decency he owes plain truth to others, since without this human society could not survive. But even as men cannot live together without truthfulness, neither can they without agreeableness, since, as Aristotle remarks (*Ethic. viii*), *No one can put up with the gloomy or disagreeable man all day long.* Thus a person is bound by a certain natural debt in decency to get along amicably with the other, except when for good cause there is need to be purposefully harsh.[51]

---

[49] *ST* I-II, 32, 6.

[50] *ST* I-II, 32, 8.

[51] *ST* II-II, 114, 2 ad 1.

While it is not clear from Sacred Scripture that Mary actually wept at the foot of the cross, reason suggests that seeing her Son in such a wretched condition and dying a horrible death, she most likely shed maternal tears. That someone cries, as St. Thomas points out, is a very human response to such a situation:

> Weeping and sobbing assuage sorrow, for two reasons. Hurtful things hurt still more if they are pent up within us, for the soul is then more concentrated upon them; but if they are released, the soul's energies are turned to things outside itself, and interior pain is thus lessened. This is why sorrow is assuaged by outwardly expressing it in tears or sobs or even words. Second, there is always pleasure in activity appropriate to one's state at the moment; weeping and lamentation are appropriate to one in pain and sorrow; therefore there is some pleasure in them. Now we have seen that all pleasure gives some relief to sorrow or pain; so sorrow will be assuaged by sobbing and lamentation.[52]

Moreover, it would be natural for Mary in the two most sorrowful events of her life, namely, the death of her husband, and the passion of her Son, to be present to them during their agony in order to bring them some consolation:

> It is natural in sorrow, to be consoled if a friend shares our grief. Aristotle suggests two reasons (*Ethic. ix*). First, sorrow weighs one down; it is a load which of course, one tries to lighten. When therefore a person sees others joining him in sorrow, it feels as if they are helping him carry the load, trying to lessen its weight on him; so the burden weighs on him less heavily, just as in the case of carrying physical weights. The second reason is a better one. When a person's friends share in his sorrow, he sees that they love him: and this fact itself is a source of pleasure . . . But we have also seen that all pleasure assuages sorrow. It follows, therefore, that sorrow is assuaged by a friend's sharing it.[53]

Mary and St. Joseph's Love

Now we are in a better position to understand certain key texts of John Paul II when he writes about Joseph and Mary's virginal love for each other and their child, Mary's child in the biological order, and Joseph's by choice and the command of God. But first we must now look at another work of John Paul II,

---

[52] *ST* I-II, 38, 2.
[53] *ST* I-II, 38, 3.

Mulieris Dignitatem, which was written in 1988 and concerns the feminine dimension of the human person. Here he further articulates the Theology of the Body in relation to womanhood:

> We must now focus our meditation on virginity and motherhood as two particular dimensions of the fulfillment of the female personality. In light of the Gospel, they acquire their full meaning and value in Mary, who as a Virgin became the Mother of the Son of God. These *two dimensions of the female vocation* were united in her in an exceptional manner, in such a way that one did not exclude the other but wonderfully complemented it.[54]

To be a mother (or a father) can be connected with virginity or celibacy. As one becomes more and more joined to Christ in virginity or celibacy, so a different kind of parenting takes place, not in the one flesh union of marriage but in the spirit, and this because one's "readiness [to love] is open *to all people, who are embraced by the love of Christ the Spouse*."[55] And just as Mary is "virgin-mother-spouse," so is the Church.[56] Logically, we can also speak of St. Joseph being a perfectly "chaste-father-spouse" as well.

Graced for Mission

While articulated in a different context, the following insight of St. Thomas pertains primarily to Mary and secondarily to St. Joseph:

> No matter what category we mention, the nearer a thing comes to its principle the more it shares its effect. Hence Dionysius can say (*Coel. Hier. iv*) that the angels have a greater share than man in the divine goodness since they are nearer to God. Now Christ in his Godhead is the authoritative principle of grace and in His humanity is the instrumental principle of grace. We read that *grace and truth have come through Jesus Christ* (Jn. 1:17). But the Blessed Virgin Mary was nearest to Christ in His humanity since He received His human nature from her. Hence it was her due to receive a fuller intensity of grace than others.[57]

---

[54] *Mulieris Dignitatem,* 17.

[55] *Ibid.*, 21. Also, John Paul II notes that a "man's consecration in priestly celibacy or in the religious state is to be understood analogously" to a woman's virginal consecration. See *Mulieris Dignitatem*, 20.

[56] See *Mulieris Dignitatem*, 22.

[57] *ST* I-II, 27, 5.

While both Mary and St. Joseph were given exceptional graces, this did not dispense them from trials against faith, hope and charity. During the flight into Egypt, hope was tried to a high degree since both had to trust in the providence of God when it seemed hopeless. Also, Mary had to have great divine love in the face of all the insults hurled at her Son from the crowds during her Son's passion and death. She had to make her Son's prayer of divine love her own, "Father, forgive them for they know not what they do" (Lk. 23:34).

Mary was intrinsically necessary for the hypostatic union to occur since it was in her very flesh, or, rather, from her genetic make-up, that Christ was formed—she gave half of the human genome to her Son while the Holy Spirit created the other half. Hence, she was given a fullness of grace beyond human imagining. Since St. Joseph was extrinsically necessary for the hypostatic union by the choice of God, to protect the legitimacy and honor of the Son of God as well as safeguard Mary from any accusation of infidelity, he, too, needed exceptional graces.[58]

Since both were filled with such intensity of grace, being married to each other and having mutual affection, it follows that they were channels of grace to one another. Aquinas makes the point that the more chaste one becomes the more one is able to go into the depths of another's soul through the virtue of mercy.[59]

Virginal or chaste love enables one to love the other predominantly for the sake of the other rather than for one's own personal usefulness or pleasure. Virginal love does not mean denial of human affection for an other but increases caring, tenderness and the other "soft" feelings and virtues. This is something sinners cannot understand or fathom because there is a tendency to project one's own lack of virtue on to others and thereby fail to understand how the great virtue of chastity does not kill feeling; on the contrary, it keeps the physical pleasures of the body in check.

In some traditions, virginal love (celibate-chaste love, too) meant aloofness, distance and coldness. As a result, St. Joseph was

---

[58] See Boniface Llamera, O.P., *Saint Joseph* (St. Louis, MO: Herder & Herder, 1962), esp. Ch.3: "St. Joseph and the Hypostatic Order."

[59] See Albert Plé, O.P., *Chastity and the Affective Life* (New York: Herder & Herder, 1966).

portrayed in many works of art and literature as being a much older man, like a grandfather to Mary, kept in the background. This view made the marriage merely an arrangement, not a friendship. John Paul II's teaching in *Redemptoris Custos,* however, presents the understanding that in their chaste love for one another Mary and St. Joseph were close friends, sharing the intimacy of the heart.

Spiritual Friendship among the Saints[60]

In a much neglected work by Paul Conner, O.P. titled *Celibate Love* we discover how certain pairs of celibates of the opposite sex developed deep friendship with each other. By a process of reasoning upon this data, one can understand how Mary and St. Joseph's friendship grew and developed. From studying the excerpts of letters between two Blesseds, Jordan (the second Master of the Order of Preachers) and Diana (a Dominican cloistered nun in Bologna), I have come to the following conclusions about their relationship:[61]

1. They enjoyed each other's company, which in turn helped both of them in their spiritual life.
2. Both possessed a holy anxiety about each other's welfare. They identified with each other.
3. They were on each other's mind from time to time.
4. Their relationship was rooted in God.
5. They felt sorrow when separated from one another.

Even though these two Blesseds of the Dominican Order were neither immaculately conceived nor sanctified in the womb, sanctifying grace took such a hold on them through their cooperation in grace that they became, in part, holy through their relationship with one another, primarily through letters, secondarily through occasional visits. So, by deduction, one can easily conclude that Mary and St. Joseph, being perfectly human, Mary immaculately conceived and St. Joseph probably sanctified in the womb, cared for one another and enjoyed each other's company. Moreover, since both were more open to God's grace and providence, they were more open to the Spirit such that they could more easily communi-

---

[60] Concerning this section, see my article "Mary and Joseph: Their Love for Each Other," *Homiletic & Pastoral Review* (October, 1981): 9-17.

[61] See Paul Conner, O.P., *Celibate Love.* (Huntington, IN: Our Sunday Visitor, 1979), 56-67.

cate with one another, which can become a difficulty when sin predominates in a marriage or in any other relationship.

Paul Conner also treats of the friendship between St. Catherine of Siena and Bartolomeo de Dominici.[62] What is interesting here is that when Bartolomeo was in St. Catherine's presence, his sexual feelings were quieted and both had a deep affection for one another. On a much higher level, such a phenomenon must have occurred between Mary and St. Joseph. When individuals are attracted to one another by reason of affinities and outlook, good affections naturally arise, a sense of tenderness and even enthusiasm. As normally happens with young and old who are seeking marriage, their affection also looks to the desire for the conjugal act, a part of possessive love that travels along with the desire to marry and have children. However, if St. Catherine, a beautiful young woman, could so quiet down such legitimate feelings in a man, much more so could Mary's presence do the same for Joseph.[63]

In addition, Conner analyzes St. Teresa of Avila's ideas of holy friendship.[64] St. Teresa is very helpful for understanding Mary and St. Joseph's love for each other since marriage is ultimately meant to be a friendship as well:

> These benefits of comfort and intercession, mutual enlightenment and restraint from sin result from truly spiritual friendship based on unselfish love. And Teresa is not here speaking of dispassionate love. She distinguishes three kinds of affection. "Illicit affections" she excludes calling them a "very hell," and finding no need to discuss them further. The second type are "lawful affections" which we have naturally for those we love—"relatives and friends." These

---

[62] *Ibid.*, 67-75.

[63] Interestingly, Fulton Sheen, commenting on why he believes St. Joseph was a young man, notes the following concerning Mary's ability to elevate St. Joseph's virility: "A woman's love always determines the way a man loves: she is the silent educator of his virile powers. Since Mary is what might be called a 'virginizer' of young men as well as women, and the greatest inspiration of Christian purity, should she not logically have begun by inspiring and virginizing the first youth whom she had probably ever met—Joseph, the Just? It was not by diminishing his power to love but by elevating it that she would have her first conquest, and in her own spouse, the man who was a man, and not a mere senile watchman!" See Fulton J. Sheen, *The World's First Love*, (San Francisco: Ignatius Press, 1996), 93.

[64] See *Celibate Love*, 75-87.

earthly affections make us either joyous or sad over a natural human good or evil that has come to our loved ones. "If their heads ache, we are unable to sit still under it and so on." "Spiritual affection," however, looks beyond this physical reaction of nature. We "reflect whether our friend's trials are not good" for him, whether he is bearing them with patience, so becoming richer in virtue and merit. We ask this patience of God, and if we see it in our friend, his trials give us "no distress"; rather, "we are gladdened and consoled."[65]

It is reasonable to presume that, like St. Teresa and her friendships, there existed between Mary and St. Joseph an even deeper spiritual friendship. Since Mary and St. Joseph were in no way self-centered or selfish, it would seem that their friendship was elevated to a very high level and transformed by the fire of charity, surpassing ordinary virtue.

Lastly, Conner analyzes the holy friendship that existed between St. Jane de Chantal and St. Francis de Sales.[66] In a letter to St. Jane, St. Francis had this to say about her:

Madame, God forces me to speak to you in confidence: His goodness and grace have always granted that whenever I am celebrating Holy Mass, I have no distracting thoughts; but for some time you have always come to my mind, *not to distract me, but to attach me more to God.*[67]

From this citation and many others, I conclude that since St. Francis' thoughts for St. Jane attach him more to God, the bond of love between them created more spiritual freedom to give himself to God and the affection he possessed for her was a detached and reasonable one.

Given this possibility with human nature, when empowered by a high degree of grace, which all the above Blesseds and Saints possessed, it is once again reasonable to assume such would be the case to an even higher degree between Mary and St. Joseph, not only in their prayers but also any other activities which they might engage in from work to play. Their affectionate bonds for each other, flowing from the marriage tie, were neither selfish nor pos-

---

[65] *Ibid.*, 76.

[66] *Ibid.*, 87-94.

[67] *Ibid.*, 89.

sessive, but, rather, gave them a deeper intimacy toward God. Since Mary was immaculately conceived and St. Joseph probably sanctified in the womb, they possessed the greatest possible intimacy that two friends could have on earth.

Conclusion

In this study, I have tried to show the meaning of John Paul II's thought concerning the theology of the body as provided in a statement in his Apostolic Letter *Mulieris Dignitatem:*

> These *two dimensions of the female vocation* [virgin and mother] were united in her [Mary] in an exceptional manner . . . *Virginity and motherhood coexist in her:* they do not mutually exclude each other or place limits on each other . . . [they] explain and complete each other.[68]

Virginity and motherhood are coordinated in Mary to a very high degree, beyond our ability to understand. Likewise, her marriage is part of her virginal and maternal commitment.

Mary's commitment to God through virginity extended itself in her commitment to her Son and her husband. Her holiness, beyond imagining, does not simply come from heaven but was also earned by fidelity to her state in life as virgin-wife-mother. She is a model for everyone, male and female, because divine love, in the final analysis, is the measure by which God will judge everyone.

Given what Mary is and has done for us, it is remarkable that before much theological work was done, Origen had the brilliance to note the following:

> The Gospel's are the first fruits of all Scripture and the Gospel of John is the first of the Gospels: no one can grasp its meaning without having leaned his head on Jesus' breast and having received Mary as Mother from Jesus.[69]

---

[68] *Mulieris Dignitatem*, 17.

[69] Origen, Commentary on St. John's Gospel I, 6 in *PG* 14, 31 as quoted in Paul Haffner, *The Mystery of Mary*, (England: Gracewing, 2004), 64.

THE VIRGIN MARY AND THE CULTURE OF LIFE

Donald DeMarco, Ph.D

The Gospel of Life

When *The Gospel of Life* (*Evangelium Vitae*) was released in 1995, John Paul's repeated references to the emergence of a "Culture of Death," received a great deal of attention. The Media, in particular, given its propensity for regarding "bad news" as "good news," assigned the "Culture of Death" a prominence that all but overshadowed the Holy Father's deeper and more important references to developing a "Culture of Life." It is not enough, said the Pope, to refrain from abortion, euthanasia, and other "crimes against life." We must work together in various spheres—including the political sphere[1]—as witnesses to the sanctity of life. "To be actively pro-life is to contribute to the *renewal of* society through the promotion of the common good."[2]

The Media, as is well known, is fond of presenting the Church as always being *against* something, and therefore casting her in a negative light. Yet, the main theme of *The Gospel of Life*, as is sufficiently evident in its title, is not "The Culture of Death," but "The Gospel of Life." Accordingly, John Paul reminds us, on the encyclical's very first page, of the redemptive implications contained in Jesus' words: "I came that they may have life, and have it abundantly" (Jn. 10:10).

---

[1] John Paul II, *The Gospel of Life* (Sherbrooke, QC: Médiaspaul, 1995), §101, 181: "There can be no *true democracy* without a recognition of every person's dignity and without respect for his or her rights. Nor can there be *true peace* unless *life is defended and promoted.*"

[2] *Ibid.*, 180.

The essential message of *The Gospel of Life*, because of its broad, humanitarian basis, is presented to all citizens of the world. And the Pope is unsparing of the *"tyrant State*, which arrogates to itself the right to dispose of the life of the weakest and most defenseless members, from the unborn child to the elderly."[3] The State, however, does not take kindly to such stinging criticism. Nor do certain critics of the left who believe the Pope to be more tyrannical than any State that consigns its children in the womb and its elderly to premature death. Hans Küng, for example, stated at a press conference that *The Gospel of Life* demonstrated the Holy Father's "dogmatic coldness and unrelenting rigorism," and that "the voice in the document is not that of a good shepherd but of a spiritual dictator."[4] Nonetheless, as political philosopher Robert P. George of Princeton University states: "People of good will—of whatever religious faith—who are prepared to consider seriously the Pope's teaching in *Evangelium Vitae* cannot now avoid asking themselves, soberly and unblinkingly, whether our regime is becoming the democratic 'tyrant state' about which he warns."[5]

Newsweek's religion editor, Kenneth Woodward, was in greater agreement with Professor George in his evaluation of the document than he was with Father Küng. He praised *The Gospel of Life* as "the clearest, most impassioned and most commanding encyclical" of John Paul II's pontificate, one that would be the Pontiff's "signature statement" in history.[6]

The Theology of the Body

Delivering the Church's "Culture of Life" message so that it is received in an undiluted and undistorted manner to a skeptical and cynical society is problematic. One way, which has always been close to the Church's heart as well as to the hearts of her people, is by means of an appeal to the dignity and value of motherhood, especially through the woman who embodies its perfection, Mary. For Mary, as Coventry Patmore reminds, in his simple but eloquent

---

[3] *Ibid.*, §20, 36.

[4] Quoted in *The Tablet*, April 8, 1996, 467.

[5] Robert P. George, *The Clash of Orthodoxies* (Wilmington, DE: ISI Books, 2001), 135.

[6] Cited in *ibid.*

phrase, is "Our only Saviour from an abstract Christ."[7] Christ is bodily because He was conceived, carried to term, and given birth through a woman's body. And even after birth, she continued to be a mother in all its bodily significance, for, as St. Augustine has pointed out, "she gave milk to our Bread."[8] Motherhood has a moral immediacy and palpable reality that people of good will are not likely to turn aside. Motherhood is a compelling moral witness to the primacy of loving unselfishness.

The great American novelist, Nathaniel Hawthorne, though not formally a Catholic, reflected this bodily significance of Mary's motherhood when he wrote: "I have always envied the Catholics that sweet, sacred Virgin Mother who stands between them and the Deity, intercepting somewhat His awful splendor, but permitting His love to stream on the worshipper more intelligibly to human comprehension through the medium of a woman's tenderness."[9]

Mary's *fiat*, her consent to be the Mother of God, embraces her bodily as well as spiritual realities. Indeed, bodily and spiritual realities that converge and are unified in her virgin motherhood. Moreover, "this mother's body," as Hans Urs von Balthasar writes, "which was already (in the overshadowing of the spirit) a bride's body, is proleptically the church body which and for which everything will be formed unto Christ, which will later be called church."[10] Mary's bodily motherhood prefigures the body of the Church. At the same time, she exercises a "spiritual motherhood with regard to all people."[11]

Throughout the 130 presentations that constitute John Paul II's Theology of the Body, we find an unremitting emphasis on the existential fact that men and women have different bodies and that the body, with its masculine/feminine polarity, is not a mere

---

[7] Coventry Patmore, "The Child's Purchase" in *The Poems of Coventry Patmore.* ed. Frederick Page. (London: Oxford University Press, 1949), 442.

[8] St. Aurelius Augustinus, *Sermons*, 184.

[9] Cited in Fulton J. Sheen *The World's First Love* (Garden City, NY: Doubleday, 1961), 197.

[10] Hans Urs von Balthasar, "Mary—Exemplar of the Church," trans. R. J. Daly and F. Lawrence (New York, NY: Crossroad, 1982), 219.

[11] John Paul II, *U.S.A.—Message of Justice, Peace and Love (Boston, MA: Daughter of St. Paul, 1979)*, 242.

"attribute" of the person, but an integral feature of his whole being. The body is something that a human being *is*.[12]

Denigration of the Body

This bodily notion of the human person needs to be reiterated again and again in the contemporary world since its trivialization and even denial is an important ingredient in the formation of the Culture of Death. A woman's body, according to leading secular feminists, is either a mere "instrument" or something of little or no ontological significance. Thus, Regula Giuliani, following the thought of Simone de Beauvoir, views men's and women's bodies as transitional: "The body has become . . . an inert object imprisoned by material, a mere instrument and tool that serves to realize mental desires more (with a male body) or less (with a female body) adequately."[13] Shulamith Firestone goes further, arguing that we must eradicate the natural basis for the male-female distinction. In her work, *The Dialectic of Sex*, which she dedicated to Simone de Beauvoir, Firestone writes: "Humanity has begun to outgrow nature: we can no longer justify the maintenance of a discriminatory sex class system on grounds of its origins in Nature. Indeed, for pragmatic reasons alone it is beginning to look as if we *must* get rid of it."[14]

According to feminist author Julia Kristeva, there is no such thing as a real woman, even though the term "woman" does have political utility: "Woman is a valid concept politically, but not philosophically. There are still many goals which women can achieve: freedom of abortion and contraception, daycare for children, equality on the job, etc. Therefore we must use 'we are women' as an advertisement or slogan for our demands. On a deeper level, however, a woman cannot 'be'."[15] For Kristeva, a woman

---

[12] John Paul II, *The Theology of the Body* (Boston, MA: Pauline Books & Media, 1997), 49.

[13] Regula Giuliani, "Der über gangene Leib," *Phänomenologische Forchungen*, n.s., 2(1997): 110.

[14] Shulamith Firestone, *The Dialectic of Sex: The Case for Feminist Revolution* (New York, NY: Bantam Books, 1971), 10.

[15] *New French Feminisms*, ed. Elaine Marks and Isabelle de Courtivran (New York, NY: Schocken Books, 1981), 157.

has no nature (*physis*), only a name (*nomos*) and that for purely political (and obviously deceptive) purposes.[16]

Finally, Andrea Stumpf, writing for the *Yale Law Review*, proposes that motherhood be reduced to an abstraction. In the case of "surrogate motherhood" where one woman carries a child for an infertile woman, a number of legal disputes have arisen about whether the mere act of gestating a child provides a sufficient basis for a claim of motherhood. Stumpf argues that we need a new legal definition of motherhood that recognizes "mental conception" as having a superior claim to motherhood than mere "biological conception." Accordingly, she writes: "The psychological dimension of procreation precedes and transcends the biology of procreation."[17] Therefore, according to Stumpf, motherhood is fundamentally in the mind: "Prior to physical conception of a child, the beginnings of a normal parent-child relationship can come from a mental conception, the desire to create a child."[18] Ironically, in her proposal for a new legal definition of motherhood, Stumpf makes no distinction between motherhood and fatherhood (since the male parent can have the "mental conception" first). By de-biologizing motherhood, even a child, presumably, could fulfill Stumpf's proposed definition of motherhood.

In contrast to Stumpf's abstract notion of motherhood, is Gerard Manley Hopkins' decisively natural and incarnate view of Mary's Motherhood, taken from two of his poems:

> All things rising, all things sizing
> Mary sees, sympathizing
> With that world of good,
> Nature's motherhood.[19]

> If I have understood
> She holds high motherhood

---

[16] See David Vincent Meconi, "Theology of the Body and Purity of Heart," *Homiletic & Pastoral Review*, April 2001.

[17] Andrea E. Stumpf, "Redefining Motherhood: A Legal Matrix for New Reproductive Technologies," *Yale Law Review* (Nov. 1986), 194.

[18] *Ibid.*, 195

[19] Gerard Manley Hopkins, "The May Magnificat," ed. John Pick, *A Hopkins Reader* (Garden City, NY: Doubleday, 1966), 70.

> Towards all our ghostly good
> And plays in grace her part
> About man's beating heart.[20]

The Culture of Life

There is a direct connection between disparaging the body and the Culture of Death. If biology is "tyranny" (or something we must be rid of) as so many secular feminists claim, then contraception, sterilization, abortion, and the eradication of corporeal pain through euthanasia are nothing more than forms of liberation from the body. Christ came to liberate us from sin. But secular feminists seek to liberate women from the tyranny of their biology so that they can live as they desire without being impeded by their body. Simone de Beauvoir, generally regarded as the intellectual matriarch of contemporary feminism, has challenged all women to rise above the "animal" act of *giving* life so they can involve themselves in the superior masculine act of *risking* life. In this way, for de Beauvoir, women will transcend the sphere of nature and enter into the more elevated human sphere:

> The worst curse that was laid upon woman was that she should be excluded from those warlike forays. For it is not in giving life but in risking life that man is raised above the animal; that is why superiority has been accorded in humanity not to the sex that brings forth but to that which kills.[21]

The Culture of Death begins with a negation of some essential element of human life—God, spirituality, reason, nature, the body—and thereby fractionalizes the human being. Thus fractionalized, he wars against the very elements he has negated. In this way, secular feminism wars against the woman's body and everything it directly implies. But it leaves them amputated, so to speak, and not well disposed to recognize the inherent appeal of a Culture of Life.

By contrast, Mary is whole and blessed in uniting herself with God both bodily and spiritually. The Culture of Life, therefore, begins with an affirmation, a *fiat*: "Be it done unto me

---

[20] *Ibid.*, "The Blessed Virgin Compared To The Air We Breathe," 71-72.
[21] Simone de Beauvoir, *The Second Sex*, trans. H. M. Parshley (New York, NY: Bantam, 1968), xxviii.

according to thy word." There are three great *fiats*: "Let there be light," at the commencement of creation; "Let there be love," preceding the Passion in the Garden of Olives; and "Let there be life," in response to the Annunciation. Light, Life, and Love also represent the three Persons of the Holy Trinity: the Father, the Son, and the Holy Spirit. Mary is the link between divine life and human life. She is the beginning of the Culture of Life.

In his splendid commentary on John Paul's Theology of the Body, Christopher West speaks of the special living-giving role that Mary has as the model of the Church and as the archetype of humanity:

> She is the one who in this life was impregnated with divine life! She is the one who in this life allowed her entire person—body and soul—to be permeated by the Holy Spirit. Hence, she is our eschatological hope. For in her, the redemption of the body is already brought to completion.[22]

Mary's *fiat* inaugurates the Culture of Life. If we look at three mysteries in particular—the Annunciation, the Visitation, and the Nativity—we can see how Mary offers us three powerful, yet distinct affirmations and exemplifications of the Culture of Life, and how they sharply contrast with their corresponding negations of life that characterize the Culture of Death. Yet, the life-connoting message of the Annunciation, Visitation and Nativity are commonly negated by contraception, abortion, and their logical extension in the form of "wrongful birth." In fact, these three negations can be found in the same person.

The Culture of Death

On September 25, 2002, the Zenit international news service reported from Rome that a Venetian court ordered a gynecologist to pay for the food and maintenance of a child until he comes of age because his birth was due to a mishap in his mother's sterilization procedure. This case, involving the curious notion of "wrong-

---

[22] Christopher West, *Theology of the Body Explained: A Commentary on John Paul II's "Gospel of the Body"* (Boston, MA: Pauline Books & Media, 2003), 252.

ful birth," illustrates three distinct choices against the life of the same human being. Initially, sterilization was used to prevent his conception. When that procedure failed, the woman's doctor recommended an abortion to end his life. Finally, when the child was born, his mother sued her doctor because she did not think that she was obliged to raise the child. The Venice Tribunal ordered the doctor to pay just over $98,000 U.S. for the child's upkeep.

In our time, the notion of "freedom of choice" is, more often than not, associated with a rejection of life. Sterilization (including contraception), abortion, and wrongful birth have become accepted in the secular world as legal and legitimate choices. The prevailing view is that a woman is not free unless she is free to oppose and even assault the very life that may and does emanate from her own flesh. This popular notion of "reproductive freedom" is viewed as a freedom from any *love* that might guide a woman's choice and any *good* that is the natural object of a loving will. It is essentially a negative freedom since its main concern is to be severed from both a loving act and a good object. In this regard, it is a false freedom, one that diminishes rather than fulfills a person. When St. Paul said, "Where the spirit of the Lord is, there is liberty" (2 Cor. 3:17), he was explaining that true freedom cannot exist in isolation and that the "spirit of the Lord," which places freedom in a context of love and goodness, ensures that freedom is consistent with the wholeness (and ultimately the holiness) of the person.

Freedom

In *Love & Responsibility*, Karol Wojtyla made the point that "man longs for love more than for freedom—freedom is the means and love is the end." Consequently, "Freedom exists for the sake of love. If freedom is not used, is not taken advantage of by love it becomes a negative thing and gives human beings a feeling of emptiness and unfulfillment."[23]

Freedom without love can lead to boredom, mischief, or desperation. Freedom cries out for love in order to give it direction, purpose, and fulfillment. When a loved one dies, we mourn the

---

[23] Karol Wojtyla, *Love & Responsibility*, trans. H. T. Willetts (New York, NY: Farrar, Straus & Giroux: 1981), 135-136.

loss of the beloved. We do not rejoice in our newly attained freedom. Freedom, in its best expression, is bound. We do not want to be unbound from people we love. Freedom is the opening of the door, but love is the dwelling place inside. And this is why human beings desire love more than they desire freedom.

No one ever conceived a child more freely and more instantly than did Mary. A woman may yearn for a child. But she must wait upon nature and her unpredictable processes. Only Mary could conceive a child through an act of freedom. Her *fiat* alone was instantly met with her conception of Christ. By uniting her will with the Divine Will, she became the Mother of God. Her freedom and her motherhood, therefore, are inseparable.

Mary's "yes" overturns Eve's "no". As St. Irenaeus has said, "Being obedient she became the cause of salvation for herself and for the whole human race. The knot of Eve's disobedience was untied by Mary's obedience: what the virgin Eve bound through her disbelief, Mary loosened by her faith."[24]

In one sense, it is easier to say "no" to love because of the weighty and worrisome responsibilities it brings in its train. A firm "no" appears to spare a person from any entanglements that would compromise his freedom. Yet "no" leaves one unfulfilled. The separation that "no" implies can never unite us with what we need. We must sooner or later say "yes" to something or someone. Mary's "yes" to become the Mother of God is an extraordinary act of freedom, but one that is supported by faith, humility, courage, fidelity and love. Mary's freedom springs from a rich and grace-filled personality. It is a freedom that is the flower of her virtue and the fulfillment of God's pledge to mankind. Mary's *fiat* is the culminating "yes" to a long concatenation of "yeses" that prepared for and preceded it.

We express our gratitude to Mary for freely permitting our Savior to come into the world by our own countless "Thy will be dones" that we recite daily in the Lord's Prayer. These modest *fiats* lead to their own little incarnations. To say "yes" to God is to live

---

[24] St. Irenaeus, *Adv. haeres.* 3, 22, 4: *PG* 7/1, 959A.

by faith, hope and charity. By accepting Mary as our mother and spiritual role model, we re-enact in our own particular way, the mysteries of the Annunciation, Visitation and Nativity.

The Annunciation

Mary the Mother of God is of paramount moral significance in today's wayward world. She represents freedom that is perfectly integrated with love and goodness. Her witness, through the Mysteries of the Annunciation, Visitation, and Nativity are a powerful repudiation of the Culture of Death's besetting negativities of contraception, abortion and wrongful birth (and, by extension, the various nuances of wrongful, burdensome, or meaningless life that provide the basis for rationalizing euthanasia for the sick and for the elderly).

The Annunciation is the antithesis of contraception and sterilization. Mary is open to conceiving Jesus. Contraception and sterilization are closed to new life. Mary is open to the Word, both spiritually and maternally. When the angel Gabriel made God's plan evident to Mary that she conceive Christ, "she uttered words," to borrow those of Bishop Fulton J. Sheen, "which are the greatest pledge of liberty and the greatest charter of freedom the world has ever heard: 'Be it done unto me according to thy word'."[25] Similarly, psychiatrist Karl Stern has said of Mary, "the stillness in the nod of *assent* was equaled in freedom only by the original freedom of the creative *act*."[26] "*Thy will be done*" is the human *fiat* that complements the *fiat* of creation. The highest freedom, epoch-making freedom, is not unfettered freedom. It is freedom that is directed by love to that which is good. It is freedom that serves life.

The Annunciation is also an Invitation and an Acceptance. It is the perfect concordance between Divine and human wills. But a concordance that bears fruit and renews the face of the earth. Through Mary's Acceptance, God and mankind are less estranged from each other. Mary's children are destined to love their divine Father more intimately. A new covenant is established, through Mary, between God and man.

---

[25] Sheen, *The World's First Love,* 26.

[26] Karl Stern, *The Flight From Woman* (New York, NY: Farrar, Straus & Giroux, 1965), 274.

The Visitation

The Visitation is the account of a moment in the ongoing pregnancies of Mary and her cousin Elizabeth. When Mary entered the home of Elizabeth, she offered her a greeting. No sooner had Elizabeth heard Mary's words, than she declared, "Blessed art thou among women and blessed is the fruit of thy womb. How have I deserved to be thus visited by the mother of my Lord." At that moment, her own child in the womb, John the Baptist, "leaped for joy" (Luke 1:39-45).

This moment represents the reciprocal affirmations of two pregnancies and their correlative two children in the womb. It is a moment of joy. It is a midpoint in time between conception and birth. Elizabeth was "advanced in years." Her conception proved that nothing is impossible with God. Mary's conception occurred without a man. Both conceptions were extraordinary, one despite advanced age, the other despite the absence of a biological father. After such extraordinary conceptions, the periods of gestation were occasions of great rejoicing as well as high expectation.

The Nativity

The Nativity is the fulfillment of Mary's pregnancy. From the standpoint of Herod, it was indeed a "wrongful birth" and, there-fore, the Holy Family needed to flee to Egypt in order to escape his sword. It was never a "wrongful birth" for Mary despite Simeon's prophecy at the Purification that her heart would be pierced by a sword, and her son's Passion to which she was a witness at the foot of the cross. Christmas brings a Savior into the world and with Him, redemption and joy to all men of good will. Has anyone ever been more *wrong* about anything than Herod was about Jesus?

The Annunciation, the Visitation and the Nativity, then, are moments when Mary illustrates her threefold acceptance of life. She conceives life freely through her *fiat*; she rejoices as the child in her womb continues to develop; she exults in the birth of her child on Christmas. Yet her *fiat* has eternal significance, for moth-erhood is indissoluble.

The Personal Unity of the Mother

John Paul II, aware of the various negations of the different stages of motherhood that abound in the contemporary world, carefully explained, drawing from his Personalism and from his Theology of the Body, that motherhood subsumes and integrates all of its different facets into one unified person.

In his Apostolic Letter, *On the Dignity of Women* (*Mulieris Dignitatem*), he alludes to detailed scientific analyses that attest to the fact that "the very physical constitution of women is naturally disposed to motherhood—conception, pregnancy and giving birth."[27] This means that there is a profound harmony in women between the biophysiological and psychological processes involved in motherhood. In the biophysiological sense, motherhood appears to be passive. But in the conception and development of new life these biophysiological processes are deeply and naturally intertwined with motherhood in its "personal-ethical"[28] sense and involves a most important creativity on the part of women. It is not the case that any of the biophysiological stages are contrary to the "woman-as-person." Rather, motherhood, in all its stages, is profoundly linked to the personal structure of the woman. Moreover, it is linked in this way to her personal dimension of a gift. In the light of this, a woman discovers herself as a mother through a sincere gift of herself.

In reading through secular feminist literature, one finds many references to a Cartesian bifurcation of the woman into the spiritual mode and the bodily mode. The former is identified as constituting the woman herself, whereas the latter is regarded as an enemy to her personal liberty, and to her identity as a human being.

Jeffner Allen, to take but one salient example of this curious bifurcation, sees motherhood as the "annihilation" of women: "Children come from patriarchal sexuality's use of woman's body as a resource to reproduce men and the world of men."[29] A woman's

---

[27] John Paul II, *Mulieris Dignitatem*, (August 15, 1988), 18.

[28] *Ibid.*

[29] Jeffner Allen, "Motherhood: The Annihilation of Women," ed. Marilyn Pearsall, *Women and Values: Readings in Recent Feminist Philosophy* (Belmont, CA: Wadsworth, 1986), 92. See also, Ellen Peck, *The Baby Trap* (New York,

escape from the tyranny of men comes through "evacuation": "I am endangered by motherhood. In evacuation from motherhood, I claim my life, body, world, as an end in itself."[30] Allen seems forgetful of the fact that she owes her existence to her mother's motherhood, which was decidedly not used simply "to reproduce men." This is not a philosophy that could survive for more than one generation.

The Word of God

Mary is blessed, as von Balthasar states, by "hearing the word of God and keeping it (Luke 11:28; 2:19-51)," in the Johannine sense of "abiding" in it.[31] In a parallel sense, she conceives the Word of God, cultivates it, and brings it out into the world to share with others. She invites us to do the same, that is, to *hear*, *cultivate*, and *express* the Word of God. She, as Mother of God, urges all of us to be mothers of the Word.

In Raniero Cantalamessa's study of Mary, *Mary: Mirror of the Church*, the preacher to the Papal household writes about how we can all become "mothers of Christ."[32] He explains that this can come about "by hearing the Word and by practicing it."[33] We hear and accept the Word (The Annunciation and conception); we nurture and cultivate the Word (The Visitation and gestation); and we deliver the Word and put it into practice (The Nativity and birth).

Cantalamessa goes on to describe two forms of "unfulfilled maternities." In the first case, a woman suffers a miscarriage or has an abortion. The woman conceives life but her maternity remains unfulfilled because she does not deliver the life she conceived. In the second instance, a woman carries a child to term, but, because of *in vitro* fertilization, gamete intrafallopian transfer, or some other similar technique in which the zygote is formed outside the mother's body, she delivers a child that she did not conceive. Mary's maternity is fulfilled on each account since she both

NY: B. Geis associates, 1971): "I married a lovely, sexy girl—then she turned into someone's mother" (Dust jacket).

[30] *Ibid.*

[31] Balthasar, *Mary—Exemplar of the Church,* 219.

[32] Raniero Cantalamessa, *Mary: Mirror of the Church*, trans. Frances Lonergan Villa (Collegeville, MN: The Liturgical Press, 1992), 70.

[33] *Ibid.*

conceived and gave birth to Jesus (significantly, the Feast of the Annunciation, March 25, is nine months prior to Christmas).

We are, all of us, men as well as women, called to experience both types of maternity on a spiritual level. Unfortunately, some hear the Word but do not give birth to it in practice. Such people have one "spiritual abortion" after another. They have faith without good works. For them, the Gospel, at best, is merely interesting reading. Then, there are those who do many good works without having conceived Christ. Such good works, however, may be tinged with hypocrisy or seeking one's own glory. In such instances, one has good works without faith.

The model that Mary provides of fulfilled maternity in both the bodily and spiritual senses is one that serves as the basis for the Culture of Life. It is a model that is reaffirmed by the words of St. Paul:

> For by grace you have been saved through faith; and this is not your own doing, it is the gift of God—not because of works, lest any man should boast. For we are His workmanship, created in Christ Jesus for good works, which God prepared beforehand, that we should walk in them (Eph. 2:8-10).

Motherhood as a Model for Life

That Mary's motherhood is the preeminent model for life has a natural and logical appeal. "Motherhood, on the human plane," writes Louis Bouyer, "is, evidently, the personal relationship which can reach the most eminent dignity and value of all."[34] Yet the beauty and creativity of motherhood does not derive from itself as a sovereign and self-sufficient principle. The mother does not convey to her child the material of her own being, but shares, equally with the father, in determining the unique nature of that being, assisting in his becoming. Motherhood is not a first principle or one that operates independently of the father. While Mary's motherhood is a model for life, its own reality and inception depends on a creative receptivity to God the Father. This willingness to be open to the

---

[34] Louis Bouyer, *The Seat of Wisdom*, trans. A. V. Littledale (Chicago, IL: Henry Regnery Co., 1960), 148.

Father requires a humility that is neither commonplace nor greatly prized in a post-modern world where self-sufficiency and radical autonomy have become ideals. Nonetheless, Mary's humble renunciation of autonomy is an essential pre-condition for her maternity.

Those who would participate effectively in establishing a Culture of Life are wise to follow Mary's humility. Only then can they begin to appreciate her maternity and how they can be fruitful by imitating it in their own individual and unique ways.

Against humility and maternity stand pride and the illusion of self-sufficiency. But the latter modes, because of their inherent and extreme negativity, are essentially sterile. Thus, they form the cornerstone of a Culture of Death.

The lofty example of unselfish, loving maternity will mean little to men if it means nothing to women. If maternity is merely a "choice," placing it on a moral par with sterility, abortion, and wrongful birth, then maternity loses its transcendent value and ceases to be a model. And in a world without moral models, without moral directives, everyone is lost.

Fulfillment through Surrender

St. Edith Stein argues that "the fallen and perverted feminine nature" can be restored to purity and health only through a surrender to God. Paradoxically, it is through this "surrender" that a woman achieves her fulfillment both as a woman and as a human being. It is not her destiny to isolate herself from others and live only for herself. Elisabeth Badinter's injunction to all women that they absolutize their egos is a formula for moral suicide.[35] Speaking to all women, St. Edith writes:

> Whether she lives as a mother in her home, in the limelight of public life or behind the silent walls of a convent, she must everywhere be a "handmaid of the Lord", as the Mother of God had

---

[35] Elisabeth Badinter, *Man/Woman: The One Is the Other*, trans. Barbara Wright (London, GB: Collins Harville, 1989), 194-195: "Self-love has become a code of ethics. The categorical imperative no longer sets out the conditions of the relationship between Ego and Other People, but those of my relationship with myself . . . We are obliged to recognize that intersubjective relations are losing their value."

been in all the circumstances of her life, whether she was living as a virgin in the sacred precincts of the Temple, silently kept house at Bethlehem and Nazareth, or guided the apostles and the first Christian community after the death of her Son. If every woman were an image of the Mother of God, a spouse of Christ and an apostle of the divine Heart, she would fulfill her feminine vocation no matter in what circumstances she lived and what her external activities might be.[36]

In his concluding words of the Second Vatican Council, Wojtyla made the urgent appeal to women that they *"Reconcile people with life."*[37] As Pope John II, in *Mulieris Dignitatem*, he spoke of their unique capacity to achieve this reconciliation:

Motherhood involves a special communion with the mystery of life, as it develops in the woman's womb. The mother is filled with wonder at this mystery of life and 'understands' with unique intuition what is happening inside her. In the light of the 'beginning,' the mother accepts and loves as a person the child she is carrying in her womb. This unique contact with the new human being developing within her gives rise to an attitude towards human beings not only towards her own child, but every human being, which profoundly marks the woman's personality.[38]

At the close of *The Gospel of Life*, John Paul, as he did so often in ending encyclicals, referred to Mary as the "bright dawn of the new world, Mother of the living," and one to whom "we entrust the *cause of life*."[39] His tribute is most fitting. Mary, indeed, is the model and mother of that new "springtime" of the Church that is also a Culture of Life and a Culture of Love. It will come to pass when we cooperate with our model in receiving, cultivating, and giving birth to the Word of God that gently knocks at the door of our hearts.

---

[36] Edith Stein, *Writings of Edith Stein*, trans. Hilda Graef (London, GB: Peter Owen, Ltd., 1956), 110-125; 161-173.

[37] *Closing Messages of the Council* (December 8, 1965): "To Women."

[38] John Paul II, *Mulieris Dignitatem* (August 15, 1988), 18: *AAS* 80 (1988), 1696.

[39] *The Gospel of Life*, 188.

THE NUPTIAL MEANING OF THE BODY IN THE MARRIAGE OF MARY AND JOSEPH

Gloria Falcão Dodd, S.T.D.

In Advent, on Marian feast days, and for pro-life events, Catholic homilists and lecturers sometimes have described Mary as an unwed mother. These speakers often draw this conclusion from Luke 1:26-27: "The angel Gabriel was sent from God to a town of Galilee called Nazareth, to a virgin betrothed to a man named Joseph, of the house of David, and the virgin's name was Mary", and from Mary's response to Gabriel in Luke 1:34: "How can this be, since I have no relations with a man?"[1] Some modern translations have even substituted "engaged" for "betrothed" because modern culture understands betrothal to mean engagement.[2] Still other translations render Mary's response to Gabriel as: "How can this be, since I have no husband?"[3] Even the official Vatican translation of John Paul II's encyclical letter *Redemptoris Mater* has been mistranslated into English. It reads: "Mary knows she has conceived and given birth to Him 'without having a husband,' ...."[4] Moreover, various devotional and scholarly books state that Mary was not yet married when Jesus was conceived at the Annunciation.[5] Some even enlarged the theme by

---

[1] *The New American Bible* (Nashville: Thomas Nelson Publishers, 1987), and *The Jerusalem Bible*, (Garden City, NJ: Doubleday and Company, Inc., 1986).

[2] *The Holy Bible: The New Revised Standard Version* (New York: Collins, 1989).

[3] *The Holy Bible: Revised Standard Version, Catholic edition* (Camden, NJ: Thomas Nelson and Sons, 1966).

[4] John Paul II, *Redemptoris Mater,* 17. In Latin, "*Novit Maria se illum concepisse et peperisse 'viro non cognito.'*"

[5] Clear statements that Mary was not married at the Annunciation: Jean Cantinant, *Mary in the Bible*, Trans. Paul Barrett (Westminster, MD: Newman

explaining that if her fiancé Joseph denied fathering the child, Mary was risking death by stoning, according to the Jewish punishement for adulterers (Dt. 22:22, Jn. 8:3-5).[6] Certain pro-life homilists have used this story to encourage unwed mothers to choose life for their unborn children and to inspire the audience to help unwed mothers. While this intent is good, and it is true that Mary is a model for everyone, the description of Mary as an unwed mother is actually false due to the fact that Mary was already married at the Annunciation.

Why does it matter whether Mary was engaged or married at the time of the Incarnation of Christ in her womb? St. Ambrose and St. Thomas Aquinas had observed that, if Mary were unwed at the Annunciation, then Jesus would be an illegitimate child. This conclusion prompted them to refute this error because, in their time, illegitimacy was such a dishonor to the child and to the mother that it would be sufficient to reject Christianity.[7] But in the modern United States where by 1991 at least thirty percent of children were born outside of marriage, the liberal culture does not consider illegitimacy as a serious, moral problem.[8] Even many Catholic speakers and

Press, 1965), 58. Carlo Carretto, *Blessed Are You Who Believed*, trans. Barbara Wall (Maryknoll, NY: Orbis Books, 1983), 10-11. Hilda Graef, *The Devotion to Our Lady* (New York: Hawthorn Books, 1963), 11. Bernard Häring, *Mary and Your Everyday Day: A Book of Meditations* (Ligouri, MO: Ligouri Publications, 1978), 54. George H. Tavard, *The Thousand Faces of the Virgin Mary* (Collegeville, MN: Liturgical Press, 1996), 7-9. *Mary in the New Testament: A Collaborative Assessment by Protestant and Roman Catholic Scholars*, Ed. Raymond E. Brown, et al (Philadelphia: Fortress Press, 1978), 115. Ambivalent or conflicting statements of Mary's marriage at the Annunciation: Andre Feuillet, *Jesus and His Mother According to the Lucan Infancy Narratives, and According to St. John: The Role of the Virgin Mary in Salvation History and the Place of Woman in the Church*, Trans. Leonard Maluf (Still River, MA: St. Bede's Publications, 1984), 103. Romano Guardini, *The Lord*, trans. Elinor Castendyk Briefs (Chicago: Henry Regnery Co., 1954), 14-15. Francis L. Filas, *Joseph: The Man Closest to Jesus: The Complete Life, Theology, and Devotional History of St. Joseph* (Boston: Daughters of St. Paul, 1962), 107-109, cited Psuedo-Origen and Maximus of Turin as Patristic ambivalence about Mary's marriage. Michael O'Carroll, "Joseph, St.," in *Theotokos: A Theological Encyclopedia of the Blessed Virgin Mary* (Collegeville, MN: Liturgical Press, 1982), 207.

[6] Cantinant, *Mary in the Bible,* 120.

[7] St. Ambrose, *De Institutione Virginis* VI, 42, in *PL* 16, 316, and *Expositio Evangeliu Secundum Lucam, II*, in *PL* 15:1552-1553. St. Thomas Aquinas, *Summa Theologica*, III, Q. 29, a. 2, c.

[8] Cf. Robert H. Bork, *Slouching Towards Gomorrah: Modern Liberalism and American Decline* (New York: Regan Books, 1996), 155.

authors see nothing wrong in their descriptions of Mary as an unwed mother.

The problem is that this error has devotional and theological implications. On the devotional level, if Jesus were illegitimately conceived, then Joseph would be only an adoptive, foster or step-father of Jesus, not Jesus' legal, and true spiritual father from the conception. Thus, Jesus' supposed illegitimacy unhinges Joseph's paternal relationship with us, the Church that is the Body of Christ, and negates Jesus' genealogy from David to Joseph (Mt. 1:1-17, Lk. 3:23-33).

To learn the truth about Mary and Joseph's marriage, this essay will study John Paul II's teachings. First, John Paul II's doctrine of Mary and Joseph's marriage will be presented. Then, John Paul II's Theology of the Body will be applied to show how the unusual marriage of Mary and Joseph fulfilled the nuptial meaning of the body. This essay will conclude with some theological and moral implications drawn from the unusual marriage of Mary and Joseph.

The True and Timely Marriage of Mary and Joseph

The marriage of Mary and Joseph has been long disputed in the Catholic tradition because the insistence on Mary's perpetual virginity seems incompatible with a true marriage. The Church Fathers maintained Mary's virginity to defend Christ's divinity. Therefore, some Fathers of the Church hesitated to state that Mary was married at the Annunciation.[9] Other Fathers tried to explain how Joseph and Mary were married even though they did not consummate their marriage. St. Hilary of Poitiers (d.368) generally called Joseph and Mary only "spouses," but also attributed to Mary the title of "wife" after giving birth to Jesus because she was the mother of Jesus, not because she had a physical union with Joseph.[10] Maximus of Turin (d.420) described Joseph as "always spouse but never husband."[11] St. Augustine (c.354-430) recognized the validity of Joseph and Mary's marriage, even though they did not have marital relations, because their marriage possessed all three blessings of marriage: 1) children,

---

[9] See O'Carroll, "Marriage, Our Lady's," in *Theotokos*, 234.

[10] See Hilary of Poitiers, *Commentarii in Evangelium Matthaei* 1, 3 in *PL* 9:921.

[11] Maximus of Turin, *Sermones* 53 in *PL* 57:639.

because of Christ; 2) fidelity, because there was no adultery, and 3) sacrament, because there was no divorce.[12] St. Thomas Aquinas acknowledged the reality of Mary and Joseph's marriage because the spouses remained continent by mutual consent and their marriage possessed the perfect form, that is: "A certain inseparable union of souls, by which husband and wife are pledged by a bond of mutual affection that cannot be sundered."[13] He explained that Mary and Joseph "...both consented to the nuptial bond, but not expressly to the bond of the flesh, save on the condition that it was pleasing to God..." and that in their marriage, they never consummated their marriage "...by the marriage act, if this be referred to carnal intercourse, by which children are begotten."[14] Because Mary and Joseph never consummated their marriage, it was unusual, but it was a true marriage because they exchanged the rights to each other's bodies, even though they chose never to exercise these rights. Both Pope Leo XIII and Pope John Paul II defended the reality of their marriage, though Leo XIII did not specify when the marriage began.[15]

Part of the Catholic theological tradition has proposed that Mary and Joseph were already married at the time of the Annunciation and Incarnation. Origen reported that St. Ignatius of Antioch had explained that Jesus was conceived and born of an "espoused" or married woman to hide the virginal conception from Satan.[16] St. Jerome and St. Thomas Aquinas reaffirmed this idea and added more reasons for Christ's conception in the womb of a married woman, such as the prevention of Mary's stoning as an adulteress.[17] Some twentieth-century Catholic scholars, such as Raymond Brown and Frederick Jelly, used rabbinic documents to propose the two stages of Jewish marriage to explain how Mary was already married to Joseph at the Annunciation.[18]

[12] St. Augustine, *De Nuptiis Et Concupiscentia*, i, in *PL* 44:121.

[13] St. Thomas Aquinas, *Summa Theologica*, III, Q. 29, a. 2, c.

[14] *Ibid.*

[15] *Quamquam Pluries* was cited by John Paul II, *Redemptoris Custos*, 7.

[16] Origen, *In Lucam Homilia 6* in *PG* 13, 1814.

[17] St. Jerome, *Commentariorum in Evangelium Matthae 1, 2*, in *PL* 26: 23-24. St. Thomas Aquinas, *Summa Theologica*, III, Q. 29, c.

[18] Raymond E. Brown, *The Birth of the Messiah: A Commentary on the Infancy Narratives in Matthew and Luke* (Garden City, NY: Doubleday and Company, Inc., 1977), 123-125. Frederick M. Jelly, *Madonna: Mary in the Catholic Tradition* (Huntington, IN: Our Sunday Visitor, 1986), 35, 41- 42, and 49.

In his 1982 series of talks titled "Life according to the Spirit," Pope John Paul II indirectly affirmed the pre-Annunciation marriage of Mary and Joseph with the statement: "...in the Nazareth conditions of the pact of Mary and Joseph in marriage and in continence, the gift of the Incarnation of the Eternal Word was realized."[19] This brief statement was clarified by John Paul II's 1989 apostolic exhortation *Redemptoris Custos*. In this document the Pope explicitly identified Mary as a married woman at the time of the Incarnation: "...at the moment of the Annunciation, Mary was 'betrothed to a man whose name was Joseph, of the house of David. ... Mary is already 'wedded' to Joseph."[20] John Paul II confirmed the scholarly theory of the two-phase marriage of Mary and Joseph: "According to Jewish custom, marriage took place in two stages: first, the legal, or true marriage was celebrated, and then, only after a certain period of time, the husband brought the wife into his own house. Thus, before he lived with Mary, Joseph was already her 'husband'."[21] Therefore, John Paul II noted that God spoke through the angel to Joseph specifically in his capacity as the husband of Mary.[22]

Moreover, the Pope commented that the conception of Jesus in Mary's womb by the power of the Holy Spirit "also confirmed in a special way the marriage bond which already existed between Joseph and Mary."[23] As the Gospel of Matthew states:

> When his mother Mary was betrothed to Joseph, before they came together, she was found to be with child through the Holy Spirit. Her husband, Joseph, being a just man and unwilling to put her to shame, resolved to send her away quietly. But as he considered this, behold, an angel of the Lord appeared to him in a dream saying: 'Joseph, son of David, do not fear to take Mary your wife, for that which is conceived in her is of the Holy Spirit ... When Joseph woke from sleep, he did as the angel of the Lord commanded him and took Mary as his wife (Mt. 1:18-20, 24).

[19] John Paul II, "Life according to the Spirit," March 24, 1982, in *The Theology of the Body: Human Love in the Divine Plan* (Boston: Pauline Books and Media, 1997), 269. Hereafter cited as *TOTB*, with proper page number and date.

[20] John Paul II, *Redemptoris Custos*, 2.

[21] *Ibid.*, 18.

[22] *Ibid.*, 3 and 18.

[23] *Ibid.*, 18.

While confirming the validity and the pre-Annunciation timing of the marriage between Mary and Joseph, John Paul II also reaffirmed the virginal quality of their marriage. "The nature of this 'marriage' is explained indirectly when Mary, after hearing what the messenger says about the birth of the child, asks, 'How can this be, *since I do not know man?*' (Lk 1:34) ... Although Mary is already 'wedded' to Joseph, she will remain a virgin, ..."[24] Already married, "Mary, however, preserved her deep desire to give herself exclusively to God. ... From the moment of the Annunciation, Mary knew that she was to fulfill her virginal desire to give herself exclusively and fully to God precisely by becoming the Mother of God's Son. ... In her divine motherhood Mary had to continue to live as 'a virgin, the wife of her husband' (cf. Lk 1:27)."[25] Joseph, too, accepted the mystery of virginity in marriage in order to correspond to Mary's virginal maternity.[26] Mary's unique vocation as the Mother of God required Joseph and Mary to remain married while sacrificing the usual conjugal act.

However, this sacrifice of physical unity did not impede the spiritual unity of Mary and Joseph in their shared faith. John Paul II identified Mary's faith as "... a kind of 'key' which unlocks for us the innermost reality of Mary, whom the angel hailed as 'full of grace'."[27] He described Mary as "the perfect realization" of "the obedience of faith," whereby "man entrusts his whole self freely to God .... The 'decisive' moment was the Annunciation, and the very words of Elizabeth: 'And blessed is she who believed' refer primarily to that very moment."[28] But in her marriage Mary was not alone in this faith.

> ... the faith of Mary meets the faith of Joseph. If Elizabeth said of the Redeemer's Mother, 'blessed is she who believed,' in a certain sense this blessedness can be referred to Joseph as well, since he responded positively to the word of God when it was communicated to him at the decisive moment. While it is true that Joseph did not respond to the angel's 'announcement' in the same way as Mary,

---

[24] *Ibid.*, 2.

[25] *Ibid.*, 18.

[26] *TOTB,* 268 [March 24, 1982].

[27] John Paul II, *Redemptoris Mater,* 19.

[28] *Ibid.*, 13.

he 'did as the angel of the Lord commanded him and took his wife.' What he did is the clearest 'obedience of faith' (cf. Rom. 1:5; 16:26; 2 Cor 10:5-6). One can say that what Joseph did united him in an altogether special way to the faith of Mary. He accepted as truth coming from God the very thing that she had already accepted at the Annunciation. ... Therefore he became a unique guardian of the mystery 'hidden for ages in God' (Eph 3:9), as did Mary, in that decisive moment which St. Paul calls 'the fullness of time,' when 'God sent forth his Son, born of woman...to redeem those who were under the law, so that we might receive adoption as sons' (Gal 4:4-5) ... Together with Mary, Joseph is the first guardian of this divine mystery. Together with Mary, and in relation to Mary, he shares in this final phase of God's self-revelation in Christ, and he does so from the very beginning. Looking at the gospel texts of both Matthew and Luke, one can also say that Joseph is the first to share in the faith of the Mother of God, and that in doing so he supports his spouse in the faith of the divine annunciation.[29]

Thus, John Paul II taught that Mary and Joseph were united by their free obedience of faith to the word of God. This acceptance of God's will joined the immaculate Mary and the just Joseph in a virginal marriage wherein they both accepted lovingly, and became parents of, the child that God miraculously sent them.

In summary, John Paul II reiterated the traditional doctrine of Mary and Joseph's valid and virginal marriage. He identified the source of Mary and Joseph's marital unity as a living faith that first listens to the word of God and then does the will of God in practice. John Paul II's papal authority confirmed the theological tradition that Mary and Joseph were already married at the time of the Annunciation, affirming that Jesus was not only born within marriage but was also conceived within marriage. Therefore, although there may have been confusion in the past, now an educated Catholic speaker or author should describe Mary as a married woman at the time of the Incarnation, and Christ as a legitimate child born within the marriage of Joseph and Mary. The proclamation of this truth reaffirms at least two Catholic doctrines: 1) the fulfillment of the Davidic prophecies, 2) Joseph's paternal patronage of the Church.

---

[29] John Paul II, *Redemptoris Custos,* 4.

How Mary and Joseph Lived the "Nuptial Meaning of the Body" in Their Marriage

This section will explain the concepts that John Paul II created for his series of talks that have come to be known as "The Theology of the Body." Interpreting Matthew 19:3-12 and Mark 10:2-12, John Paul II understood Christ's references to Genesis 1-2 ("in the beginning") to teach the truth about human beings in general and marriage in particular. The Genesis accounts of man's origins are then complemented by Jesus' teaching that "Blessed are the Pure of Heart," from the Sermon on the Mount. John Paul II concluded this theology of the body with an exegesis on Pauline doctrines of life according to the Spirit, also adding some reflections on Paul VI's encyclical *Humanae Vitae*. For our purposes, after a brief synthesis has been presented, the concepts will be applied to the marriage of Mary and Joseph. In particular, this section will study how Mary and Joseph experienced an original solitude, an original unity, and a redemption of the body in order to live the nuptial meaning of the body in their marriage.

John Paul II started his Theology of the Body by presenting the three fundamental human experiences of the original human couple. Constituted in "original solitude," man possessed a knowledge of himself being alone before God and above the animals as the only embodied person with self-determination.[30] The original solitude included the male's loneliness for the woman.[31]

The second fundamental human experience, the "original unity" of man and woman, was revealed by Adam's joy when he saw Eve for the first time: "This one, at last, is bone of my bone and flesh of my flesh!" (Gen. 2:23). This original unity was based on the nuptial meaning of their male and female bodies.[32] Pope John Paul II created the phrase, "the nuptial (spousal) meaning of the body," to refer to the capacity of embodied human persons, who are created male and female in the image of the loving and life-giving God. The nuptial meaning of the body reveals that human happiness is obtained only by men and women who express their love in a mutual self-giving that is fruitful.[33] In brief, this nuptial meaning of the

---

[30] See *TOTB*, 35-39 [October 10 and 24, 1979].

[31] See *TOTB*, 35.

[32] See *TOTB*, 42-48.

[33] *TOTB*, 46-47 [November 11, 1979] and 58-63 [January 2 and 9, 1980].

body refers to "the capacity of expressing love, that love in which the person becomes a gift and—by means of this gift—fulfills the meaning of his being and existence."[34] Adam and Eve experienced this mutual gift-giving in a marriage that was indissoluble.[35]

The third fundamental human experience for Adam and Eve was "original innocence," expressed by the phrase "naked without shame." This original innocence was the interior freedom "from the constraint of their own bodies and sex," to enjoy the whole truth about embodied man, male and female.[36] This truth is: 1) man (male and female) is "the only creature in the world that the Creator willed 'for its own sake;'" and 2) each human person "can find himself only in the disinterested giving of himself."[37] Adam and Eve accepted each other as unique and unrepeatable, as willed 'for his own sake' by the Creator, constituted in the mystery of the image of God through masculinity or femininity that both includes and goes beyond the purely physical dimension of sexuality.[38] Thus, the man receives and accepts the woman "for her own sake" while the woman receives and accepts the man "for his own sake" as a gift from God as well as a mutual self-donation from the other spouse.[39] In particular "the woman is entrusted to his eyes, to his consciousness, to his sensitivity, to his heart," while the man is enriched by the woman's acceptance of him in his masculinity.[40] The Pope commented that the responsibility rests especially on the man to accept femininity as a gift.[41]

Unfortunately this original innocence was lost after the original sin. Shame entered the relationship of man and woman because they realized that their dignity as persons can be violated by being used as an object of lust.[42] By Christ's resurrection from the dead and the gift of the Holy Spirit, the human body has been redeemed and therefore

---

[34] *Ibid.*, 63 [July 23, 1980].

[35] See *TOTB,* 48 [November 21, 1979].

[36] See *TOTB,* 51-57 [November 28 and December 19, 1979] and 66-72 [January 30 and February 6, 1980].

[37] *TOTB,* 64 [January 16, 1980].

[38] *Ibid.*, 65 [January 16, 1980].

[39] See *TOTB,* 60 [January 2, 1980] and 70-71 [February 6, 1980].

[40] *TOTB,* 71 [February 6, 1980].

[41] See *TOTB,* 128-129 [July 30, 1980].

[42] See *TOTB,* 55 [December 19, 1979] and 70 [February 6, 1980] and 75 [February 20, 1980].

empowered to overcome lust and to live the nuptial meaning of the body either in celibacy for the sake of the kingdom of God or the sacrament of matrimony.[43] In matrimony, "man and woman ... become gifts to one another through their masculinity and femininity, also through their physical union."[44] Note the distinction between the gift and physical union as a type of gift. As a fruit of the gift of the Holy Spirit, the couple's mutual attraction spiritually matures into a mutual deference out of reverence for Christ and the wife's respect for the husband (Eph. 5:21, 33) so that they show a "disinterested tenderness" toward each other.[45] The "disinterested" quality does not mean a lack of interest but rather a lack of selfishness. The redemption of the body empowers spouses to live the fullness of their mutual self-donation in both its love-giving and life-giving dimensions. As embodied persons, the spouses are to be responsible parents. This responsibility is shown differently by each couple who must discern for themselves the number of children they are called to have.

Having defined the basic concepts used in the Theology of the Body, these concepts can now be applied to the marriage of Mary and Joseph. Just as original solitude allowed Adam to come to a "consciousness" of who and what he was as an embodied person, so Mary's question to Gabriel—"How can this be, since I do not know man?" (Lk. 1:34)—showed her knowledge of human biology and of herself as an embodied person already committed to virginity, having free will in choosing whether or not to accept God's plan. It was precisely because God respected her human intellect and free will that the angel Gabriel had been sent to inform her of God's will and to gain her consent to the Incarnation.

The angel's greeting formed Mary's "consciousness" of who and what she was as an individual, having the full freedom to choose her response to the angel. "Full of grace" is the translation of the Greek word "*kecharitomene*," a word that is better translated as "having been fully graced". Gabriel had greeted Mary as if "*kecharitomene*" were her proper name.[46] Catholic theology has understood this

---

[43] See *TOTB*, 270-275 [March 31 - April 7, 1982].

[44] *TOTB*, 274 [April 7, 1982].

[45] See *TOTB*, 371 [May 30, 1984] and 378-380 [July 4, 1984].

[46] Cf. A Feuillet, "La Vierge Marie dans le Nouveau Testament," in *Maria: Études sur la Sainte Vierge*, vol. VI, Ed. D'Hubert du Manoir (Paris:

to mean that Mary has been uniquely graced more than any other human person. Although different from Adam's loneliness, as he experienced an existential difference when surrounded by the animals, Mary could have felt a loneliness based on the difference in grace when surrounded by others who suffered a lack of grace by reason of original sin and their own actual sins. Just as Adam longed for a human companion, Mary would have longed for a grace-filled companion who would love God with an intensity close to her own and who would love her in a way that would respect her vocation to virginity.

With such a unique and difficult vocation, Mary and Joseph must have both rejoiced to have found a spouse willing to receive and accept the other as a gift in a virginal marriage. In John Paul II's application of the nuptial meaning of the body to the marriage of Mary and Joseph, the Roman Pontiff wrote the following: "At the culmination of the history of salvation, when God reveals His love for humanity through the gift of the Word, it is precisely the marriage of Mary and Joseph that brings to realization in full 'freedom' the 'spousal gift of self' in receiving and expressing such a love."[47] The gift that Mary received was Joseph, "a just man," whose faith matched hers to form a virginal community of love in their marriage, reflecting the spiritual self-donation of persons in the Trinity, without the usual physical embodiment in marital relations. Their unusual marriage "...conceals within itself, at the same time, the mystery of the perfect communion of the persons, of the man and the woman in the conjugal pact, and also the mystery of that singular continence for the kingdom of heaven."[48] How? After being assured by Gabriel that the conception of this son would not violate her commitment to virginity, due to the fact that the Holy Spirit would overshadow her, Mary's self-knowledge as a married woman enabled her to accept God's plan freely (Lk. 1:35-38). Mary understood the procreative dimension of the nuptial meaning of her body in her marriage. It was precisely because Mary already had received St. Joseph as her husband and had been entrusted to him that she was able to say "yes" to bearing a child.

Beauchesne 1962), 32.

[47] John Paul II, *Redemptoris Custos,* 7.

[48] *TOTB,* 268 [March 24, 1982].

As a valid marriage must be, Mary and Joseph's total and mutual self-gift was open to the children that God would send them. By their marriage, Joseph was a gift to Mary enabling her to become the virginal mother of the Messiah, while Mary was a gift to Joseph, making him the spiritual father of the Messiah.

Joseph's obedience to God's message to take Mary into his home showed that Joseph "loved the Virgin of Nazareth and was bound to her by a husband's love."[49] Joseph's obedience of accepting into his home both Mary and the child conceived by the Holy Spirit (cf. Mt. 1:24) showed that "his love as a man was also given new birth by the Holy Spirit," who molded Joseph's love to perfection.[50] "This bond of charity was the core of the Holy Family's life, first in the poverty of Bethlehem, then in their exile in Egypt, and later in the house of Nazareth."[51]

Commenting on the verse "Joseph...took his wife; but he knew her not, until she had borne a son" (Mt. 1:24-25), John Paul II noted another kind of closeness in marriage:

> The deep spiritual closeness arising from marital union and the interpersonal contact between man and woman have their definitive origin in the Spirit, the Giver of Life (cf. Jn 6:63). Joseph, in obedience to the Spirit, found in the Spirit the source of love, the conjugal love which he experienced as a man. And this love proved to be greater than this 'just man' could ever have expected within the limits of his human heart.[52]

Thus, guided and strengthened by the Holy Spirit, Joseph discerned that he and Mary were not called to have marital relations:

> Through his complete self-sacrifice, Joseph expressed his generous love for the Mother of God, and gave her a husband's 'gift of self.' Even though he decided to draw back so as not to interfere in the plan of God which was coming to pass in Mary, Joseph obeyed the explicit command of the angel and took Mary into his home, while respecting the fact that she belonged exclusively to God.[53]

---

[49] John Paul II, *Redemptoris Custos*, 19.
[50] *Ibid.*
[51] *Ibid.*, 21.
[52] *Ibid.*, 19.
[53] *Ibid.*, 20.

Their mutual self-donation in marriage enriched both Joseph and Mary. In regard to this, John Paul II stated: "Since marriage is the highest degree of association and friendship, involving by its very nature a communion of goods, it follows that God, by giving Joseph to the Virgin, did not give him to her only as a companion for life, a witness of her virginity and protector of her honor: he also gave Joseph to Mary in order that he might share, though the marriage pact, in her own sublime greatness."[54] Thus, the mutual self-donation of marriage brought Joseph so spiritually close to Mary and through her, to Jesus, that Joseph is second only to Mary in human holiness.

The primacy of the interior life is also exemplified in the marriage of Mary and Joseph. Mary's reflection on what God had done in her life was recorded by Luke in terms of keeping or treasuring all these things in her heart (cf. Lk. 2:19, 51). Scripture does not record a single word spoken by Joseph, but rather his silent and obedient actions reveal his "deep contemplation."[55] It was precisely "his profound interior life" that empowered him to make the extremely difficult decisions of accepting Mary and Jesus as his family and of renouncing "the natural conjugal love that is the foundation and nourishment of the family."[56] Within the family life, Joseph then developed a deep and reciprocal love for Jesus that empowered him to love the truth and to live the demands of love.[57]

Accepting God's will for them to have Christ but not to have physical or biological children together did not inhibit Mary and Joseph's spiritual parenting. When Joseph followed "the light of the Holy Spirit who gives Himself to human beings through faith, he certainly came to discover ever more fully the indescribable gift that was his human fatherhood."[58] Joseph taught Jesus how to be a good man and a good Jew. As a just Jewish man, Joseph took time off from his work to observe the weekly Sabbath day of prayer and rest. He fulfilled his religious obligations as a Jewish father by

[54] *Ibid.*, quoting Leo XIII, *Quamquam pluries* (August 15, 1889).
[55] John Paul II, *Redemptoris Custos,* 25.
[56] *Ibid.*, 26, quoting Paul VI's discourse of March 19, 1969, as recorded in *Insegnanmenti*, VII (1969), 1268.
[57] John Paul II, *Redemptoris Custos,* 27.
[58] *Ibid.*, 21.

ensuring that the first-born son was circumcised on the eighth day after His birth, by naming Him, by ransoming this first-born son at the temple in Jerusalem, and by taking the twelve-year-old Jesus on His first obligatory journey to Jerusalem for the Passover.[59] The spiritual fathering of Jesus made Joseph a spiritual father of the mystical body of Christ, and therefore earned Joseph the title of the "Universal Patron of the Catholic Church."[60] Mary, too, educated Jesus and set a good example by traveling every year with Joseph to Jerusalem for the Passover (cf. Lk. 2:22-41). Mary's spiritual maternity of Christ expanded to include the entire mystical body of Christ (cf. 1 Cor. 12:12-31 and Rev. 12:17) so that she is "a mother to us in the order of grace."[61] The procreative dimension of Mary and Joseph's marriage showed both their conjugal chastity by permanent continence and also their generosity in accepting the many spiritual children that God chose to send them.

Like Adam and Eve in their original innocence, Mary had been so completely redeemed in her Immaculate Conception that she was a perfectly integrated person who, unlike Adam and Eve, then freely chose to remain sinless.[62] She possessed the interior peace to accept fully her own body and her husband's body as temples of the Holy Spirit. Although Joseph suffered the effects of original sin, Joseph also knew that Mary had conceived by the Holy Spirit, and therefore her body was a temple of the Holy Spirit *par excellence*. As a "just man" whose holiness was second only to Mary's, Joseph would have made the effort to cooperate with God's grace to attain a full integration of his sensual pleasure and emotional delight in Mary as a person to love, not an object to be used.

In the redemption of the body brought by Christ to humanity, Mary and Joseph's marriage received a sacramental quality. In this context, John Paul II quoted Pope Paul VI:

---

[59] *Ibid.*, 11-15.
[60] *Ibid.*, 28, footnote 42, citing "Sacror. Rituum Congreg., Decr. *Quemadmodum Deus* (December 8, 1870): *Pii IX P.M. Acta*, pars I, vol. V, 283.
[61] *Lumen Gentium*, 61.
[62] See Eamon R. Carroll, "Mary in the Documents of the Magisterium," in *Mariology*, vol. 1, ed. Juniper Carol (Milwaukee: Bruce Publishing Co., 1955), 15-17.

In this great undertaking which is the renewal of all things in Christ, marriage—it too purified and renewed—becomes a new reality, a sacrament of the New Covenant. We see that at the beginning of the New Testament, as at the beginning of the Old, there is a married couple. But whereas Adam and Eve were the source of evil which was unleashed on the world, Joseph and Mary are the summit from which holiness spreads all over the earth. The Savior began the work of salvation by this virginal and holy union, wherein is manifested His all-powerful will to purify and sanctify the family—that sanctuary of love and cradle of life.[63]

How did Mary and Joseph express their conjugal love in a virginal marriage? There were two primary ways: affection and work. As integrated persons who saw each other with interior peace as images of God, Mary and Joseph would have felt disinterested tenderness and respect for each other as well as the accompanying "deep satisfaction, admiration, disinterested attention to the visible and at the same time the invisible beauty of femininity and masculinity, and finally a deep appreciation of the disinterested gift of the other."[64] Their signs of affections probably included compliments, small gifts such as flowers, or doing the other person's chores.

Secondly, "work was the daily expression of love in the life of the Family of Nazareth."[65] Joseph worked as a carpenter with Jesus at his side. Joseph showed his love for his wife and for Jesus by doing manual labor to provide for the family's daily needs. Joseph moved to Egypt to protect Jesus, even though the move would have hurt the profits of his carpentry business. As a carpenter, Joseph's shop was probably in the home where he was able to help Mary or Jesus whenever needed. Mary, too, did the customary work of a wife and mother by cooking, cleaning, spinning thread, weaving cloth, and making the family's clothes. The seamless garment that Jesus had worn was most likely made by his Mother (cf. Jn. 19:23). Thus, Mary and Joseph showed their love for each other through work that served God first and then the family.

Thus, John Paul II's Theology of the Body has provided a new vocabulary and fresh insights into understanding Mary and Joseph's

---

[63] John Paul II, *Redemptoris Custos,* 7.
[64] *TOTB,* 418 [November 21, 1984].
[65] John Paul II, *Redemptoris Custos,* 22.

marriage. Mary and Joseph lived their nuptial meaning of the body
in the freedom of the redemption of the body. They had the interior
freedom from lust to choose to marry each other and then to remain
continent for their entire marriage. At the same time, their marriage
was precisely what allowed Mary to live the procreative dimension
of the nuptial meaning of the body by physically bearing Jesus as her
Son. The physical generation of the body of Christ then provided the
specific shape of Mary and Joseph's spiritual generation of Jesus
both by educating Him and then by caring for the mystical body of
Christ. Although a unique vocation to a virginal commitment within
marriage, Mary and Joseph remain an instructive model for all married couples to live the redemption of their bodies.

Mary and Joseph as a Model for Married Couples

The Theology of the Body provides a new perspective from
which to view how Mary and Joseph serve as a model for married
couples. Just as Mary and Joseph lived the fundamental human
experiences of solitude, unity, and redemption of the body, all married couples can draw inspiration from how Joseph and Mary handled these experiences. Although miraculous and unrepeatable
with a virginal conception, Joseph and Mary's marriage was a real
marriage between two concrete spouses. The Holy Family's example provides some principles that all married couples can follow.

Like Joseph and Mary, all married couples are called to the
obedience of faith. In an individual's original solitude, this obedience
begins first with a discernment of God's will, to determine whether
God is calling an individual to give himself in a loving self-donation
to an individual in marriage, or to give himself exclusively to God in
celibacy for the kingdom of heaven. If marriage is a person's vocation, then the person should prepare for it by acquiring a self-knowledge of embodied persons. Because they are embodied, those dis-
cerning marriage should know the basics of biology, as Mary and
Joseph did. It is useful for engaged couples today to learn natural
family planning as part of their education of conjugal chastity.[66] As

---

[66] Pontifical Council for the Family, "Preparation for the Sacrament of Marriage,"
May 13, 1996, in *Enchiridion on the Family: A Compendium of Church Teaching
on Family and Life Issues from Vatican II to the Present* (Boston: Pauline Books
and Media, 1994), 763.

persons with an intellect and free will, those seeking a spouse should choose someone who shares the same faith. This education and careful selection prepares an individual to become "one flesh" both spiritually and physically in the mutual self-donation of the conjugal act that is necessary to consummate a marriage.[67]

In modern culture, some husbands and wives fear the responsibility and sacrifices required of parenting, while other parents believe they have a right to be a parent. Mary and Joseph's marriage emphasizes that children are a gift from God. When given a child, parents can trust that God will also give all the graces necessary to be good spiritual parents who also educate their children in everything necessary for their bodily and spiritual welfare.

The Holy Family's example of work as an expression of love is another important lesson for families today. Seeing work as an expression of love would subordinate work to the service of the family. Prioritizing the family over career would empower couples to choose to rent rather than buy a home, or to buy a smaller home, if necessary, allowing one parent to stay home with the children before they go to school, and allowing the working parent to live close enough to work that he or she still would have sufficient time to eat a shared meal and to pray with the family daily. At home, the necessary household chores would become a labor of love. This perspective would lighten the difficulties of work both figuratively and literally, allowing the couple to build a community of love.

Mary and Joseph's marriage reveals how the true vocation of married couples is the same vocation of everyone—a vocation to be loved and to love: "The family has the mission to guard, reveal and communicate love, and this is a living reflection of and a real sharing in God's love for humanity and the love of Christ the Lord for the Church his bride."[68] Thus, it is primarily the charity of the Holy Family that makes it a model for all families.[69] It is by receiving God's love first that the couple is then able to love in a true reflection of the God of love: "The love of God also molds—in a

---

[67] See *TOTB,* 355 [January 5, 1983].
[68] John Paul II, *Redemptoris Custos,* 7, quoting John Paul II, *Familiaris Consortio* (November 22, 1981), 17: *AAS* 74 (1982): 100.
[69] *Ibid.,* 21.

completely unique way—the love of husband and wife, deepening within it everything of human worth and beauty, everything that bespeaks an exclusive gift of self, a covenant between persons, and an authentic communion according to the model of the Blessed Trinity."[70] Mary and Joseph showed how it was possible to live this love in an eschatological and miraculous way. Although in different ways, each according to its own vocation, every couple can imitate Mary and Joseph's total self-giving love that is inscribed in the nuptial meaning of the body.

Conclusion

Hopefully this essay has eliminated the confusion about the marriage of Mary and Joseph. They were indeed married before the Annunciation, and Jesus was conceived within their virginal marriage. It was precisely Mary's understanding of the nuptial meaning of her body that gave her the freedom to consent to the conception of a child in her womb. By their permanent and loving abstinence within marriage, Mary and Joseph give hope to married couples to live their vocations to mutual self-donation even when periodic or even permanent abstinence is required. The marriage of Mary and Joseph provides lessons in love for married couples.

Thus, Mary is still a model for unwed mothers, even though she was married. She is an example, not because she was like us in some particular detail, but rather because she said "yes" to God's will. By accepting her unique vocation, Mary and Joseph lived according to the nuptial meaning of the body and found the joy we are all called to have here on earth and later in heaven.

---

[70] Paul VI, *Humanae Vitae*, 19.

JOHN HENRY NEWMAN'S MARIOLOGY:
A KEY TO UNLOCKING
JOHN PAUL II'S THEOLOGY OF THE BODY

Fr. Nicholas L. Gregoris, S.T.D.

Introduction

Perhaps it is a truism that Pope John Paul II was the first theologian to propose a theology of the body *per se*, doing so in a
series of catechetical talks delivered at his Wednesday audiences
from September 5, 1979 to November 28, 1984.[1] The Holy Father's
unique contribution has immensely enhanced the study of
Christian anthropology in general and of moral theology in particular. The Pope's writings have become the manifest impetus for
authors like Christopher West, who has successfully enunciated
and elaborated on John Paul II's Theology of the Body in simpli-
fied language quite accessible, most especially to parents and
young people of the contemporary English-speaking world.[2]

What are some essential aspects of this theology of the body?
John Paul II underscored its solid scriptural foundations with exegesis of key biblical passages. He emphasized its perennial value in

---

[1] Cf. John Paul II, *The Theology of the Body: Human Love in the Divine Plan*
(Boston: Pauline Books and Media, 1997). Also, Karol Wojtyla, *Love and
Responsibility* (San Francisco: Ignatius Press, 1993).

[2] Cf. Christopher West, *Theology of the Body Explained* (Boston: Pauline *Books
& Media*, 2003). Also, by the same author, *Good News about Sex & Marriage*:
Answers to Your Honest Questions About Catholic Teaching (Ann Arbor,
Michigan: Servant/Charis Books, 2000).

regard to God's original plan for the unity and harmony of creation. He demonstrated the intrinsic cohesiveness of the Theology of the Body with regard to the dictates of the human conscience, the natural law and divine positive law, not to mention the Ten Commandments and Gospel principles taught by Our Lord in the Sermon on the Mount. John Paul II, in delineating the various strata of Pauline theology, stressed the fundamental unity of the human person as a body-soul composite called to live according to the law of grace, that is to say, the law and promptings of the Holy Spirit.

John Paul II reflected profoundly on the God-centered mystery of truth and freedom as intrinsically associated with human rationality and personhood. The Roman Pontiff highlighted the philosophical, theological, moral, ethical and psychological significance of human body language, gender differentiation and the complementarity of the sexes. He fleshed out a theology of the body that posits an indelible ascetical and nuptial meaning of the body. John Paul II recalled God's original plan, His constant will and law that an indissoluble bond should exist between a man and woman in the sacramental covenant of marriage designed to mirror on earth the intra-Trinitarian communion of life and love. The Holy Father was indefatigable in his defense of the fundamental, God-given dignity, beauty, goodness and sacredness of human sexuality and of every human life from conception to natural death. Following the insights of Saint Thomas Aquinas, the Supreme Pontiff explained how the Theology of the Body relates to the mystery of grace building on and perfecting nature.

John Paul II also unpacked sound definitions and concrete implications of moral acts, identifying objective criteria for the formation of a good conscience and the debilitating marks of a bad conscience. John Paul II distinguished good habits from bad habits and meditated on man's propensity toward living a life of virtue or vice in his daily struggle to deny himself, taking up his cross and following in Our Lord's footsteps. In doing so, man is called with the help of God's grace preceding, accompanying and following his every good thought, word and deed (work) to overcome his heart's evil inclinations, and even human suffering whether physical or spiritual or otherwise, so as to be more closely configured to Christ, who in His human nature was like us in all things save sin.[3]

Furthermore, John Paul II examined the mystical core of spousal love and the conjugal act, addressing the practical need for responsible parenthood, and outlining a course for developing a healthy spirituality of marriage rooted in prayer and regular recourse to the Sacraments of Penance and the Holy Eucharist.

Moreover, John Paul II expounded on the moral consequences of evil, sin and concupiscence for individuals and society, doing so *vis à vis* complex theological doctrines, ecclesiastical disciplines, moral and ethical issues, like co-suffering, virginity, chastity, celibacy, continence, fornication, artificial contraception, *in vitro* fertilization, direct sterilization, abortion and euthanasia. Subsequently, the papal Magisterium has been forced to lend added contour to the Theology of the Body by dealing with other moral and ethical crises, like partial-birth abortion, embryonic stem-cell research, cloning, same-sex unions, and assisted suicide.[4]

The Pontiff explicated the salvific significance of the Theology of the Body in relation to man's aspirations for purity and holiness of life, his deep-seated hope for meaningful relationships in a communion of persons (*communio personarum*). This communion of persons necessarily involves the total gift of self to another person, that is intended to be centered on God in all its physical and spiritual dimensions. John Paul II likewise taught us about man's eschatological longing stemming from the fact that his personal existence bears within itself seeds of immortality and

---

[3] Cf. Hebrews 4:15.

[4] In order to understand better John Paul II's catechetical talks on the theology of the body, the reader is strongly recommended to study, for example, the following magisterial documents: Pope Paul VI's Encyclical on the regulation of birth, *Humanæ Vitæ* (July 25, 1968); Pope John Paul II's Apostolic Exhortation on the family, *Familaris Consortio* (November 22, 1981); his Marian Encyclical, *Redemptoris Mater* (March 25, 1987); Apostolic Letter on the dignity and vocation of women, *Mulieris Dignitatem* (August 15, 1988); Encyclical regarding fundamental questions on the Church's moral teaching, *Veritatis Splendor* (August 6, 1993); Encyclical on the value and inviolability of human life, *Evangelium Vitæ* (March 25, 1995); his Catechetical talks on Mary, Mother of God, presented at General Audiences from September 6, 1995 to November 12, 1997.

not just the imprint of immorality stemming from original and actual or personal sin.

In sum, John Paul II's Theology of the Body is rooted in the theological virtues of faith, hope and charity and in the beatitudes, with special emphasis given to the beatitude regarding purity of heart. This theology reassures a fallen humanity that at every stage of human existence God desires that all men be saved and come to the knowledge of the truth.[5] It teaches us that God continues to orient man—mind, body, soul and spirit (to use Pauline categories)—toward resurrection unto eternal life; toward the reunion of each individual with his own unique glorified body and soul in an everlasting communion with the Triune God, his Creator, Redeemer and Sanctifier; in whose image and likeness all men are created; in whom "we live and move and have our being."[6]

John Paul II articulated quite lucidly and insightfully the Marian underpinnings of the Theology of the Body. Hence, it is clear that an authentically Catholic Theology of the Body cannot be apprehended without reference to the mystery of the Blessed Virgin Mary and her singular cooperation in the Father's plan for our eternal salvation accomplished in her divine Son through the working of the Holy Spirit. This salvation of man's entire being is now being brought to fulfillment primarily through the sacramental instrumentality of the Mystical Body of Christ, the Church, which constitutes the communion of saints, wherein Mary holds the highest position of honor as our spiritual Mother, Mediatrix, Advocate and Queen.[7]

A most poignant passage illustrating the interconnectedness of John Paul II's Mariology with the Theology of the Body can be found in his Apostolic Letter, *Mulieris Dignitatem*. The Holy Father wrote:

> The dignity of every human being and the vocation corresponding to that dignity find their definitive measure in *union with God*. Mary, woman of the Bible, is the most complete expression of this

---

[5] 1 Timothy 2: 4.
[6] Acts 17: 28.
[7] Pope John Paul II, *Redemptoris Mater*, 40. 2.

dignity and vocation. For no human being, male or female, created in the image and likeness of God, can *in any way* attain fulfillment apart from this image and likeness.[8]

   With this background in mind, the present essay attempts to
flesh out a rudimentary Theology of the Body in the Mariological
writings of the Venerable John Henry Cardinal Newman. In doing
so, another principal aim of the essay is to discover how John Paul
II's own writings can shed light on Newman's thought. The reader
must bear in mind that Newman, living in nineteenth-century
Europe, did not, by any means, possess either the precise terminology delineating a systematic theology of the body or the need
to address in a direct fashion many of the moral questions that
plagued the previous century and which continue to uproot the
twenty-first century from its Judeo-Christian moral moorings.
However, Newman's prophetic vision did afford him an uncanny
sense of how, for example, the spirit of liberalism in religion and
in society were setting mankind on a wrong path, a path that would
eventually drive man farther away from his innate desire for eternal happiness, rather than closer toward it.[9]

---

[8] Pope John Paul II, *Familiaris Consortio*, 5.

[9] Cf. Wilfrid Ward, *The Life of John Henry Newman: Based on His Life in the
English Church* [Volume 2] (London: Longmans, Green & Co., 1913), 40-461
passim. On the morning of May 12, 1879, Newman was elevated to the Sacred
College of Cardinals in a secret consistory held by Pope Leo XIII. That afternoon
at the Vatican Cardinal Newman delivered his famous *biglietto* speech. In that
speech, Newman graciously accepted the Holy Father's appointment, which
Newman rightly considered to be the crowning of his many achievements, most
especially his outstanding contributions as an intellectual and spiritual convert
from Anglicanism. Furthermore, he used the occasion to summarize many of his
heartfelt beliefs and prophetic prognostications about the state of the Church and
society in the modern world: "I rejoice to say, to one great mischief I have from
the first opposed myself. For thirty, forty, fifty years I have resisted to the best of
my powers the spirit of Liberalism in religion. Never did Holy Church need
champions against it more sorely than now, when, alas! it is an error overspread-
ing, as a snare, the whole earth. . . Liberalism in religion is the doctrine that there
is no positive truth in religion, but that one creed is as good as another, and this
is the teaching which is gaining substance and force daily. It is inconsistent with
any recognition of any religion, as true. It teaches that all are to be tolerated, for
all are matters of opinion. Revealed religion is not a truth, but a sentiment and a
taste; not an objective fact, not miraculous; and it is the right of each individual
to make it say just what strikes his fancy. Devotion is not necessarily founded on
faith. Men may go to Protestant Churches and to Catholic, may get good from
both and belong to neither. They may fraternize together in spiritual thoughts and

1) The Dogma of the Immaculate Conception

A logical starting place for our purpose is the dogma of the Immaculate Conception. This dogma, as Newman both heralded and enthusiastically embraced it long before it was dogmatically defined in 1854, intends, *inter alia*, to focus our attention on Eden, that garden paradise of primordial delights in which the first man and first woman were not only created by a loving and providential God but also justly admonished and punished by Him after the fall.[10]

In his *Meditations and Devotions*, Newman reflects on Mary's title of *Rosa Mystica* (Mystical Rose). He begins by stating that the different elements of the created universe manifest particular attributes of God:

> All that God has made speaks of its Maker; the mountains speak of His eternity; the sun of His immensity; and winds of His Almightiness. In like manner flowers and fruits speak of His sanctity; His love and His Providence . . . by flowers and fruits, are meant, in a mystical sense, the gifts and graces of the Holy Spirit, so by a garden is meant mystically a place of spiritual repose, stillness, peace, refreshment and light.[11]

It is in this Mystical Garden, reminiscent of the Garden of Eden that Newman sees as firmly planted the Mystical Rose, who is Mary, the New Eve. Mary is the fairest fruit of God's creation. She blossoms because she is filled with the graces of the Holy Spirit and because of her particular nearness to the Tree of Life— the Cross of her Son. She is near the Tree of Redemption from the very moment of her Immaculate Conception.

In fact, she is the first fruit of the Redemption, having experienced redemption in anticipation by means of a prevenient grace. She is the first to drink of the delightful waters flowing from the side of the pierced Savior. Furthermore, as Newman argues, the

---

feelings, without having any views at all of doctrines in common, or seeing the need of them. Since, then, religion is so personal a peculiarity and so private a possession, we must of necessity ignore it in the intercourse of man with man . . . The general [nature] of this great *apostasia* is one and the same everywhere; but in detail, and in character, it varies in different countries."

[10] Cf. Genesis 3:8-24.

[11] John Henry Newman, *Meditations and Devotions* (New York: Longmans, Green & Co., 1907), 21.

beauty of Mary's holiness enhances the beauty of the garden of the New Creation because she is not only created without original sin but, as Newman poetically puts it, "in those blessed gardens, as they may be called, she lived by herself, continually visited by the dew of God's grace and growing up a more and more heavenly flower, till at the end of that period she was meet for the inhabitation in her of the Most Holy."[12]

Newman's discussion of this fundamental dogma leads him to consider the notion of the preternatural gifts of Adam and Eve that our first parents possessed before the fall. In other words, Newman emphasizes the importance of our having been created according to the Father's original plan for our beatitude as persons full of original holiness and justice. Therefore, Newman lauds Mary as the S*peculum Iustitiæ* (Mirror of Justice). For Newman, Mary reflects perfectly as a human creature that original justice and holiness in which our first parents participated as the first married couple, and which original sin marred but did not shatter completely.[13]

Certainly, Newman's meditations on the Marian titles *Virgo Purissima* (Virgin Most Pure) and *Virgo Prædicanda* (Virgin to Be Preached), which are part of a series of meditations by Newman on the doctrine of the Immaculate Conception, are meant to enhance our love of Mary's purity as well as the extraordinary gift of integrated holiness—body and soul—that forms the essence of her being from its inception.[14] Mary's sinlessness from the moment of conception is, as Newman reflects in his meditation

---

[12] *Ibid.*, 22.

[13] *Ibid.*, 32.

[14] Cf. John Henry Newman, *Discourses to Mixed Congregations* (New York: Longmans & Green Co., 1909), 352: "Mary then is a specimen, and more than a specimen, in the purity of her soul and body, of what man was before his fall, and what he would have been, had he risen to his full perfection." Newman, relying on the patristic use of the antithetical parallelism between Eve and Mary, so dear to Fathers like St. Justin Martyr and St. Irenæus of Lyon, writes: "And thus she [Mary] is a better Eve. Eve, too, in the beginning may be called the May of the year. She was the first-fruits of God's beautiful creation. She was the type of all beauty; but alas! she represented the world also in its fragility. She stayed not in her original creation. Mary comes as a second and holier Eve, having the grace of indefectibility and the gift of perseverance from the first, and teaching us how to use the gifts without abusing them." [John Henry Newman, *Sermon Notes* (New York: Longmans, Green & Co., 1914), 79.]

Virgo Purissima, her divine "prerogative," "the foundation of all those salutary truths which are revealed to us concerning her."[15]

Newman also underscores this truth in his meditation, *Virgo Prædicanda*. The reader should easily detect how Newman reasons along patristic lines. He likewise follows the logic laid out by medieval theologians like Saint Anselm of Canterbury and his disciple Eadmer of Canterbury, which was brought to fruition in the theology of Blessed John Duns Scotus and later adopted in the dogmatic definition of the Immaculate Conception by Blessed Pope Pius IX. Newman writes:

> Wherefore, when all seemed lost, in order to show what human nature, His work, was capable of becoming; to show how utterly He could bring to naught the utmost efforts, the most concentrated malice of the foe, and reverse all the consequences of the Fall, Our Lord began, even before His coming, to do His most wonderful act of redemption, in the person of her who was to be His Mother. By the merit of that Blood which was to be shed, He interposed to hinder her incurring the sin of Adam, before He had made on the Cross atonement for it. And therefore we *preach* her who is the subject of this wonderful grace.[16]

Mary is the New Eve for she was, as Newman says, "a child of Adam and Eve as though they had never fallen," one who "inherited the gifts and graces (and more than these) which Adam and Eve possessed in Paradise." Thus, even though we neither share in the privilege of Mary's Immaculate Conception nor enjoy the gift of pristine holiness, Newman urges us, as sons and daughters of Adam and Eve fallen from grace yet redeemed by Christ, to join our voices with "all holy souls" in entreating the *Virgo Purissima*: "Virgin Most Pure, conceived without original sin, Mary, pray for us."[17]

According to Newman, the dogma of the Immaculate Conception points to God as having predestined us, but not predetermined us, for eternal life, which constitutes a full share, body and soul, in God's own blessedness, a definitive entering into the Triune Godhead's own communion of eternally reciprocated life and love.

---

[15] *Meditations and Devotions*, 9.
[16] *Ibid.*, 11.
[17] *Ibid.*, 9.

The Supreme Pontiff commented thus in his catechesis delivered on January 30, 1980:

> Happiness is being rooted in love. Original happiness speaks to us of the beginning of man, who emerged from love and initiated love. That happened in an irrevocable way, despite the subsequent sin and death. In His time, Christ will be a witness to this irrevocable love of the Creator and Father, which had already been expressed in the mystery of creation and in the grace of original innocence. The common beginning of man and woman, that is, the original truth of their body in masculinity and femininity, to which Genesis 2:25 draws our attention, does not know shame. This beginning can also be defined as the original and beautifying immunity from shame as a result of love.[18]

Newman, in his 1865 letter to the Reverend Edward B. Pusey, an Anglican professor of New Testament Greek and former member of the Oxford Movement—once spearheaded by Newman—offers an apologetical response to the latter's queries about Catholic Marian doctrine and devotion.[19] In the course of Newman's brilliant apologetic, he tackles the thorny issue of the dogma of the Immaculate Conception.

At one point, Newman is careful to distinguish between the Protestant notion of original sin as a positive almost tangible reality and the Catholic notion of original sin as a negation, an absence or privation of the good, which must be ultimately identified with God Himself. This difference in perspective on original sin is for Newman one of the main premises upon which Protestants base their objection to the dogma of the Immaculate Conception. If we forget that holiness and goodness are man's original state and solely focus on original sin and its effects, we can fall short in appreciating why God chose to create Mary as the Daughter of Eve Unfallen.[20] Newman writes:

---

[18] John Paul II, "The Mystery of Man's Original Innocence" (General Audience of January 30, 1980) in *Theology of the Body*, 67.

[19] Newman's *Letter to Pusey* is a response to the latter's previous missive entitled "*Eirenicon*," a work aimed at fostering ecumenical unity and "peace."

[20] Cf. John Henry Newman, *Certain Difficulties Felt by Anglicans in Catholic Teaching* [Volume II] (New York: Longmans, Green & Co., 1907-1908), 48: "[…] we deny that she had original sin; for by original sin we mean, as I have already said,

Mary may be called, as it were, the daughter of Eve unfallen. . . .I have drawn the doctrine of the Immaculate Conception as an imme-diate inference, from the primitive doctrine that Mary is the Second Eve . . . . If Eve was raised above human nature by that indwelling moral gift we call grace, is it rash to say that Mary had even a greater grace? . . . .And if Eve had this supernatural inward gift from the very first moment of her personal existence, is it possible to deny that Mary too had this gift from the very moment of per-sonal existence? I do not know how to resist the inference. Well, this is simply and literally the doctrine of the Immaculate Conception. I say the doctrine of the Immaculate Conception is in its substance this, and nothing more or less than this (putting aside the question of degrees of grace). And it really does seem to me bound up in the doctrine of the Fathers that Mary is the Second Eve.[21]

Newman's theology of the Immaculate Conception is premised on a solid Catholic anthropology: The truth that God does not view man merely from the perspective of his present sin-ful state of being but primarily as a creature who from the begin-ning was infused with every good, gracious and perfect gift. Of course, Catholic theology has always taken seriously original sin and its dire consequences for man, but never to the point of declar-ing human nature corrupt, only severely debilitated. At the same time, it holds that man is ever capable, by means of God's sancti-fying, healing and saving grace, of recuperating varying degrees of that lost innocence, original holiness and justice that allowed man to live in harmony with God, his neighbor, and the rest of creation before the fall. In other words, we are certainly damaged goods; we are not, however, destroyed goods.

something negative, viz; this only, the *deprivation* of that supernatural unmerited grace which Adam and Eve had on their first formation—deprivation. Mary could not merit, any more than they, the restoration of that grace; but it was restored to her by God's free bounty, from the very first moment of her existence, and thereby, in fact, she never came under the original curse, which consisted in the loss of it. And she had this special privilege, in order to fit her to become the Mother of her and our Redeemer, to fit her mentally, spiritually for it, so that by the aid of the first grace, she might grow in grace, that, when the Angel of the Lord was at hand, she might be 'full of grace,' prepared as far as a creature could be prepared to receive Him into her bosom. I have drawn the doctrine of the Immaculate Conception, as an immediate inference, from the primitive doctrine that Mary is the Second Eve. This argument seems to me to be conclusive." This second volume of this work of Newman is commonly referred to as the *Letter to Pusey*.
[21] *Difficulties of Anglicans*, II, 45-49 *passim*.

These tenets of Catholic anthropology espoused by Newman are a cornerstone of Pope John Paul II's Theology of the Body as explained in the General Audience of September 12, 1979. The Holy Father wrote:

> To this mystery of his creation ("In the image of God He created him"), corresponds the perspective of procreation, ("Be fertile and multiply, fill the earth"), of that becoming in the world and in time, of that *fieri* which is necessarily bound up with the metaphysical situation of creation: of contingent being (*contingens*). Precisely in the metaphysical context of the description of Genesis 1, it is necessary to understand the entity of the good, namely, the aspect of value. Indeed, this aspect appears in the cycle of nearly all the days of creation and reaches its culmination after the creation of man: "God saw everything that He had made, and behold, it was very good" (Genesis 1:31). For this reason it can be said with certainty that the first chapter of Genesis has established an unassailable point of reference and a solid basis for a metaphysic and also for an anthropology and an ethic, according to which *ens et bonum convertentur* (being and the good are convertible). Undoubtedly, all this has a significance for theology, and especially for the theology of the body.[22]

Mary's singular privilege should inculcate in us not only a special reverence or devotion toward her, who is our Mother in the order of grace,[23] but also the realization that the original sin from which she was preserved from the first moment of her existence (i.e., her conception) is that same sin from which we are cleansed at the baptismal font. In both instances is affirmed the awesome initiative of God's omnipotent and providential love for His creatures. In John Paul II's General Audience entitled "Christ's grace preserved Mary from sin," given on June 5, 1996, one learns that:

> No one fails to see how the affirmation of the exceptional privilege granted to Mary stresses that Christ's redeeming action does not only free us from sin, but also preserves us from it. This dimension of preservation, which in Mary is total, is present in the redemptive intervention by which Christ, in freeing man from sin, also gives him the grace and strength to conquer its influence in his life. In this

---

[22] John Paul II, "Analysis of the Biblical Account of Creation" (General Audience of September 12, 1979) in *Theology of the Body*, 29.
[23] Cf. *Lumen Gentium*, 62.

way the dogma of Mary's Immaculate Conception does not obscure but rather helps wonderfully to shed light on the effects in human nature of Christ's redemptive grace. Christians look to Mary, the first to be redeemed by Christ and who had the privilege of not being subjected even for an instant to the power of evil and sin, as the perfect model and icon of that holiness (cf. *Lumen Gentium*, 65) which they are called to attain in their life, with the help of the Lord's grace.[24]

The dogma of the Immaculate Conception extols Mary as the Daughter of Eve Unfallen. Mary's constitution in the fullness of grace should instill in us a holy nostalgia, a desire to be ever more fully conformed and configured to the divine image and likeness in which we were created. The path of return to God was trod in a most admirable way by the Daughter of Eve Unfallen who, by her word and example, taught us that nothing that is unclean can come before God's all-holy presence.

In his meditation, "A Short Service for Rosary Sunday," Newman reflects on the theological significance of Mary's fullness of bodily and spiritual sanctity as evocative of man's eschatological longing that both fulfills and surpasses the happiness of Adam and Eve in the Garden of Eden. By devoutly remembering Mary's name and invoking her intercessory power, the believer is drawn into an earthly web of grace that prepares him for entering into that great cloud of witnesses of the new and everlasting Jerusalem. For example, Newman proffers this ethereal musing:

> Who can repeat her very name without finding in it a music that goes to the heart, and brings before him thoughts of God and Jesus Christ, and heaven above, and fills him with the desire of those graces by which heaven is to be gained?. . . .We will take our part in praising thee in our own time and place with all the redeemed of Our Lord, and will exalt thee in the full assembly of the saints and glorify thee in the Heavenly Jerusalem.[25]

Mary, therefore, is the first fruits, as it were, of the redemptive sacrifice of Our Lord Jesus, who purchased us for God, body and

---

[24] Pope John Paul II, "Christ's Grace Preserved Mary from Sin," (General Audience of June 5, 1996) in *A Catechesis on Mary, Mother of God: Theotókos, Woman, Mother, Disciple* (Volume Five) (Boston, Massachusetts: Pauline Books & Media, 2000), 99.

[25] *Meditations and Devotions*, 261f.

soul, at the price of shedding His royal and innocent blood which He derived from the veins of His Immaculate Mother, now gloriously reigning as the Queen of heaven and earth. The Marian prayer with which Newman concludes his sermon, "The Glories of Mary for the Sake of Her Son," should serve well to summarize what has been said thus far to introduce the next section of this essay:

> Such thou art, Holy Mother, in the creed and in the worship of the Church, the defense of many truths, the grace and smiling light of every devotion. In thee, O Mary, is fulfilled, as we can bear it, an original purpose of the Most High. He once had meant to come on earth in heavenly glory, but we sinned; and then He could not safely visit us, except with a shrouded radiance and a bedimmed Majesty, for He was our God. So He came Himself in weakness, not in power, and He sent thee, a creature, in His stead, with a creature's comeliness and luster sued to our state. And now thy very face and form, dear Mother, speak to us of the Eternal; not like earthly beauty, dangerous to look upon, but like the morning star, which is thy emblem, bright and musical, breathing purity, telling of Heaven, and infusing peace. O harbinger of day! O hope of the pilgrim! lead us still as thou hast led; in the dark night, across the bleak wilderness, guide us on to Our Lord Jesus, guide us home.[26]

2) The Dogmas of the Virginal Conception and the Divine Motherhood (Maternity) of the Blessed Virgin Mary

We can begin with the basic affirmations of the creeds and the liturgy of the Church which Newman cherished in expounding the dogmas they encapsulate according to the logic adhered to in the theological principle: "*Lex orandi, lex credendi*" ("the law of praying is the law of believing"). Thus, for example, we profess in the heart of the Nicene-Constantinopolitan Creed, "For us men and for our salvation He became man by the power of the Holy Spirit and was born of the Virgin Mary." Newman is also fond of citing the following expression from the *Te Deum*, "You did not abhor the Virgin's womb."[27] Furthermore, Newman explains:

---

[26] Cf. *Discourses Addressed to Mixed Congregations,* 358f.

[27] John Henry Newman, *Parochial and Plain Sermons* [Volume II] (New York: Longmans & Green Co., 1907-1909), 29. Newman links these two sources together in his Sermon III, "The Incarnation": "[…] the *Te Deum* and Athanasian Creed—are especially suitable in divine worship, inasmuch as they kindle and elevate the religious affections. They are hymns of praise and thanksgiving; they give

As in the beginning woman was formed out of man by Almighty power so now, by a like mystery, but a reverse order, the new Adam was fashioned from the woman. He was, as had been foretold, the immaculate "seed of the woman," deriving His manhood from the substance of the Virgin Mary; as it is expressed in the articles of the Creed, "conceived by the Holy Ghost, born of the Virgin Mary."[28]

Throughout several of his sermons and discourses, not to mention his *Meditations and Devotions*, the Anglican and Catholic Newman alike does not tire of reflecting on the Incarnation as that mystery of "divine condescension," whereby an *admirabile commercium* ("a marvelous exchange") takes place between God and man. Relying on Fathers of the Church like Saints Athanasius of Alexandria and Gregory of Nazianzen, Newman asserts that: "God became man so that men might become gods."[29]

This process of apotheosis or divinization prompted Newman to ponder the mystery of how God has elevated our fallen human nature, all our human faculties and affections, and the natural state of marriage, together with the entire human family, through the mystery of the Incarnation brought about through the ministration of the humble Virgin of Nazareth.

Newman describes the unfathomable depths of the communion of persons shared by the Virgin Mother Mary and her divine Son. At the same time, he upholds their intimate union as paradigmatic of every mother-son relationship. Newman views this bond between mother and child as one that should be cultivated according to God's providential design. Thus, grace and nature are meant to work harmoniously in the communion of persons from conception to death.

He took the substance of His human flesh from her, and clothed in it He lay within her, and He bore it about with Him after birth, as a sort of pledge and witness that He, though God, was hers. He was nursed and tended by her; He was suckled by her; He lay in

glory to God as revealed in the Gospel, just as David's psalms magnify His attributes displayed in nature, His wonderful works in the creation of the world, and His mercies towards the house of Israel."

[28] *Parochial and Plain Sermons*, II, 31.

[29] Cf. John Henry Newman, *Select Treatises of Saint Athanasius in Controversy with Arians* [2 volumes], (New York: Longmans Green & Co., 1903).

her arms. As time went on, He ministered to her for thirty years, in one house, with an uninterrupted intercourse, and with only the saintly Joseph to share with Him. She was the witness of His growth, of His joys, of His sorrows, of His prayers; she was blest with His smile, with the touch of His hand, with the whisper of His affection, with the expression of His thoughts and feelings, for that length of time.[30]

The divinization of man is a process that occurs through the cooperation of the Virgin Mary from whom Our Lord derived His Sacred Humanity which, both Saint Thomas Aquinas[31] and Cardinal Newman tell us, is the primary instrument of our eternal salvation. Newman stresses time and again that the divine maternity is a bulwark of the Church's theology of the Incarnation. As history proves, so Newman argues, those who began by denying Mary's divine maternity ended up denying Our Lord's divinity. Far from throwing Our Lord's divinity into the shade, Mary's divine maternity highlights it. She is the presidium of the hypostatic union so that her body-soul composite safeguards Jesus' body-soul composite.[32]

In his *Discourses to Mixed Congregations*, Newman impresses his listeners with an argument in favor of the *nexus myste-*

---

[30] *Discourses to Mixed Congregations*, 362.

[31] See, for example, Saint Thomas Aquinas, *Summa Theologiæ*, III, q. 19. art. 4. & *pars* III, q. 22. art. 3.

[32] In his Anglican sermon, "The Reverence Due to the Virgin Mary," Newman praises Mary as an object of singular divine predilection in view of her singular office as Mother of the Redeemer and Mother of the redeemed. Her merits in effect safeguard Christ's own unique position in the divine economy of salvation, and likewise assist us in our cooperation in the same. Newman preached this homily on "Lady's Day," as the feast of the Annunciation was commonly termed in England (March 25, 1832): "But further, she is doubtless to be accounted blessed and favoured in herself, as well as in the benefits she has done for us. Who can estimate the holiness and perfection of her, who was chosen to be the Mother of Christ? If to him that hath, more is given, and holiness and divine favour go together (and this we are told), what must have been the transcendent purity of her, whom the Creator Spirit condescended to overshadow with His miraculous presence? What must have been her gifts, who was chosen to be the only near-earthly relative of the Son of God, the only one whom He was bound by nature to revere and instruct day by day, as He grew in wisdom and in stature? This contemplation runs to a higher subject, did we dare follow it; for what, think you, was the sanctified state of that human nature, of which God formed His sinless Son; knowing as we do, 'that which is born of the flesh is flesh,' and 'none can bring a clean thing out of an unclean thing?'" [*Parochial and Plain Sermons*, II, 131f.]

riorum (the linking together of the mysteries of faith) in the divine economy of salvation by which the essential truths concerning the *Theotokos* and her cooperation in this economy are never separated from the truths we hold about her Son:

> You see, then, my brethren, in this particular, the harmonious consistency of the revealed system, and the bearing of one doctrine upon another; Mary is exalted for the sake of Jesus. It was fitting that she, as being a creature, though the first of creatures, should have an office of ministration. She, as others, came into the world to do a work, she had a mission to fulfill; her grace and her glory are not for her own sake, but for her Maker's; and to her is committed the custody of the Incarnation; this is her appointed office. . . . As she was once upon earth, and was personally the guardian of her Divine Child, as she carried Him in her womb, folded Him in her embrace, and suckled at her breast, so now, and to the latest hour of the Church, do her glories and the devotion paid to her proclaim and define the right faith concerning Him as God and Man.[33]

The apex of Divine Revelation is, of course, the mystery of the Incarnation, at the heart of which is found together with the Word of God made flesh, a woman named Mary: "Her [Mary's] very image is as a book in which we may read at a glance the mystery of the Incarnation and the mystery of Redemption."[34] Mary is no ordinary creature but the bearer of a unique privilege, insofar as her relationship to the mystery and event of the Incarnation is incomparably more intimate than any other creature. She is the *Theotokos* (God–bearer) and her divine motherhood is the most fundamental of all her privileges: "As soon as we apprehend by faith the great fundamental truth that Mary is the Mother of God, other wonderful titles follow in its train."[35] Newman explains:

> It is this awful title which both illustrates and connects together the two prerogatives of Mary, on which I have been lately enlarging, her sanctity and her greatness. It is the issue of her sanctity; it is the origin of her greatness. What dignity can be too great to attribute to her who is so closely bound up, as intimately one, with the Eternal Word, as a mother is with a son? . . . What fullness and

---

[33] *Discourses to Mixed Congregations*, 349.
[34] *Meditations and Devotions*, 261. Newman's source for this phrase is a homily attributed to St. Epiphanius of Salamis, wherein he compares Mary to the incomparable book in which the Word is read. (cf. *PG* 94:1029).
[35] *Meditations and Devotions*, 62.

redundance of grace, what exuberance of merits must have been hers, when once we admit the supposition, which the Fathers justify, that her Maker really did regard those merits, and take them into account, when He condescended "not to abhor the Virgin's womb"? Is it surprising then that on the one hand she should be immaculate in her conception? Or on the other hand that she should be honoured with an Assumption, and exalted as a queen with a crown of twelve stars, with the rulers of day and night to do her service? Men sometimes wonder that we call her Mother of life, of mercy, of salvation; what are all these titles compared to that one name, Mother of God?[36]

Newman upholds the Church's teaching that Mary can be rightly venerated under the title of Mother of God (e.g., *Mater Dei, Dei Genetrix*) because the Church regards her neither as a goddess, nor as the author of Our Lord's divine essence, as was misunderstood by Nestorius and his followers, but rather as the pure Mother of Christ's whole person. Clarifications of subsequent ecumenical councils (e.g., Constantinople II) are treated in Newman's thought as integral to a full and proper explanation of the Church's orthodox Christology. These councils infallibly teach that Our Lord's human and divine natures correspond to His possession of both a human and a divine intellect and of both a human and divine will, which function with complete integrity in subordination to the will of the Father and the promptings of the Holy Spirit, so that any action attributed to His sacred humanity is automatically attributed to His divine person eternally united to the Godhead, thereby following the theological principle known as *communicatio idiomatum* or "the communication of idioms."

This theological groundwork provided by the Church's earliest ecumenical councils serves undoubtedly to ground Catholic Marian doctrine and devotion in a proper understanding of human personhood. Because Newman regards Mary's intimate association with the whole spectrum of Our Lord's redemptive life and ministry, the doctrine of Mary's divine maternity becomes the *raison d'être* of all of Our Lady's other titles and functions (offices) in the history of salvation. If Mary is understood by Newman as

---

[36] *Difficulties of Anglicans*, II, 62f.

an integral part of the Incarnation and Paschal Mysteries, one can likewise speculate that Newman would have affirmed Mary as a central node of an authentic Catholic Theology of the Body.

Furthermore, at the most basic level, the mystery of the Annunciation, for example, reveals that Our Lady is "pro-life" at the very core of her being. Not only does her joyful consent (*fiat*) reveal her openness to life but likewise her canticle of praise, the *Magnificat*, acts as a prolonged commentary on her pro-life stance during the joyful mystery of the visitation of her cousin Elizabeth, who (once sterile) has now become pregnant in her old age with John the Baptist. While Mary's conception of Our Lord is purely virginal, Elizabeth's comes about through the normal course sanctified by the same one, true and living God of Abraham, Isaac and Jacob, who looks upon Mary and Elizabeth in their lowliness (*tapeinosis*).

Mary at the house of Zechariah and Elizabeth sings about the *magnalia Dei* or the *mirabilia Dei* (the great/marvelous things of God) who has performed a life-affirming miracle within her that enlightens the whole history of salvation and encompasses the whole of her being: "My soul proclaims the greatness of the Lord; my spirit rejoices in God my Savior. . . ." John Paul II's reflection on the *Magnificat* in *Redemptoris Mater* reveals a similar appreciation of Mary's role of cooperation in the economy of salvation as the New Eve:

> In the *Magnificat* the Church sees uprooted that sin which is found at the outset of the earthly history of man and woman, the sin of disbelief and of "little faith" in God. In contrast with the "suspicion" which the "father of lies" sowed in the heart of Eve, the true "Mother of the Living," boldly proclaims the *undimmed* truth about God: the holy and almighty God, who from the beginning is *the source of all gifts*, He who 'has done great things' in her, as well as in the whole universe. In this act of creation God gives existence to all that is. In creating man, God gives him the dignity of the image and likeness of Himself in a special way as compared with all earthly creatures. Moreover, in His desire to give, *God gives Himself in the Son*, notwithstanding man's sin: "He so loved the world that He gave His only Son" (John 3:16). Mary is the first wit-

ness of this marvelous truth, which will be fully accomplished through "the works and words" (cf. Acts 1:1) of her Son and definitively through His Cross and Resurrection.[37]

Mary's response at the Annunciation and Visitation is characterized by Newman not as indicative of her having been a passive spectator in the economy of salvation; on the contrary, she exercised free-will, reasons of both heart and intellect (mind), in consenting to the Word of God and in bearing witness to it through evangelization. Friedel, in reflecting on Newman's Mariology, comments thus:

> God ever demands a reasonable service and the voluntary cooperation of creatures in His works; He forces no will, but requires acquiescence in His designs. Though the Incarnation was to be of such tremendous significance for the whole human race, nevertheless as for man's fall, so for the restoration, He allowed the accomplishment of His Will to rest solely on the *fiat* of a young maiden.[38]

Mary of Nazareth's response to the Angel, as Newman reflects, does not elicit sentiments of a mere biological virginity reduced to a mere biological instrumentality for the sake of bringing Jesus into the world. Rather, Our Lady's *fiat* is indicative of her free and loving personal agency that allows for the enfleshment of God.

In the *Letter to Pusey*, Newman considers the mystery of Mary's cooperation at the moment of the Annunciation as one that parallels in antithetical fashion the very real cooperation, not just notional, that Eve exerted in the cause of our fall. As Virgin Mother, Mary's maternity is one that encompasses her entire being, body and soul. Her *fiat*, or yes to God's plan of salvation, constituted an on-going consent that allowed the Holy Spirit to make his indwelling a fountain of physical and spiritual benefits for Mary as an individual believer. These benefits then redounded to us who are likewise saved by the actions of the God-Man, whose coming is facilitated by her singular *amen* to the divine economy of grace. The Theology of the Body is, therefore, viewed by Newman as inexorably linked to the life of the Spirit. The virtues of faith and

---

[37] Pope John Paul II, Encyclical, *Redemptoris Mater*, 37.
[38] Francis J. Friedel, *The Mariology of Cardinal Newman* (New York: Benziger Brothers, 1928), 191.

obedience, of submitting one's will to God's will, are essential components of a Marian theology of the body, and, therefore, paradigmatic for each one of us in our relationship with the Lord.

Newman writes about the patristic view thus:

> They declare that she was not a mere instrument in the Incarnation such as David or Judah may be considered; she cooperated in our salvation not merely by the descent of the Holy Ghost upon her body; but by specific holy acts, the effects of the Holy Ghost within her soul; but as Eve forfeited privileges by the fruits of grace; as Eve was disobedient and unbelieving; that as Eve was a cause of ruin to all; that as Eve made room for Adam's fall, so Mary made room for Our Lord's reparation of it; and thus, whereas the free gift was not as the offense, but much greater, it follows that, as Eve cooperated in effecting a great evil, Mary cooperated in effecting a much greater good.[39]

Furthermore, he explains in his sermon, "Our Lady in the Gospel," that virtue is at the heart of Mary's predestination to become the Mother of the Word-made-flesh. God is so respectful of the tremendous gift of human free-will that He does not and will not coerce us into becoming or being virtuous. Newman understands that virtues must be honed in cooperation with God who aims to save us as whole persons. Here, one is reminded of Saint Augustine's famous adage: "*Qui ergo fecit te sine te non te justificat sine te*," "He who made you without you does not justify you without you."

Newman reflects:

> For when the Angel appeared to her and declared to her the will of God, they say that she displayed especially four graces, humility, faith, obedience and purity. Nay, these graces were, as it were, preparatory conditions to her being made the minister of so high a dispensation. So that if she had not had faith, and humility, and purity, and obedience, she would not have merited to be God's Mother. Thus it is common to say that she conceived Christ in mind before she conceived Him in body, meaning that the blessedness of faith and obedience preceded the blessedness of being a Virgin Mother. Nay, they even say that God waited for her consent before

---

[39] *Difficulties of Anglicans*, II, 36.

He came into her and took flesh of her. Just as He did no mighty work in one place because they had not faith, so this great miracle, by which He became the Son of a creature, was suspended til she was tried and found meet for it—til she obeyed.[40]

Thanks to Mary's love and responsibility by which, first and foremost, she conceives the Word of God in her mind through reasoned faith, she is declared by Saints Augustine and John Chrysostom and the Venerable Newman as being more blessed spiritually than in actually conceiving Christ in her womb.[41] In effect, all three hail Mary as having a two-fold blessedness, a blessedness rooted in her faithful discipleship of Christ and in her divine maternity or virginal motherhood of the Word-made-flesh who pitches his tent in our midst.[42]

John Paul II, in his catechesis on the Theology of the Body given at the General Audience of March 12, 1980, wrote:

The whole exterior constitution of woman's body, its particular aspect, the qualities which, with the power of perennial attractiveness, are at the beginning of the knowledge, which Genesis 4:1-2 speaks of ("Adam knew his wife Eve"), are in close union with motherhood. The Bible (and subsequently the Liturgy), with its characteristic simplicity, honors and praises throughout the centuries "the womb that bore you and the breasts that you sucked" (Luke 11:27). These words constitute a eulogy of motherhood, of femininity, of the female body in its typical expression of creative love. In the Gospel these words are referred to the Mother of Christ, Mary, the Second Eve. The first woman, on the other hand, at the moment when the maternal maturity of her body was revealed for the first time, when she conceived and bore, said: "I have begotten a man with the help of the Lord."[43]

---

[40] John Henry Newman, *Faith and Prejudice*, 89.

[41] Cf. *Faith and Prejudice*, 86.

[42] Cf. John 1:14. In this verse of John's Prologue, the Greek word "*eskenosin*," meaning: "He pitched his tent," is employed. This word's significance, harkening back to the Old Testament theology of God's abiding presence in the midst of His Chosen People Israel in relation to the portable meeting tent (tabernacle), ark of covenant, Temple of Jerusalem, is somewhat lost in translations like "and dwelt among us."

[43] John Paul II, "The Mystery of Woman Revealed in Motherhood" (General Audience of March 12, 1980) in *Theology of the Body*, 82.

Newman treats these points thus:

> What is the highest, the rarest, the choicest prerogative of Mary? It is
> that she was without sin. When a woman in the crowd cried out to
> Our Lord, "Blessed is the womb that bore thee!" He answered, "More
> blessed are they who hear the Word of God and keep it." Those words
> were fulfilled in Mary. She was filled with grace *in order* to be the
> Mother of God. But it was a higher gift than her maternity to be thus
> sanctified and thus pure. Our Lord indeed would not have become
> her Son *unless* He had first sanctified her; but still, the greater
> blessedness was to have that perfect sanctification.[44]

To this end, Newman offers a prolonged exegesis of Luke
11:27-28 in his Catholic sermon, "Our Lady in the Gospel," and
also cites in the *Letter to Pusey* the Father of the Church, St. Peter
Chrysologus, who declares that Mary's *fiat* to virginal motherhood
has a "price" and a "hire" in terms of our salvation.[45] Consequently,
Newman notes that Mary's cooperation, both physical and spiritual, is meritorious both for her own salvation and for ours. In citing
St. Jerome in that same *Letter to Pusey*, Newman concurs that
death came to us through Eve and life, on the other hand, came to
us through Mary.

In reflecting on the Virgin Mary's prudent and sapiential
question addressed to the Angel, "*Quomodo istud fiet mihi quia
non cognosco vir?*" Newman, following certain strains of traditional piety now formidably backed up by certain biblical exegesis,
posits the notion that Mary's consent to become the *Theotokos* presupposes her having made a vow of virginity; she does not know
man in the biblical sense,[46] but like all the pious, humble women of
her time (*anawim*) would have been open to becoming the mother
of the Promised Messiah according to the natural course. However,
as *Lumen Gentium* teaches, citing the third canon of the Lateran
Council held in A.D. 649, Christ in being born of Mary by the

---

[44] *Meditations and Devotions*, 10.
[45] Cf. *Difficulties of Anglicans*, II, 43.
[46] Cf. John Paul II, "Analysis of Knowledge and Procreation," (General Audience
of March 5, 1980) in *Theology of the Body*, 78: "In this way, through the term
knowledge used in Genesis 4:1-2 and often in the Bible, the conjugal relationship
of man and woman—that they become, through the duality of sex, 'one flesh'—
was raised and introduced into the specific dimension of persons. Genesis 4:1-2
speaks only of knowledge of the woman by the man, as if to stress above all the

power of the Holy Spirit did not violate Mary's virginity but rather consecrated it.[47] This teaching of the Second Vatican Council is one already anticipated in the doctrinal and devotional writings of the Venerable Newman, who has been dubbed by many a theologian and pope as a precursor or prophet of the Council.[48] Newman reflects on the title, *Janua Cæli* (Gate of Heaven):

> Therefore, weighing well the Angel's words before giving answer to them—first she asked whether so great an office would be a forfeiture of that Virginity which she had vowed. When the Angel told her no, then, with full consent of a full heart, full of God's love to her and to her own lowliness, she said, "Behold the handmaid of the Lord; be it done to me according to thy word." It was by this consent that she became the *Gate of Heaven*.[49]

Mary was not an incubator of the Christ-Child. Rather, she had a real, not just notional, relationship with the One whom she carried in her womb for the nine-month gestation period. Her personal relationship with the Word-made-flesh is unsurpassed among human creatures. Newman goes to great lengths to use vivid, biological language to describe the reality of the Incarnation (Christ's Sacred Humanity), for he derived His manhood from her. Because of the mystery of the Incarnation, "the flesh is the hinge of our salvation" (*caro cardo salutis*), according to the third-century Latin Christian writer Tertullian. Newman's theology of the Incarnation seconds the truth of this adage. He speaks of Christ as having taken from Mary all those elements that make up His perfect human nature.

In a beautiful passage taken from his Anglican sermon, "The Mystery of the Divine Condescension," Newman reflects on Mary's union with Christ, from the crib of Bethlehem to the cross of

---

activity of the latter. It is also possible, however, to speak of the reciprocity of this knowledge, in which man and woman participate by means of their body and their sex. Let us add that a series of subsequent biblical texts, as, moreover, the same chapter of Genesis (cf. Genesis 4:17, 4:25), speak with the same language. This goes up to the words Mary of Nazareth spoke in the Annunciation: 'How can this be, since I know not man?' (Luke 1:34)."

[47] Cf. *Lumen Gentium* 57.

[48] Cf. Jean Guitton, *Il Secolo che Verrà: Conversazioni con Philip Guyard,* trans. Antonietta Francavilla (Milan: Bompiani, 1999), 141. Also, *L'Osservatore Romano* (28 October 1963).

[49] *Meditations and Devotions*, 37f.

Calvary, as one that is both maternal and spousal; in so doing, he relates this theology to the nuptial imagery of the Canticle of Canticles (5:10-16) that also foreshadows the spousal relationship between Christ and his Mystical Bride, the Church, mentioned in Saint Paul's Epistle to the Ephesians 5:21-33.

Thus, Newman exhorts his congregation:

> Think not you, my brethren, that to Mary, when she held Him in her maternal arms, when she gazed on the pale countenance and the dislocated limbs of her God, when she traced the wandering lines of blood, when she counted the weals, bruises, and the wounds, which dishonoured her virginal flesh, think you not that to her eyes it was more beautiful than when she first worshipped it, pure, radiant, and fragrant, on the night of His Nativity? *Dilectus meus candidus et rubricandus*, as the Church sings; "My beloved is white and ruddy; His whole form doth breathe of love, and doth provoke to love in turn; His drooping head; His open palms; and His breast are all bare. My beloved is white and ruddy; choice out of thousands; His head is of the finest gold; His locks are branches of palm-trees, black as a raven. His eyes are doves upon the brooks of water, which are washed with milk, and sit beside the plentiful streams. His cheeks are as beds of aromatical spices set by the perfumers; His lips are lilies dropping choice myrrh. His hands are turned and golden, full of jacinths; His throat is most sweet, and He is all lovely. Such is my beloved, and He is my friend, O ye daughters of Jerusalem."[50]

In other words, to paraphrase an expression of Adam in the Genesis story, Jesus is bone of Mary's bone and flesh of Mary's flesh. One could also add to this, given what Newman says in the previous text, that Jesus is blood of Mary's blood, blood being that element of man which according to biblical theology was believed to contain the life, the very soul of a living man (*nefesh*).[51] Newman explains this theology of the body in his discourse to Mixed Congregations, entitled "On the Fitness of the Glories of Mary":

> She had no chance place in the divine Dispensation; the Word of God did not merely come to her and go from her; He did not pass through her, as He visits us in Holy Communion. It was no heavenly body which the Eternal Son assumed, fashioned by angels, and brought down to this lower world: no; He imbibed, He absorbed into

---

[50] *Discourses to Mixed Congregations*, 302f.
[51] Cf. *Summa Theologiæ*, III, q. 31. art. 5.

His divine Person, her blood and the substance of her flesh; by becoming Man of her, He received her lineaments and features, as the appropriate character in which He was to manifest Himself to mankind. The child is like the parent, and we may well suppose that by His likeness to her was manifested her relationship to Him. Her sanctity comes, not only of her being His Mother, but also of His being her Son: "If the first fruits be holy," says Saint Paul, "the mass is also holy; if the mass be holy, so are the branches."[52]

John Paul II, in his General Audience on November 14, 1979, shed further light on these mysteries of our faith in his Theology of the Body when he wrote:

The words of Genesis 2:24 bear witness to the original meaning of unity, which will have in the revelation of God an ample and distant perspective. This unity through the body—"and the two will be one flesh"—possesses a multiform dimension. It possesses an ethical dimension, as is confirmed by Christ's answer to the Pharisees in Matthew 19 (cf. Mark 10). It also has a sacramental dimension, a strictly theological one, as is proved by St. Paul's words to the Ephesians which refer to the tradition of the prophets (Hosea, Isaiah, Ezekiel).

This is so because, right from the beginning, that unity which is realized through the body indicates not only the "body," but also the "incarnate" communion of persons—*communio personarum*—and calls for this communion. Masculinity and femininity express the dual aspect of man's somatic constitution. "This at last is bone of my bones and flesh of my flesh." Furthermore, through the same words of Genesis 2:23, they indicate the new consciousness of the sense of one's own body. It can be said that this sense consists in mutual enrichment. Precisely this consciousness, through which humanity is formed again as the communion of persons, seems to be the layer which in the narrative of the creation of man (and in the revelation of the body contained in it) is deeper than his somatic structure as male and female. In any case, this structure is presented right from the beginning with a deep consciousness of human corporality and sexuality, and that establishes an inalienable norm for the understanding of man on the theological plane.[53]

---

[52] *Discourses to Mixed Congregations*, 368f. Cf. Romans 11:16.
[53] John Paul II, "By the Communion of Persons Man Becomes the Image of God" (General Audience of November 14, 1979) in *Theology of the Body*, 47f.

In his *Meditations and Devotions*, Newman is careful to balance his understanding of the intimacy between the Divine Son and Mother by saying that it did not reside merely on the physical plane but encompassed also the fact that Our Lord's intellectual and spiritual growth according to His human nature would have been attained in no small measure due to Mary's influence. Of course, conversely this also holds true, for as Newman speculates, the divine intimacy of the thirty years of Jesus' hidden life would have been a privileged *locus theologicus* in the life of the Virgin. This is why Newman has a particular fondness for considering Mary under her title of *Sedes Sapientiæ*, (Seat of Wisdom).[54] In Newman's estimation, Mary far surpassed in knowledge of the Incarnate Lord the knowledge of all the philosophers, saints and angels combined. Hers is not a mere speculative or book knowledge but one that derives from a unique experience of a prolonged, daily intercourse, a sacred conversation (*cor ad cor loquitur*, "heart speaks to heart,"—Newman's cardinalatial motto) with the Son of God made man. As Our Lord's filial devotion and obedient submission to the Father's Will and to Mary and Joseph at the Holy House of Nazareth allowed Him to grow in wisdom, age and grace before God and men, so too did Our Lady make steady progress in her own pilgrimage of faith, exemplifying the obedience of faith as Our Lord's most perfect disciple.

Along these lines, in his fifteenth sermon[55] before the University at Oxford, Newman (on the threshold of conversion to Catholicism) began by reflecting on how Mary may be considered to be exemplary of both the lay man and theologian, indeed a paradigm of the Doctors of the Church, in relationship to the mysteries of faith which she not only experienced first-hand in the flesh but likewise pondered in the depths of her heart as those mysteries unfolded before her eyes.

---

[54] Cf. *Meditations and Devotions*, 33-35.

[55] Cf. John Henry Newman, *Fifteen Sermons Preached before the University at Oxford* [between 1826 and 1843] (New York: Longmans, Green & Co, 1909), 312f. This sermon was preached on the feast of Our Lady's Purification, 2 February 1843. It is entitled, "The Theory of Development in Religious Doctrine" and deals primarily with the relationship between faith and reason and was considered as the foundational text for his *magnum opus*, *An Essay on the Development of Christian Doctrine*. See the edition of Newman's *Essay* with a foreword by renowned Newman scholar Ian Ker (South Bend, Indiana: University of Notre Dame Press, 1989).

3) The Dogma of Mary's Perpetual Virginity

Cardinal Newman sides most definitely with Saint Jerome in his doctrinal positions in favor of Mary's perpetual virginity, assimilating for himself Jerome's timeless arguments against the heretical notions of Jovinian, Bonossus and Helvidius in the fifth century.[56] He also appropriates the patristic distinctions in speaking of Mary as *virgo ante partum, in partu et post partum* (a virgin before giving birth, in giving birth, and after giving birth). Even prior to these considerations, however, one would be remiss not to remark about how Newman both as an Anglican and a Catholic refers to Mary by the simple yet profound title "the Virgin." One could argue in a straightforward manner that if Mary were not truly and perpetually a virgin calling her "the Virgin," would defy all logic.

In commenting on Justin's *Dialogue with Trypho*, Newman contrasts the sterility of Eve's virginity to the fruitfulness of Mary's virginity. Both virgins offer consent. However, Mary the Virgin consents to the Word of God and thus makes manifest a cornucopia of virtues, manifold fruits of faith, hope and charity. On the other hand, the virgin Eve consents to the word of satan, which consent brings death in its wake (e.g., the fratricide of Abel by Cain) while Mary's *fiat* brings immortal life and light to the world in the person of the Logos Incarnate.

Mary's perpetual virginity stands for the totality and irrevocability of one's Christian commitment. In no uncertain terms, Newman identifies Mary's response to the Angel as an avowal of virginity, predisposing her to be the *Janua Cæli* through which, as Newman writes, "Our Lord passes from heaven to earth." We discover in this meditation a significant example of his spiritual exegesis of the Sacred Text, especially insofar as he shows the interconnectedness between the Old and New Testaments and the fulfillment of the Old in the New. In this instance, Newman focuses on the words of the prophet Ezekiel (44:1-3), which he interprets, according to the Tradition, as a prophecy of the virgin birth. Hence, the use of the title *Janua Cæli* for the Blessed Mary ever-Virgin:

[56] Cf. *Difficulties of Anglicans*, II, 66. See *Select Treatises on Saint Athanasius*, II, 205f. Also, Friedel, *Mariology*, 229.

The prophet Ezechiel, prophesying of Mary, says, "the gate shall be closed, it shall not be opened, and no man shall pass through it, since the Lord God of Israel has entered through it—and it shall be closed for the Prince, the Prince Himself shall sit in it." Now this is fulfilled, not only in Our Lord having taken flesh from her, and being her Son, but, moreover, in that she had a place in the economy of Redemption; it is fulfilled in her spirit and will, as well as in her body.[57]

John Paul II commented on the relationship between the doctrine of Mary's perpetual virginity and the Theology of the Body in a series of seventy Marian catechetical discourses which he delivered at his General Audiences from September 6, 1995 to November 12, 1997. In his General Audience of December 6, 1995, the Pope stated:

In looking attentively at Mary, we also discover in her the model of virginity lived for the Kingdom. The virgin *par excellence*, in her heart she grew in her desire to live in this state in order to achieve an ever deeper intimacy with God. For women called to virginal chastity, Mary reveals the lofty meaning of so special a vocation. Thus she draws attention to the spiritual fruitfulness which it produces in the divine plan: a higher order of motherhood, a motherhood according to the Spirit (cf. *Mulieris Dignitatem*, 21).[58]

The Pope reflects on Mary's intention to remain a virgin in a Jewish culture that emphasized God's blessings on child-bearing (cf. Genesis 1:28: "Be fertile and multiply; Fill the earth and subdue it.") and the divine curse on sterility and infertility to the detriment of any real notion of sacred virginity as a divinely willed state of life (vocation) thus: "The extraordinary case of the Virgin of Nazareth must not let us fall into the error of tying her inner dispositions

---

[57] *Meditations and Devotions*, 36. See *Lumen Gentium*, 64 as regards the Church's virginal maternity: "She herself is a virgin, who keeps whole and entire the faith given to her by her spouse. Imitating the mother of her Lord, and by the power of the Holy Spirit, she keeps with virginal purity an entire faith, a firm hope and a sincere charity. . . . The Church indeed, contemplating her hidden sanctity, imitating her charity and faithfully fulfilling the Father's will, by receiving the Word of God in faith becomes a mother. By her preaching she brings forth to a new and immortal life the sons who are born to her in Baptism, conceived of the Holy Spirit and born of God."

[58] Pope John Paul II, "Mary Sheds Light on the Role of Woman" (General Audience of December 6, 1995) in *A Catechesis on Mary, the Mother of God*, 47.

completely to the mentality of her surroundings, thereby eliminating the uniqueness of the mystery that came to pass in her."[59]

John Paul II explained how Mary's choice of virginity, which is a particular fruit of the Holy Spirit's activity, inspires consecrated virginity when he stated: "Mary's virginal life inspires in the entire Christian people esteem for the gift of virginity and the desire that it should increase in the Church as a sign of God's primacy over all reality and as a prophetic anticipation of the life to come."[60]

During the General Audience held on August 21, 1996, which was entitled, "Mary and Joseph Lived the Gift of Virginity," the Holy Father explained that the Blessed Mother and Saint Joseph were given the grace to live according to the charism of virginity without in any way diminishing the authenticity of their marriage, so much so that Joseph, for example, though certainly not the biological father of Jesus, exercised a real fatherhood in his regard.[61]

Drawing inspiration from John Paul II, we can finally return to Newman's thought by asking the question: If everything in Mary's personhood is centered on Christ the God-Man, then must not our persons also be Christ-centered, no matter what our vocation in life since the universal call to holiness also implies a universal call to chastity? This central tenet of our Catholic Faith is illustrated by Newman's meditation for "Saturday," dedicated to the contemplation of Mary as the model of virgins. He invites us to imagine Mary as "robed in white, like the lily," bringing our attention to her purity. Newman then instructs us to address the Virgin in these words:

> Thou, Mary, art the Virgin of Virgins. To have a virginal soul is to love nothing on earth in comparison to God, or except for His sake. That soul is virginal which is ever looking for its Beloved Who is in Heaven, and which sees Him in whatever is lovely upon

[59] Pope John Paul II, "Our Lady Intended to Remain a Virgin" (General Audience of July 24, 1996) in *A Catechesis on Mary, the Mother of God*, 118.

[60] Pope John Paul II, "Mary's Choice Inspires Consecrated Virginity" (General Audience of August 7, 1996) in *A Catechesis on Mary, the Mother of God*, 125.

[61] Cf. Pope John Paul II, "Mary and Joseph Lived the Gift of Virginity" (General Audience of August 21, 1996) in *A Catechesis on Mary, the Mother of God*, 127-129.

the earth, loving earthly friends very dearly, but in the proper place, as His gifts, and His representatives, but loving Jesus alone with sovereign affection, and bearing to lose all, so that she may keep Him . . . O Mary, when will you gain for me some little of this celestial purity, this true whiteness of soul, that may fix my heart on my true love?[62]

4) The Dogma of the Assumption

In his Discourse to Mixed Congregations, entitled, *"On the Fitness of the Glories of Mary,"* Newman focuses on the appropriateness of this dogma in relationship to the dogma of the Immaculate Conception and the saving effects of the Paschal Mystery, which include eschatological hope. He affirms his belief that Mary's Assumption, body and soul, into the glories of Heaven is the logical consequence of the divine privilege of being conceived without original sin, of possessing that original holiness and sanctity in which she faithfully persevered until her earthly course was completed. In citing Psalm 16, Newman infers the fulfillment of both Our Lord's and Mary's bodily incorruption and resurrection. Moreover, Newman views this psalm as prophetic in its eschatological outlook as it implies that on the Last Day the Lord will communicate to all his faithful ones a bodily and spiritual incorruptibility. Thus, we will be inserted definitively into the Paschal Mystery, whose joys the Ascended Christ shares as the first-born of many brothers. In the mystery of the Assumption, Jesus communicated to Mary her own particular share in these paschal joys as a reward for her perfect discipleship, which we in turn are exhorted by Newman to imitate.

John Paul II, in his Encyclical *Redemptoris Mater*, relying on the insights of Pope Pius XII and the Second Vatican Council, reflected on the implications of the dogma of the Assumption for the eschatological hopes of all Christian believers:

Through her mediation, subordinate to that of the Redeemer, Mary contributes *in a special way to the union of the pilgrim Church* on earth with the eschatological and heavenly *reality* of the Communion of Saints, since she has already been "assumed into heaven." . . . . By the mystery of the Assumption there were

---

[62] *Meditations and Devotions*, 221f.

definitively accomplished in Mary all the effects of the one mediation of *Christ the Redeemer of the world* and *risen Lord*: "In
Christ shall all be made alive. But each in his own order: Christ
the first fruits, then at His coming those who belong to Christ"
(1 Corinthians 15:22-23). In the mystery of the Assumption is
expressed the faith of the Church, according to which Mary is
"united by a close and indissoluble bond" to Christ, for, if as
Virgin and Mother she was singularly united with Him *in His first
coming*, so through her continued collaboration with Him she
will also be united with Him in expectation of the second;
"redeemed in an especially sublime manner by reason of the merits of her Son," she also has that specifically maternal role of
mediatrix of mercy *at His final coming*, when all those who
belong to Christ "shall be made alive," when "the last enemy to
be destroyed is death" (1 Corinthians 15:26).[63]

It is Newman's theological opinion that Mary's physical
death could not have been a consequence of any sin whatsoever
(either original or personal) but was a means of participating more
fully in the mystery of Our Lord's dying and rising. Without apply-
ing the term prevenient grace to the doctrine of the Assumption,
Newman certainly suggests a divine and providential logic that
makes of these two doctrines two sides of the same coin.

Of course, it must be stated here that the Catholic Church
(including the present *Catechism of the Catholic Church*)[64] has
never taught Mary's death as a dogma of divine and catholic faith;
it remains a theological opinion that has received particular attention, most akin to that given it by Newman and the Magisterium of
Pope John Paul II.[65] In the Apostolic Constitution, *Munificentissimus Deus* (1950),[66] Pope Pius XII carefully avoided any mention
of Mary's death, not only because its doctrinal development had not

---

[63] Pope John Paul II, *Redemptoris Mater*, 41.1—41.2. *passim*.

[64] Cf. *Catechism of the Catholic Church*, 996.

[65] Cf. Pope John Paul II, "Mary was Witness to Whole Paschal Mystery" (General
Audience of May 21, 1997) in *A Catechesis on Mary, Mother of God*,194-196;
See also, "Mary and the Human Drama of Death," (General Audience of June 25,
1997) in which the Holy Father writes: "The experience of death personally
enriched the Blessed Virgin: by undergoing mankind's common destiny, she can
more effectively exercise her spiritual motherhood towards those approaching the
last moment of their life." [*A Catechesis on Mary, the Mother of God*, 202]

[66] Cf. Pope Pius XII, *Munificentissimus Deus* in *Acta Apostolica Sedis* 42 (1950),
757,768.

yet been fully ascertained but also perhaps to show respect for the Eastern theology of Mary's dormition or "falling asleep" (in Latin, *dormitio*; in Greek, *koimesis*). The theologies of East and West are by no means mutually exclusive. Newman appears to be perfectly comfortable in highlighting either or both in any given passage of his Catholic writings. In this sense Newman is truly appreciative of another concern of John Paul II's, "breathing with both lungs."

The devotional expression of sleeping the sleep of peace, which can be offered as a translation of the words "*et dormiunt in somno pacis*," used in the second memento of the Roman Canon does not preclude theological speculation concerning the physical death of Mary. What must be doctrinally affirmed in either case is that Mary's body, like Our Lord's, underwent no corruption whatsoever when she had run out her earthly course; that Mary was assumed body and soul into the glories of Heaven as Our Lord had previously ascended to Heaven by virtue of His innate power as the Son of God; that as Christ our Captain has preceded us and so too our Blessed Mother into this final state of beatitude, possessing a glorified body and soul in the unity of their respective persons, so shall all those who are saved stand before God in His heavenly kingdom after the General Judgment on the Last Day. This, in essence, is the teaching of Catholic eschatology as it relates to Mary's Assumption.

If this, then, is the Catholic teaching about the state of our bodies and souls on the Last Day, must one not assert that the doctrine of Our Blessed Mother's Assumption is a key that unlocks the Theology of the Body? For example, in a General Audience entitled, "Mary Is the First Creature to Enjoy Eternal Life" (July 9, 1997), John Paul II explicitly linked the dogma of the Assumption to the theology of the body: "Mary entered into glory because she welcomed the Son of God in her virginal womb and in her heart. By looking at her, the Christian learns to discover the value of his own body and to guard it as a temple of God, in expectation of the Resurrection. The Assumption, a privilege granted to the Mother of God, thus has immense value for the life and destiny of humanity."[67]

---

[67] Pope John Paul II, "Mary is the First Creature to Enjoy Eternal Life," (General Audience of July 9, 1997) in *A Catechesis on Mary, the Mother of God*, 208.

5) Mary's Co-suffering, the Exemplar of Christian Co-suffering as Integral to Newman's and John Paul's Theology of the Body

Newman's Anglican sermon, "Use of Saints' Days," delivered on the occasion of the Feast of All Saints, reminds us of the importance that co-suffering has in the living out of the Christian ideal of holiness, which the martyrs attained in an extraordinary way.[68] An integral part of Newman's notion of sainthood is the saint's ability to unite his sufferings to those of the Savior without, however, finding in this "privilege" a cause of pride or an excuse to seek out suffering for its own sake—which is contrary to the Divine Will for our happiness. Suffering is, after all, an essential consequence of original sin and actual sin that has redemptive value only because the sinless Savior who knew not sin became sin for us, so that we might become the very righteousness of God, according to the teaching of Saint Paul. Newman explains:

> Let us not forget, that, as we are called to be saints, so we are, by that very calling, called to suffer; and, if we suffer, must not think it strange concerning the fiery trial that is to try us, not to be puffed up by our privilege of suffering, nor bring suffering needlessly upon us, nor be eager to make out we have suffered for Christ, when we have suffered for our faults, or not at all.[69]

Newman's sermon, "Bodily Suffering," reinforces the all-important lesson of the Gospels and of the Pauline Epistles, that uniting our sufferings to Christ is carried out not only for own sakes, but on behalf of the Body of Christ, the Church. Therefore, out of the sufferings of Christ, is created a communion, a sacred solidarity, which gives us the "privilege" of sharing in God's work of salvation.[70] Suffering in union with Christ is not the masochism that non-believers might sometimes suppose, leading some atheists, for

---

[68] Newman gives a shorthand definition of martyrdom, highlighting it as a privileged means of co-suffering (*compassio*) for the sake of the Mystical Body of Christ, the Church, in his *Sermon IV* on the feast of St. Stephen's martyrdom: "A martyrdom is a season of God's especial power in the eye of faith, as great as if a miracle were visibly wrought. It is a fellowship of Christ's suffering, a commemoration of His Death, a representation filling up in figure, 'that which is behind of His afflictions, for His Body's sake which is the Church.'" (*Parochial and Plain Sermons*, II, 47)

[69] *Parochial and Plain Sermons*, II, 402.

[70] In his sermon, "Watching," Newman writes: "He watches with Christ, who ever

example, to proclaim God's non-existence, or some agnostics to throw up the perennial question to imply perhaps the existence of a sadistic God at best: "Why do good people suffer if God truly exists and He is supposed to be all-loving, all-merciful?"

John Paul II's theology of co-suffering, integral to a Catholic theology of the body, can be appropriately illustrated in several texts. In *Salvifici Doloris*, the Pontiff writes:

> Human suffering has reached its culmination in the Passion of Christ. And at the same time has entered into a completely new dimension and new order: it has been linked by love. In the Cross of Christ not only is the Redemption accomplished through suffering, but also human suffering itself has been redeemed.[71]

Again, the Holy Father explicated his theology of co-suffering, and therefore his Theology of the Body, in direct relationship to Mary's role as Mother of the Redeemer and spiritual Mother of the redeemed in *Redemptoris Mater*:

> Simeon's words seem like a second Annunciation to Mary, for they tell her of the actual historical situation in which the Son is to accomplish His mission, namely in misunderstanding and sorrow. While the announcement on the one hand confirms her faith in the accomplishment of the divine promises of salvation, on the other hand it also reveals to her that she will have to live the obedience of faith in suffering, at the side of the suffering Savior, and that her motherhood will be mysterious and sorrowful. . . . Through this faith Mary is perfectly united with Christ in His self-emptying. At the foot of the Cross, Mary shares through faith in the deepest "kenosis" of faith in human history. Through faith the Mother shares in the death of her Son, in His redeeming death; but in contrast with the faith of the disciples who fled, hers was far more enlightened. On Golgotha, Jesus through the Cross definitely confirmed that He was the "sign of contradiction" foretold by Simeon. At the same time, there was also fulfilled on Golgotha the words which Simeon had addressed to Mary: "And a sword will pierce through your own heart."[72]

---

commemorates and renews in his own person Christ's Cross and Agony, and gladly takes up that mantle of affection which Christ wore here, and left behind Him when He ascended." (*Parochial and Plain Sermons*, IV, 323f)
[71] Pope John Paul II, *Salvifici Doloris*, 18-19.
[72] Pope John Paul II, *Redemptoris Mater*, 16, 2 & 18, 3.

The response of John Paul II's echoed that of Cardinal Newman. Suffering and pain are a part of the sinful human condition, but only the Cross truly gives to our suffering and pain their redemptive merit and provides, by means of it, a greater good and the hope of an eternal consolation. In fact, Newman, remaining precisely within the ambit of a theology of merit, ponders Christian co-sufferers as "choice instruments" and "active servants" of salvation who, by participating in the uniquely meritorious sufferings of the Cross, likewise gain merit "because they are brought near to Him."[73]

Of all those most intimately associated with Our Lord and His Cross and therefore the greatest beneficiary of the infinite merits flowing from His sufferings, Newman speaks of the Blessed Mother who, "had not clasped Him to her breast for many weeks, ere she was warned of that fateful penalty: 'Yea, a sword shall pierce through thy own soul also.'"[74]

Co-suffering is a theme that pervades Newman's theology and spirituality, receiving a particular application to the life of the Virgin in his *Meditations and Devotions*.[75] For instance, Newman writes: "When then, He was mocked, bruised, scourged, and nailed to the Cross, she felt as keenly as if every indignity and torture inflicted on Him was struck at herself. She would have cried out in agony at every pang of His. This is called her *compassion* or her suffering with her Son, and it arose from this that she was the '*Vas insigne devotionis*' (Vessel of Singular Devotion)."[76] He goes on: "But He, who bore the sinner's shame for sinners, spared His

---

[73] *Parochial and Plain Sermons*, III, 140.

[74] *Parochial and Plain Sermons*, III, 140f.

[75] The Reverend Vincent Blehl, S.J. (the late postulator of Newman's cause), observes: "The seventy pages of meditations on *The Litany of Loreto for the Month of May*, which Newman composed, are models of theological accuracy and of heartfelt personal love and devotion." [*The White Stone: The Spiritual Theology of John Henry Newman* (Petersham, Massachusetts: St. Bede's Publication, 1993), 119.] Furthermore, the theology of Newman on Mary's *compassio*, or redemptive co-suffering, anticipates the teachings of the *Catechism of the Catholic Church* 618, which reads: "In fact, Jesus desires to associate with His redeeming Sacrifice those who were to be its first beneficiaries. This is achieved supremely in the case of His Mother, who was associated more intimately than any other person in the mystery of His redemptive suffering."

[76] *Meditations and Devotions*, 51.

Mother, who was sinless, this supreme indignity. Not in the body, but in the soul, she suffered a fellow-passion; she was crucified with Him; the spear that pierced His breast pierced through her spirit."[77]

To answer the question, "How does the compassion of Mary (*compassio Mariæ*) relate to the compassion or co-suffering of Christians (*compassio Christianorum*)?" one might turn to Newman's meditation on Mary's title of *Consolatrix Afllictorum* (Consoler of the Afflicted). He begins by recalling the co-suffering of the Apostle Saint Paul and how he was comforted by Our Lord, so that, in turn, he could learn how to comfort others, particularly his fellow Christians in their afflictions. Newman says, in effect, that if this is the case with Saint Paul, how much greater must be the ability of Our Blessed Mother—who, in a singular way, suffered with Our Lord—to comfort all others who suffer. Newman unequivocally identifies Mary as our spiritual Mother. He explains the rationale for the appellation *Consolatrix Afflictorum* since he determines that its precise *raison d'être* is, in fact, this spiritual, filial rapport between Mary and all believers, according to his understanding of John 19:25-27:

> And this too is why the Blessed Virgin is the comforter of the afflicted. We all know how special a mother's consolation is, and we are allowed to call Mary Our Mother from the time that Our Lord from the Cross established the relation of mother and son between her and Saint John. And she especially can console us because she suffered more than mothers in general.[78]

Newman concludes his sermon, "Our Lady in the Gospel," with the following exhortation that reveals the depths of his appreciation of Mary as Our Sorrowful Mother. Newman underscores how Our Lady's intimate association to the Paschal Mystery of her divine Son should act as a harbinger of our own future blessedness if, like her, we allow God's grace to sanctify and save us even by means of physical and spiritual suffering. Suffering, therefore, is as closely related to Newman's spirituality and Theology of the Body as one finds it to be in the spirituality and Theology of the Body of Pope John Paul II.

---

[77] *Ibid.*, Cf. *Sermon Notes*, 104-105.
[78] *Meditations and Devotions*, 56.

Depend upon it, the way to enter the sufferings of the Son is to enter into the sufferings of the Mother. Place yourselves at the foot of the Cross, see Mary standing there, looking up and pierced with the sword. Let her be your great pattern. Feel what she felt and you will worthily mourn over the Death and Passion of your and her Saviour. Have her simple faith, and you will believe well. Pray to be filled with the grace given to her. Alas, you must have many feelings she had not, the feeling of personal sin, of personal sorrow, of contrition, and self-hate, but these will in a sinner naturally accompany the faith, the humility, the simplicity, which were her great ornaments. Lament with her, believe with her, at length you will experience her blessedness of which the text speaks. None indeed can have her special prerogative, and be the Mother of the Highest, but you will have a share in that blessedness of hers which is greater, the blessedness of doing God's will and keeping His commandments.[79]

Conclusion

Pope John Paul II made known on numerous occasions his admiration for the person and work of the Venerable John Henry Cardinal Newman.[80] Both of them belong to the school of theological thought which takes most seriously the mystery of the Incarnation, taking the line from the Epistle to the Hebrews as a kind of template for theological reflection: "A body you have prepared for me" (10:6).

This, of course, is even given a name by John Paul II –"the Theology of the Body." As we have noted repeatedly in this essay,

---

[79] *Faith and Prejudice*, 95f.

[80] The Pope never missed commemorating a Newman milestone—anniversaries of his birth, cardinalate, death. Newman is cited in the *Catechism of the Catholic Church* four times; this is significant since all other individuals quoted are canonized saints or agents of the Magisterium. Pope John Paul drew on Newman's wisdom in crafting *Ex Corde Ecclesiæ* and *Fides et Ratio*; he also had recourse to Newman by using his Way of the Cross for Good Friday of 2001. The Holy Father likewise presented the Venerable Cardinal as a model for the prelates elevated to the Sacred College during the Consistory of 2001, the bicentennial of Newman's birth. (Newman was born on February 21, 1801 and died on August 11, 1890). Cf. Pope John Paul's Letter to the Church in England on the occasion of the hundredth anniversary of Newman's elevation to the Sacred College of Cardinals in *L'Osservatore Romano*, English Edition (21 May 1979), 5; Pope John Paul II, "Message of His Holiness to the Most Reverend G.P. Dwyer" in *L'Osservatore Romano*, English Edition (14 May 1980); Letter of Pope John Paul II to Archbishop Vincent Nichols of Birmingham, England, marking the second centenary of Newman's birth as found in Origins (15 March 2001), 631-632.

Newman exhibits the same orientation as the Holy Father, without having a name for it, as is often the case. Here we can recall the amusing scene in Molière's *Le Bourgeois Gentilhomme*, as the *nouveau riche* character is instructed in literature. His tutor explains the difference between prose and poetry, leading the silly man to declare, "And to think that I have been speaking prose my whole life but never knew it!" In many ways, Newman and others in the Catholic Tradition have been teaching the Theology of the Body for centuries without knowing it.

It cannot be forgotten that Newman's movement into the Catholic Church began as a result of a serious study of the Arian heresy, the fourth-century assault on the doctrine of the Incarnation. We can say, without exaggeration, that the enfleshment of God provided impetus for Newman's conversion. By examining the principal Marian doctrines through the prism of the Incarnation and using the lenses provided by Newman and John Paul II, we see how similar themes emerge and are handled in similar fashion by both: the centrality of the Incarnation, first of all; the place of Mary within the economy of salvation; the return to Eden as a starting point for theology and life; the complementarity of the sexes; body-soul unity; the meaning of "bodiliness," as opposed to merely "having a body"; the dignity of women; how consecrated virginity/celibacy fits into the nuptial (spousal) meaning of the body; how suffering of whatever kind can have salvific meaning when offered up to Christ Crucified and Risen in union with the Immaculate Heart of Mary, Our Sorrowful Mother.

Hopefully, we have benefited from investigating how the Venerable John Henry Cardinal Newman and the late great Pope John Paul II relied on the principle *caro cardo salutis* (the flesh is the hinge of salvation), with both seeing how the Blessed Virgin is integral to the proper interpretation of that principle and thus for advancing the Theology of the Body.

THE ANTHROPOLOGICAL SIGNIFICANCE
OF THE DOGMA OF THE IMMACULATE CONCEPTION

Fr. Paul M. Haffner, S.T.D.

In this essay I aim to show how a reflection on Mary conceived without original sin sheds light on the anthropology of Our Lady. I offer a brief exposé of the history of the doctrine of the Immaculate Conception, then I examine how Mary is also free of the consequences of original sin like concupiscence and the sting of death.

Consideration of the anthropological significance of the Immaculate Conception of Our Lady starts with a New Testament perspective. The angel Gabriel greeted Mary with the words "Rejoice, you who enjoy God's favour!" (Lk. 1:28), in Greek *"chaire kecharitomene"*. Just as Mary pondered the meaning of this greeting (Lk. 1:29), so also the Church has deepened her understanding of Mary's fullness of grace. Luke presents this greeting with an alliterative play on words. The same basic root (*charis* or "grace") is present in both the expression for "Rejoice" and also "you who enjoy God's favour", in order to highlight the special nature of God's gift of grace to Mary.[1] Moreover, the past perfect participial form of the verb, *"charitoo"* present in *kecharitomene*, is causative, indicating a change or transformation in the recipient, prior to the grace of maternity. Thus, foreseen from all eternity, God had prepared Mary to be the mother of Jesus Christ in the plenitude of grace, a "grace upon grace" (Jn. 1:16). In St.

---

[1] See P. Haffner, *The Mystery of Mary* (Leominster/Chicago: Gracewing /Hillenbrand Books, 2004), 56-58.

Paul's Letter to the Ephesians 1:3-8, we find the second and only other occurrence in the New Testament of the transformative meaning of the verb *charitoo* (Eph. 1:6), as the grace which makes us "holy and faultless." The idea that God "chose us in Christ before the world was made to be holy and faultless before Him in love, marking us out for Himself beforehand, to be adopted sons, through Jesus Christ" (Eph. 1:4-5) can be applied to the mystery of the preparation of Mary to be the Mother of God. In the angel's greeting the expression "full of grace" serves almost as a name: it is Mary's name in the eyes of God. In Semitic usage, a name expresses the reality of the persons to which it refers. As a result, the title "full of grace" expresses the deepest dimension of the personality of the young woman of Nazareth as fashioned by grace and as the object of divine favour.[2]

The Early Centuries

During the early centuries, there was an increasing awareness and understanding of Mary's holiness. Many reflected on the meaning of the biblical expression "full of grace."[3] The Fathers of the Church first focused on the Christological faith of the Church and, in relation to this, they went on to deal with the holiness of Christ's Mother. The theological concerns of this early Patristic period were different from those of later development, but nevertheless, the doctrine concerning Mary's holiness was already present in a form which required further elaboration. In Eastern Christendom, the

---

[2] See Pope John Paul II, *Discourse at General Audience* (15 May 1996), 2.

[3] In Patristic tradition there is a wide and varied interpretation of this expression. See, for example Origen, *In Lucam homiliae*, VI, 7 in *Sources Chrétiennes* (*SC*) 87, 148; Severianus of Gabala, *In mundi creationem*, Oratio VI, 10 in *Patrologia Graeca* (*PG*) 56, 497f.; Basil of Seleucia, *Oratio 39, In Sanctissimae Deiparae Annuntiationem*, 5 in *PG* 85, 441-46; St. Sophronius of Jerusalem, *Oratio 11, In Sanctissimae Deiparae Annuntiationem*, 17-19 in *PG* 87/3, 3235-3240; St. John Damascene, *Homilia in Dormitionem*, 1, 70: *SC* 80, 96-101; St. Jerome, *Epistola 65*, 9 in *Patrologia Latina* (*PL*) 22, 628;St. Ambrose, *Expositio Evangelii secundam Lucam*, II, 9 in *Corpus Scriptorum Ecclesiasticorum Latinorum* (*CSEL*) 32/4, 45f.; St. Augustine, *Sermo 291*, 4-6 in *PL* 38, 131 8f.; Idem, *Enchiridion*, 36, 11 in *PL* 40, 250; St. Peter Chrysologus, *Sermo 142* in *PL* 52, 579f.; Idem, *Sermo 143* in *PL* 52, 583; St. Fulgentius of Ruspe, *Epistola 17*, VI 12 in *PL* 65 ,458; Later, in the Middle Ages, these Fathers were followed, for example, by St. Bernard, *In laudibus Virginis Matris, Homilia III*, 2-3 in *S. Bernardi Opera*, IV, 1966, 36-38.

awareness that Mary was the first to fully participate in the grace of Christ's Paschal Mystery was expressed in the Greek word *Panagía*, meaning "the All-Holy One". It seems that the first Father to use this expression was the Alexandrian thinker Origen, as he commented on the angel's greeting to Mary: "This greeting is reserved only to Mary. Because, if she had known that such a greeting had been addressed to others (she was well-versed in the Law, and was All-Holy, and had meditated on the prophecies), it would not have startled her as a special greeting."[4]

Early Christian belief always associated Mary with Jesus in the divine plan. The Patristic writers of East and West referred to Mary as the "new Eve," who co-operated with Christ, the "new Adam". The Fathers expressed the holiness of Mary by seeing her as the New Eve, an expression with great anthropological impor-tance. Mary, the New Eve, like the New Adam, was conceived immaculate, just as the First Adam and Eve were created immac-ulate. The Fathers contrasted the disobedience of the first Eve with the obedience offered by Mary, the second Eve. Because she is the New Eve, she shares the fate of the New Adam. Whereas the first Adam and Eve died and returned to dust, the New Adam and Eve were lifted up physically into heaven. In the writings of Justin the Martyr (165 AD), we find the earliest illustration of Mary as the new Eve.[5] Tertullian developed this theme also slightly later, around the year 210.[6] Also, around the year 200, in St. Irenaeus, Mary is portrayed as bringing into the world Christ who is Life, whereas Eve brought death, and Mary's humility and obedience is contrasted with Eve's pride and disobedience:

> Consequently, then, Mary the Virgin is found to be obedient, say-ing, 'Behold, O Lord, your handmaid; be it done to me according to your word.' Eve, however, was disobedient, and, while still a vir-gin, she did not obey. Just as she, who was then still a virgin although she had Adam for a husband…having become disobedi-ent, was made the cause of death for herself and for the whole human race; so also Mary, betrothed to a man but nevertheless still a virgin, being obedient, was made the cause of salvation for her-

---

[4] Origen, *Commentary on Luke*, 6 in *PG* 13, 1816.
[5] St. Justin Martyr, *Dialogue with Trypho the Jew*, 100 in *PG* 6, 710-711.
[6] Tertullian, *The Flesh of Christ* 17, 4 in *PL* 2, 782.

self and for the whole human race. . . . Thus, the knot of Eve's disobedience was loosed by the obedience of Mary. What the virgin
Eve had bound in unbelief, the Virgin Mary loosed through faith.[7]

Mary's sinlessness was expressed in terms of the privilege
accorded to her of being exempted from the pains in childbirth.
This privilege was recorded early, by the writer of *The Odes of
Solomon*, a collection of ancient Christian hymnody, who remarks:
"So the Virgin became a mother with great mercies. And she
laboured and bore the Son, but without pain, because it did not
occur without purpose. And she did not seek a midwife, because
He caused her to give life."[8] Various other early Christian writers
strongly suggested Mary's sinlessness in general terms. Even
before the expressions "original sin" and "Immaculate Conception" had been defined, early Patristic passages implied these doctrines. Before the year 250, Hippolytus alluded in beautiful terms
to the holiness of Mary: "The Lord was without sin, made of
imperishable wood, as regards His humanity; that is, of the virgin
and the Holy Spirit inwardly, and outwardly of the word of God,
like an ark overlaid with purest gold."[9]

Around the year 390, St. Ambrose remarked: "Come, then,
and search out Your sheep, not through Your servants or hired men,
but do it Yourself. Lift me up bodily and in the flesh, which is fall-
en in Adam. Lift me up not from Sarah but from Mary, a virgin not

---

[7] St. Irenaeus, *Against the heresies* Book 3, chapter 22, n.4 in *PG* 7, 958-959. This
idea is also found in the context of Irenaeus' theme of recapitulation: "The Lord
then was manifestly coming to his own things, and was sustaining them by means
of that creation that is supported by himself. He was making a recapitulation of
that disobedience that had occurred in connection with a tree, through the obedience that was upon a tree. Furthermore, the original deception was to be done
away with—the deception by which that virgin Eve (who was already espoused
to a man) was unhappily misled. That this was to be overturned was happily
announced through means of the truth by the angel to the Virgin Mary (who was
also [espoused] to a man). . . . So Eve disobeyed God, yet Mary was persuaded
to be obedient to God. In this way, the Virgin Mary might become the advocate
of the virgin Eve. And thus, as the human race fell into bondage to death by
means of a virgin, so it is rescued by a virgin. Virginal disobedience has been balanced in the opposite scale by virginal obedience. For in the same way, the sin of
the first created man received amendment by the correction of the First-
Begotten" (*ibid.*, Book 5, chap. 19, n.1 in *PG* 7, 1175-1176).
[8] *Odes of Solomon*, 19
[9] St. Hippolytus, *Commentary on Psalm 22* in *PG* 10, 863.

only undefiled, but a virgin whom grace had made inviolate, free of every stain of sin."[10] Around the year 400, St. Augustine was also noted for his belief in the sinlessness of Our Lady: "We must except the Holy Virgin Mary, concerning whom I wish to raise no question on the subject of sins, out of honour to the Lord; for from Him we know what abundance of grace for overcoming sin in every particular was conferred upon her who had the merit to conceive and bear Him who undoubtedly had no sin."[11] While having no doubts about the holiness of Mary in terms of the absence of personal sin, St. Augustine is not clear as to an affirmation of her freedom from original sin. In part, this is due to the fact that he strenuously opposed the Pelagians who also maintained Mary's holiness, which was for them a result of her own efforts. St. Augustine proposed that Mary was holy in as much as she was redeemed by her Son, she was "freed by grace in virtue of her rebirth."[12]

Some Eastern Fathers had acknowledged a purification brought about by grace in Mary before the Incarnation, but many writers were not altogether clear when this took place. St. Cyril of Jerusalem linked Our Lady's deliverance from sin with the event of the Annunciation when "the Holy Spirit coming upon her sanctified her so as to enable her to receive Him through whom all things were made."[13] St. Gregory Nazianzen seems to place the sanctification of Mary at some point before the Incarnation of her Son: "Conceived by the Virgin, who first in body and soul was purified by the Holy Spirit, for it was needful both that Childbearing should be honoured, and that Virginity should receive a higher honour."[14] Other Eastern Fathers, like St. Ephraem the Syrian (around 350) seem to have indicated a prior purification of Mary through the agency of the Holy Spirit: "Most holy Lady, Mother of God, alone most pure in soul and body, alone exceeding all perfection of purity ..., alone made in your

---

[10] St. Ambrose, *Commentary on Psalm 118:*22-30.

[11] St. Augustine, *Nature and Grace* 36, 42.

[12] St. Augustine, *Opus Imperfectum contra Julianum* Book 4, n. 122 in *PL* 45, 1418: "quia ipsa conditio solvitur gratia renascendi."

[13] St. Cyril of Jerusalem, *Cathecheses*, 17, 6 in *PG* 33, 976.

[14] St Gregory Nazianzen, *Oratio* 38, n. 13 in *PG* 36, 325. See also Idem, *Oratio* 45, n.9 in *PG* 36, 633.

entirety the home of all the graces of the Most Holy Spirit, and hence exceeding beyond all compare even the angelic virtues in purity and sanctity of soul and body .... Therefore you are altogether immaculate."[15] St. Ephraem refers to Mary as immaculate in many places: "My Lady most holy, all-pure, all-immaculate, all-stainless, all-undefiled, all-incorrupt, all-inviolate immaculate robe of him who clothes Himself with light as with a garment ... sweet-smelling rose, flower unfading, shining white lily, alone most immaculate."[16] However, elsewhere, Ephraem seems to have proposed that Christ regenerated His Mother through baptism.[17] However, the sanctification and purification of Our Lady of which these Fathers speak need have no connection with sin, whether original or actual. Theologically these descriptions could be classified as an increase of grace given to Mary in view of her Motherhood. This sanctification would therefore have as its object not forgiveness, but rather more intimate union with God.[18]

Then, in the East, it became clearer that the sinlessness of the Mother of God went back further than just before the Incarnation. This increasing clarity is connected with the Council of Ephesus in the year 431, which, as shall be seen, is a moment of capital importance for the understanding of the Divine Motherhood.[19] For example, around the year 450, Theodotus of Ancyra declared that Mary was "a virgin, innocent, spotless, free of all defect, untainted, undefiled, holy in soul and in body, like a lily sprouting among thorns,

---

[15] St. Ephraem the Syrian, *Precationes ad Deiparam* 1-2 in *Enchiridion Marianum Bliblicum Pastristicum* (*EM*) 338-339. See also *Nisibene Hymns* 27, 8 in *EM* 429: "You alone and your Mother are more beautiful than any others, for there is no blemish in you nor any stains upon your Mother." See also *Hymns on the Nativity* 15, 23: "Let women praise her, the pure Mary, that as in Eve their mother great was their reproach, lo! in Mary their sister, greatly magnified was their honour."

[16] St. Ephraem the Syrian, *Oratio ad Deiparam* in *EM* 341.

[17] See St. Ephraem, *Hymn 11 on the Nativity of Christ in the Flesh* in S. Ephraem Syrus, *Opera omnia quae extant graece, syriace, latine* vol. 2 (Roma: Vatican, 1740), pp. 429-430, where we read how Mary addresses Christ as follows: "For I am Your sister, of the house of David the father of us both. Again, I am Your Mother because of Your Conception, and I am Your Bride because of your sanctification. I am your handmaid and your daughter, from the Blood and Water by which you have purchased me and baptised me."

[18] See W.J. Burghardt, "Mary in Eastern Patristic Thought" in J.B. Carol (ed.), *Mariology* vol. 2 (Milwaukee: The Bruce Publishing Company, 1955), 135.

[19] See Haffner, *The Mystery of Mary*, 115-116.

uninstructed in the vices of Eve."[20] Furthermore, in the middle of the fifth century, St. Proclus of Constantinople wrote: "As He formed her without any stain of her own, so He proceeded from her contracting no stain."[21] Proclus also beautifully described Mary as the heavenly orb of a new creation, "in whom the ever-shining Sun of justice, has put to flight from her entire soul all the night of sin."[22]

Doctrinal reflection on the perfect holiness of Mary in relation to her Son considered that this perfection had to go back to the beginning of her existence. The turning point came when Bishop Theoteknos of Livias in Palestine, who lived between 550 and 650, moved in the direction of this original purity. In presenting Mary as "holy and all-fair", "pure and stainless", he referred to her birth in these words: "She is born like the cherubim, she who is of a pure, immaculate clay."[23] This last expression, recalling the creation of the first man, fashioned of a clay not stained by sin, attributes the same characteristics to Mary's birth: the Virgin's origin was also "pure and immaculate", that is, without any sin. The comparison with the cherubim also emphasizes the outstanding holiness that characterized Mary's life from the very beginning of her existence.

In the eighth century, St. Andrew of Crete was the first theologian to relate the new creation to Mary's birth:

> Today humanity, in all the radiance of her immaculate nobility, receives its ancient beauty. The shame of sin had darkened the splendour and attraction of human nature; but when the Mother of the Fair One par excellence is born, this nature regains in her person its ancient privileges and is fashioned according to a perfect model truly worthy of God .... The reform of our nature begins today and the aged world, subjected to a wholly divine transformation, receives the first fruits of the second creation.[24]

---

[20] Theodotus of Ancyra, *Homily* 6, 11 (*In sanctam Mariam Dei genitricem et in sanctam Christi nativitatem*) in *PG* 77, 1427.

[21] St. Proclus of Constantinople, *Homily 1*, 3 in *PG* 65, 683.

[22] Idem, *Homily 6*, 17 in *PG* 65, 758.

[23] Theoteknos of Livias, *Encomium in Assumptionem Beatae Mariae Virginis*, 5-6 as found in A. Wenger, *L'Assomption de la Très Sainte Vierge dans la tradition byzantine du VIe au Xe siècle* (Paris: Institut Français d'Etudes Byzantines, 1955), 272-291.

[24] St. Andrew of Crete, *Sermon I on the Birth of Mary* in *PG* 97, 810.

His image of the new creation is further reinforced in another place: "The Virgin's body is ground which God has tilled, the first fruits of Adam's soil divinized by Christ, the image truly like the former beauty, the clay kneaded by the divine Artist."[25] St. John Damascene, also in the eighth century, expressed a belief in Mary's freedom from original sin in a way which approaches the doctrine of the Immaculate Conception: "O most holy daughter of Joachim and Anne, hidden from the principalities and powers, and from the fiery arrows of the Evil One. You set your dwelling place in the wedding chamber of the Holy Spirit and were conserved without stain as the bride of God, because with this nature of yours you became the Mother of God."[26] St. John Damascene also stressed the supernatural influence of God upon the generation of Mary by her parents St. Joachim and St. Anne. He proposes that, during the generation, they were filled and purified by the Holy Spirit, and freed from concupiscence: "O most blessed loins of Joachim from which came forth a spotless seed! O glorious womb of Anne in which a most holy offspring grew."[27]

Consequently according to John Damascene, even the human element of her origin, the material of which she was formed, was pure and holy.

In the West, after the Council of Ephesus, there was also increasing clarity concerning the original sinlessess of Mary. St. Maximus of Turin, writing around the middle of the fifth century affirmed: "In her there sprouts no thorn of sin; because she was the shoot born not of the thorn, but from the stock, as the prophet affirms: 'A shoot will spring from the stock of Jesse, a new shoot will grow from his roots' (Is 11:1): and this stock was Mary, pure, fine and virginal, who brought forth Christ as a flower from the integrity of her body."[28] Later, about a century after the Council of Ephesus, St. Fulgentius of Ruspe (468-533) centered Mary's sinlessness in a Christological key:

---

[25] St. Andrew of Crete, *Sermon I on the Dormition of Mary* in *PG* 97, 1067.

[26] St. John Damascene, *Homily on the Nativity of the Blessed Virgin Mary*, 7 in *PG* 96, 671.

[27] St. John Damascene, *Homily on the Nativity of the Blessed Virgin Mary*, 2 in *PG* 96, 663: "O lumbos Ioachim beatissimos, ex quibus mundissimum semen iactus est! O praeclaram Annae vulvam, in qua tacitis accrementis ex ea auctus atque formatus fuit fetus sanctissimus."

[28] St. Maximus of Turin, *Homily* 38 in *PL* 57, 310.

Man disregarded God and abandoned Him; God, loving men, came towards men... A woman with a corrupt soul, deceived the first man; an untouched Virgin conceived the Second. Through the wife of the first man, the devil's malice depraved his soul after seducing it; in the Mother of the Second Man, the grace of God conserved the integrity of her body and soul: it bestowed a firm faith to her soul and completely eradicated concupiscence from her body.[29]

During the Patristic period, the Eastern Fathers tended to see Mary as the beginning of a new race, while the Western Fathers saw her as an enclave protected from the contamination of sin.

The Immaculate Conception

Following St. Augustine in the West, many Fathers and Doctors believed in Mary's perfect holiness and the absence of any personal sin in her because of her dignity as Mother of the Lord. Nonetheless, they could not understand how the affirmation of an immaculate conception could be squared with the doctrine of the universality of original sin and the need of redemption for all of Adam's descendants. A feast of the Conception of Mary (or Conception by St. Anne), which started in the monasteries of Palestine at least as early as the seventh century, was not based on the full understanding of Our Lady's freedom from sin expressed in the later feast of the Immaculate Conception. This feast in the course of centuries became the Feast of the Immaculate Conception, as theological refinement brought about clear ideas regarding the preservation of Mary from all stain of original sin. The earlier feast also appeared during the sixth and seventh centuries in the Greek Church as a celebration in honour of the conception of Our Lady by St. Joachim and St. Anne on December 9th, and by the tenth and eleventh centuries it had become firmly established as a holyday.[30] Probably the feast passed to Naples, which lay on an important trade route from Greece. A marble calendar dating from the ninth century testifies that the feast was celebrated at Naples.

---

[29] St. Fulgentius of Ruspe, *Sermo II de duplice nativitate Christi*, 6 in *PL* 65, 728.
[30] See St. Andrew of Crete, *In conceptionem Sanctae Annae* in PG 97, 1307. This text for the feast of Our Lady's conception probably dates from the seventh or eighth century.

The feast passed by way of Naples to the West, where it first took root in Ireland. Around the year 800, there is a record of a Feast of Our Lady's Conception being celebrated in Ireland. The first definite knowledge of the feast in the West comes from England from a calendar of Old Minster, Winchester, dating from about 1030, and in another calendar of New Minster, Winchester, composed between 1035 and 1056. The feast was also kept at Worcester, Exeter, Canterbury, and in the surrounding localities. The feast was endorsed by episcopal authority and was observed by the Saxon monks with considerable solemnity. The establishment of the feast in England took place before the Norman Conquest in 1066. The Normans on their arrival in England tended to oppose and change English customs, and so the Feast of Our Lady's Conception, which appeared to the invaders a peculiar Saxon devotion, was abolished in several places. However, it lived on in the hearts and minds of the faithful, and at the first favourable opportunity the feast was restored in a monastic setting.

St. Anselm, Archbishop of Canterbury (1033-1109), was said to have written a specific treatise *De Conceptu virginali et originali peccato*,[31] which set down theological principles leading to a greater understanding of the doctrine of the Immaculate Conception. St. Anselm first pointed out that the seed could not "contain" sin, but only the will could cause sin.[32] He then makes the parallel between the creation of Eve from Adam and the Incarnation of Christ from Mary.[33] Hence, it is clear that the stain of sin could not at all have been pres-

---

[31] St. Anselm of Canterbury, *The Virgin Conception and Original Sin*, in *Complete Philosophical and Theological Treatises of Anselm of Canterbury* translated by J. Hopkins and H. Richardson (Minneapolis: The Arthur J. Banning Press, 2000), 427-465. This treatise was possibly composed by his friend and disciple, the Saxon monk Eadmer of Canterbury.

[32] See St. Anselm of Canterbury, *The Virgin Conception and Original Sin*, chapter 7, in *Complete Philosophical and Theological Treatises of Anselm of Canterbury*, 439: "For even if an infant be begotten by a corrupt concupiscence, there is no more fault in the seed than there is in the spittle or the blood should someone malevolently expectorate or malevolently shed some of his own blood. For what is at fault is not the spittle or the blood but the evil will."

[33] See St. Anselm of Canterbury, *The Virgin Conception and Original Sin*, chapter 11 in *Complete Philosophical and Theological Treatises of Anselm of Canterbury*, 443: "For just as the clay of the earth had not received a nature or a will by whose operation the first man would be produced from it (even though the clay was that from which the first man could be created by God), so it was not by the operation of human nature and the human will that a woman was made from

ent in that which the Son of God took to Himself from the Virgin Mary.[34] St. Anselm was acquainted with the Feast through the Saxon monks of Canterbury, and the Greeks with whom he came in contact during exile in Campania and Apulia (1098-99). However, St. Anselm probably had no hand in introducing the Feast into England. After the Norman Conquest, it was Anselm the Younger, the nephew of St. Anselm, who re-introduced the Feast.

An important theological development came about around 1120, when Eadmer, a monk of Canterbury, wrote the first treatise on the Immaculate Conception, and protested against the suppression of its liturgical celebration. Wishing to promote the restoration of this feast, the devout monk rejected the Augustinian objections to the privilege of the Immaculate Conception, based on the doctrine of the transmission of original sin in human generation. Eadmer countered the Augustianian objection by writing that the Holy Spirit could not be absent from the special beginnings of Mary: "Where the Spirit is, there is freedom from sin."[35] Eadmer proposed that God chose Mary from all eternity to be His dwelling-place. Based on the idea of the house built by Wisdom for itself (Prov. 9:1-16), Eadmer pointed out that God could not have allowed Mary to be stained by sin. "The foundations" of His palace "would be weak if the conception of Mary were in any way corrupted by the stain of sin."[36] Instead, Mary became a tabernacle of the Holy Spirit. Eadmer also fittingly employed the image of a chestnut "which is conceived, nourished and formed beneath its bur and yet is protected from being pricked by it." Even beneath the bur of an act of generation which in itself must transmit original sin, Eadmer argued, Mary was preserved from every stain by the explicit will of God who "was obviously able to do this and wanted to do so. Thus if he willed it, he did it."[37]

---

a man's rib or that a man was made from a woman alone. Rather, God, by His own power and will, created one man from the clay, created another man from a woman alone, and created a woman from a man alone."

[34] See St. Anselm of Canterbury, *The Virgin Conception and Original Sin*, chapter 8 in *Complete Philosophical and Theological Treatises of Anselm of Canterbury*, 439.

[35] Eadmer, *Tractatus de conceptione Beatae Mariae Virginis*, 9, in *PL* 159, 305.

[36] Eadmer, *Tractatus de conceptione Beatae Mariae Virginis*, 13, in *PL* 159, 306.

[37] Eadmer, *Tractatus de conceptione Beatae Mariae Virginis*, 10, in *PL* 159, 305. The famous expression is "potuit plane et voluit; si igitur voluit, fecit."

Despite the reflections of Eadmer, the great theologians of the 13th century followed St Augustine according to the following argument: the Redemption accomplished by Christ would not be universal if the condition of sin were not common to all human beings. If Mary had not contracted original sin, she could not have been redeemed. Redemption in fact consists in freeing those who are in the state of sin. In particular, St. Bernard opposed the doctrine of the Immaculate Conception and the celebration of the Feast in France in a forceful letter.[38] St. Bernard held, following Augustine and Jerome, that in marital union there was always some taint of sin, which made it difficult for him to envisage how Mary could have been conceived immaculate: "Could sanctity have been associated with conception in the embrace of marriage, so that she was conceived and sanctified at the same time? That is not reasonable. How could there have been sanctity without the sanctifying Spirit? How could the Holy Spirit be associated in any way with sin? How could sin not have been present where concupiscence was not absent?"[39]

Richard of St. Victor wrote a treatise answering St. Bernard, pointing out that the flesh of Mary needed no purification as it was sanctified before conception. St. Albert the Great followed St. Bernard in rejecting the doctrine of the Immaculate Conception. He observed: "We say that the Blessed Virgin was not sanctified before animation, and the affirmative contrary to this is the heresy condemned by St. Bernard in his epistle to the canons of Lyons."[40] St. Thomas Aquinas also followed this line. However, both St. Albert and St. Thomas were not opposed to a purification of Mary after animation.

In reality, St. Thomas progressed in his view of the question. At the time of his Commentary on the Sentences of Peter Lombard, St. Thomas inclined to favour this privilege for Mary.[41] At the time of the

---

[38] See St. Bernard, *Letter* 174 in *PL* 182, 333-336.

[39] St. Bernard of Clairvaux, *Letter 174 to the Canons of Lyons*, 7 in *PL* 182, 335: "An forte inter amplexus maritales sanctitas se ipsi conceptioni immiscuit, ut simul et sanctificata fuerit, et concepta? Nec hoc quidem admittit ratio. Quomodo namque aut sanctitas absque Spiritu sanctificante, aut sancto Spiritui societas cum peccato fuit? aut certe peccatum quomodo non fuit, ubi libido non defuit?"

[40] St. Albert the Great, *III Sententiarum*, distinction iii, part I, ad 1, Q. i.

[41] St. Thomas Aquinas, *In I Sententiarum*, d. 44, q.1, a.3, ad 3: "Item, videtur quod nec beata virgine: quia secundum Anselmum, decuit ut virgo quam deus unigen-

Summa Theologiae, he found no way of holding it together with the doctrine of universal redemption: "If the soul of the Blessed Virgin had never incurred the stain of original sin, this would be derogatory to the dignity of Christ, by reason of His being the universal Saviour of all... But the Blessed Virgin did indeed contract original sin, but was cleansed therefrom before her birth from the womb."[42] St. Thomas found a solution in having Mary purified as soon as possible in the womb of St. Anne, a view which fitted in with his Aristotelian concept of animation:

> The sanctification of the Blessed Virgin cannot be understood as having taken place before animation... because the sanctification of which we are speaking, is nothing but the cleansing from original sin... Now sin cannot be taken away except by grace, the subject of which is the rational creature alone. Therefore before the infusion of the rational soul, the Blessed Virgin was not sanctified.[43]

Thus, he taught the purification of Our Lady in the womb:

> Nothing is handed down in the canonical Scriptures concerning the sanctification of the Blessed Mary as to her being sanctified in the womb; indeed, they do not even mention her birth. But as Augustine, in his treatise on the Assumption of the Virgin, argues with reason, since her body was assumed into heaven, and yet Scripture does not relate this; so it may be reasonably argued that she was sanctified in the womb. For it is reasonable to believe that she, who brought forth "the Only-Begotten of the Father full of grace and truth," received greater privileges of grace than all others: hence we read (Lk 1:28) that the angel addressed her in the words: "Hail full of grace!"[44]

At the end of his life he returned to his first position, which involved stronger adherence to a doctrine of the freedom from original sin of Mary, but without specifying when she was freed from this.[45]

---

ito filio suo praeparavit in matrem, ea puritate niteret, qua major sub deo nequit intelligi. Sed nihil potest deus facere quod sibi in bonitate vel puritate aequetur. Ergo videtur quod nihil melius beata virgine facere possit."

[42] St. Thomas Aquinas, *Summa Theologiae*, III, q.27, a.2.

[43] *Ibid.*

[44] St. Thomas Aquinas, *Summa Theologiae*, III, q.27, a.1.

[45] St. Thomas Aquinas, *In salutationem angelica*, a.1: "Nam ipsa omne peccatum vitavit magis quam aliquis sanctus post Christum. Peccatum enim aut est originale, et de isto fuit mundata in utero; aut mortale aut veniale, et de istis libera fuit."

The problem of St. Thomas and other medieval authors in grasping a doctrine of Immaculate Conception is also connected with their (now outdated) Aristotelian view of ensoulment, namely the idea that the human embryo receives the rational soul some weeks after conception.

Even in the Franciscan school before Blessed John Duns Scotus, great doctors like St. Bonaventure did not hold Mary's freedom from original sin. Nevertheless his treatment of the question represented an advance towards that of Scotus. He proposed that the flesh of Our Lady was sanctified after the process of animation had taken place.[46]

The great breakthrough bringing greater understanding of the Immaculate Conception came with William of Ware and his pupil, Blessed John Duns Scotus. They were able to distinguish between a prevenient grace and a restorative grace, both of which were fruits of the Redemption. In particular, Scotus made the decisive step forward. Thus he introduced into theology the concept of Redemption by preservation, according to which Mary was redeemed in an even more wonderful way: not by being freed from sin, but by being preserved from sin. Scotus indicated that "it is a more excellent benefit to preserve from evil, than to permit someone to fall into evil, even if one is freed from it afterwards. Therefore, if Christ merited grace and glory for many souls, and Christ is the Mediator for all of these, why could not someone be in debt to Him for her innocence?"[47] He proposed that the freeing of Mary from the stain of sin required, as a precondition, the creation and infusion of her soul, but that in terms of time, the sanctification and the animation were simultaneous.[48] Scotus also resolved the problem of how to square the Immaculate

---

[46] See St. Bonaventure, *Commentary on Book III of The Sentences*, d.2, a.1, q.1: "It must be said, that the flesh of the Blessed Virgin had not been sanctified before animation; not because God could not have purified the flesh of the Virgin before He could have animated it, but because sanctification has existence through some gratuitous, superadded gift, which indeed does not have existence in the flesh, but in the soul."

[47] Bl. John Duns Scotus, *Questions in Libro III Sententiarum*, d.3, q.1, in *Opera Omnia* (Hildesheim: Georg Olms, 1968), vol. 7/1, 92-93: "imo excellentius beneficium est preservare a malo, quam permittere incidere in malum, et ab eo postea liberare. Videtur enim quod cum Christus multis animabus meruerit gratiam, et gloriam, et pro his sint Christo debitores, ut mediatori; quare nulla anima erit ei debitrix pro innocentia?"

[48] *Ibid.*, 94-97.

Conception of Mary with the issue of the universality of original sin. Christ is the perfect Mediator and perfect Redeemer, and thus it would be most fitting for Him, not only to preserve His Mother from all stain of actual sin, but also from original sin.[49] Thus Scotus held that Christ, the perfect Mediator, exercised the highest act of mediation precisely in Mary, by preserving her from original sin. Scotus proposed the famous formulation concerning God's power to preserve Mary from all stain of original sin, made popular by his disciple Francis de Mayronis: "it was possible, it was fitting, therefore it was accomplished."[50]

The controversy regarding the Immaculate Conception of Our Lady continued, with the opponents of this doctrine being mainly Dominicans. In 1439, the dispute was discussed at the Council of Basle which in its thirty-sixth session decreed the Immaculate Conception to be a doctrine which was pious, consonant with Catholic worship, Catholic faith, right reason, and Holy Scripture; nor, said they, was it henceforth allowable to preach or declare to the contrary.[51] This session of the Council was held at a time when the Council was no longer in communion with the Pope, so that its decrees are not binding. Sixtus IV decreed on February 28, 1476, that the feast be adopted in the entire Latin Church and granted an indulgence to all who would assist at Mass and the Divine Offices of the solemnity.[52] As dissent still rumbled on after this decree, in 1483 Pope Sixtus IV published a constitution in which he punished with excommunication all those of either opinion who charged the opposite opinion with heresy.[53] In 1546, the Council of Trent discussed the question of

[49] Bl. John Duns Scotus, *Reportata Parisiensia*, Book 3, d.3, q.1, in *Opera Omnia* (Hildesheim: Georg Olms, 1969), vol. 11/1, 432-433, in particular p. 433:"Mediator perfectus praevenit omne peccatum actuale.Hoc concedunt omnes de beata Virgine: sed redemptio universalis est contra originale quam contra actuale: igitur ex hoc quod redemptor universalis, perfectius et immediatius praevenit originale, quam actuale."

[50] Bd. John Duns Scotus, *Tractatus de Conceptione Mariae Virginis*, chapter V: "Potuit, decuit, ergo fecit."

[51] See J. D. Mansi, *Sacrorum Conciliorum nova et amplissima collectio,* 29, 183.

[52] See Pope Sixtus IV, Constitution *Cum Praeexcelsa* in J. Neuner and J. Dupuis (*ND*), *The Christian Faith in the Doctrinal Documents of the Catholic Church.*Sixth edition. (New York: Alba House, 1996), 704.

[53] See *Idem*, Constitution *Grave nimis* in H. Denzinger (*DS*), *Enchiridion Symbolorum,*1425-1426.

original sin, but made it clear that "it was not its intention to include in this decree dealing with original sin the Blessed and Immaculate Virgin Mary, Mother of God."[54] However, this decree did not define the doctrine, and so the theological opponents of the mystery, although much reduced in numbers, did not yield. In particular, the Jansenists opposed the theology of the Immaculate Conception. In 1567, Pope St. Pius V condemned a position of a Jansenist author, Michel du Bay, that "no one but Christ is without original sin; hence the Blessed Virgin died on account of the sin inherited from Adam, and all her afflictions in this life were, like those of the rest of the just, punishment for actual or original sin."[55] Nevertheless, in the fifteenth and sixteenth centuries, many European universities only admitted students who would swear an oath to do the utmost to defend and assert the Immaculate Conception of Mary.

In 1617, Pope Paul V decreed that no one should dare to teach publicly that Mary was conceived in original sin, and five years later, Gregory XV imposed silence, both in the written and the spoken word, even in private, upon the adversaries of the doctrine until the Holy See should define the question. At the request of King Philip IV of Spain, Alexander VII promulgated on 8 December 1661, the famous Brief *Sollicitudo omnium Ecclesiarum*.[56] He formulated the doctrine that belief of Mary's soul, "in the first instant of its creation and in the first instant of the soul's infusion into the body, was, by a special grace and privilege of God, in view of the merits of Jesus Christ, her Son and the Redeemer of the human race, preserved free from all stain of original sin."[57] He forbade all further discussion against the common and pious sentiment of the Church in this doctrine.

---

[54] Council of Trent, Session V, *Decree on Original Sin* in *ND* 705.
[55] Pope St. Pius V, Bull *Ex omnibus afflictionibus* in *ND* [708]. Later in 1690, under Pope Alexander VIII, another Jansenist proposition was condemned which implied that at the Presentation of Our Lord in the temple, His Mother needed purification from sin. See *DS* 2324: "The offering which the Blessed Virgin Mary made in the temple on the day of her purification with two young turtledoves, one as a holocaust, the other as a sin offering, is sufficient evidence that she needed purification, and that her Son, who was presented, was also marked with the stain of His Mother, according to the words of the Law."
[56] Alexander VII, Brief *Sollicitudo omnium Ecclesiarum* in *DS* 2015-2017.
[57] *Ibid.*, §1 in *DS* 2015.

Portugal in particular played a great part in fostering the doctrine of the Immaculate Conception. During the reign of King Dom João IV (which began in 1640), in thanksgiving for the miracle of Portugal's reacquisition of its liberty after sixty years of Spanish occupation, the King consulted Parliament, the University of Coimbra and all of the Bishops concerning this question and all of these institutions approved the initiative of offering the Kingdom of Portugal to the Blessed Virgin Mary under the Title of the Immaculate Conception. Following this act, all the subsequent Kings of Portugal never again wore a crown, since Our Lady had been proclaimed the Reigning Sovereign of Portugal. This devotion has its headquarters in the Shrine of the Castle of Vila Viçosa, where King Dom João IV had lived and where the image he had crowned still exists. There also exists at Vila Viçosa a Confraternity of Our Lady of Conception and the Duke of Braganza is Grand Master of the Order of Our Lady of Conception. In all Castles in Portugal and at the gates of all Portuguese cities there was placed a plaque in stone proclaiming this act of consecration of Portugal to the Immaculate Conception. This decision of the Portuguese nation which crowned Mary Immaculate as Queen of Portugal has never been revoked by any legislative act of Parliament, and thus continues to this day to be legally in force.[58]

Finally, in 1849, Pope Blessed Pius IX consulted the bishops regarding the faith of the Church concerning the doctrine of the Immaculate Conception, and also whether a dogmatic definition in this regard would be opportune. The response was affirmative on both counts, and so, on December 8, 1854, Blessed Pius IX solemnly defined the doctrine of the Immaculate Conception in these words:

> We declare, pronounce, and define: the doctrine which holds that the most Blessed Virgin Mary was, from the first moment of her conception, by a singular grace and privilege granted by Almighty God and in view of the merits of Jesus Christ, the Saviour of the human race, preserved immune from all stain of original sin, is a doctrine revealed by God and therefore to be believed firmly and constantly by all the faithful.[59]

---

[58] Dom Duarte, Duke of Bragança, Foreword in P. Haffner, *The Mystery of Mary*, .xi-xii.

[59] Pope Bl. Pius IX, Bull *Ineffabilis Deus* in *DS* 2803: "Declaramus, pronuntiamus et definimus doctrinam quae tenet beatissimam Virginem Mariam in primo

Freedom from Concupiscence

Concupiscence is an effect of original sin, and so it is logical that Our Lady was free from this effect. Thus, not only was Our Lady free from original and actual sin, but was also preserved from this consequence of original sin. This freedom from concupiscence in Our Lady implies, from the viewpoint of the Theology of the Body, a more complete human nature, a most integrated person. Concupiscence consists of three aspects, slavery to the pleasure of the senses, inordinate desire of earthly goods and the disordered affirmation of self against the dictates of reason (1 Jn. 2:16).[60] St. Thomas Aquinas applied the passage from the Song of Songs "You are wholly beautiful, my beloved, and without a blemish" (Song. 4:7) as an indication that concupiscence, the seed of sin (*fomes peccati*), which implies a blemish at least in the flesh, was not present in the Blessed Virgin Mary. The Angelic Doctor examined various opinions concerning the absence of concupiscence in Mary.

Some authors held that concupiscence was entirely taken away when the Blessed Virgin was sanctified in the womb. Others said that it remained as far as it caused a difficulty in doing good, but was taken away as far as it causes a proneness to evil. Others again, that it was taken away as to the personal corruption, by which it makes us quick to do evil and slow to do good: but that it remained as to the corruption of nature, inasmuch as it is the cause of transmitting original sin to the offspring. Lastly, others said that, in her first sanctification, concupiscence remained essentially, but was fettered; and that, when she conceived the Son of God, it was entirely taken away.

Saint Thomas pointed out that sensual concupiscence is said to be inordinate, in so far as it rebels against reason, and this it does by inclining to evil, or hindering from good. Consequently it necessarily inclines to evil, or hinders from good. Thus to say that concupiscence was in the Blessed Virgin Mary without an inclination to evil, is to combine two contradictory statements. Similarly, it is contradictory to say that it remained as to the corruption of nature, but not as to the personal corruption, for if it were entirely taken away as to personal

---

instanti suae conceptionis fuisse singulari Omnipotentis Dei gratia et privilegio, intuitu meritorum Christi Jesu Salvatoris humani generis, ab omni originalis culpae labe praeservatam immunem, esse a Deo revelatam, atque idcirco ab omnibus fidelibus firmiter constanterque credendam."

corruption, it could not remain as to the corruption of nature. The only possibilities remaining are either that concupiscence was entirely taken away from her by her first sanctification or that it was fettered. St. Thomas maintains that the Holy Spirit effected a twofold purification in the Blessed Virgin Mary. The first was preparatory to Christ's conception: which did not cleanse her from concupiscence. The second purification effected in her by the Holy Spirit, when He purified her entirely from concupiscence. The Angelic Doctor held just as before the Resurrection of Christ in His immortal Flesh, nobody obtained immortality of the flesh, so it seems unfitting to say that before Christ appeared in sinless flesh, His Virgin Mother's or anyone else's flesh should be without concupiscence. Therefore it seems better to say that by the sanctification in the womb of her mother, the Virgin was not freed from concupiscence in its essence, but that it remained fettered. Afterwards, however, at the conception of Christ's flesh, in which for the first time immunity from sin was to be conspicuous, it is to be believed that entire freedom from concupiscence redounded from the Child to the Mother.[61] Nowadays, given the insight of Blessed John Duns Scotus into the prevenient and preventative aspects of the Redemption, it seems more reasonable to suppose that Mary enjoyed complete freedom from concupiscence from the first moment of her conception.

Freedom from Death?

Death is another unfortunate consequence of original sin: "If death came to many through the offence of one man, how much greater an effect the grace of God has had, coming to so many and so plentifully as a free gift through the one man Jesus Christ!" (Rm. 5:15; cf. Rm. 5:17; 1 Cor. 15:21). The question thus arises, since Our Blessed Lady was free from original sin and its consequences like concupiscence, what was the nature of her passing this life, and concretely whether she died or not. This issue examines whether she experienced the separation of the soul from the body. The dogma of the Assumption of the Mother of God leaves open the question of whether or not she died. A minority of theologians hold that she did not in fact suffer death. In the late fourth century, we find the earliest

[60] See *Catechism of the Catholic Church*, 377.
[61] See St. Thomas Aquinas, *Summa Theologiae*, III, q.27, a.3.

known, non-Apocryphal mention of the close of Mary's life, in the writings of St. Epiphanius (315-403), Bishop of Constantia, on the island of Cyprus:

> Whether she died or was buried we do not know.... Say she died a natural death. In that case she fell asleep in glory, and departed in purity, and received the crown of her virginity. Or say she was slain with the sword according to Simeon's prophecy. Then her glory is with the martyrs, and she through whom the divine light shone upon the world is in the place of bliss with her sacred body. Or say she left this world without dying, for God can do what He wills. Then she was simply transferred to eternal glory.[62]

St. Epiphanius genuinely may have not known, or else he was being careful not to play into the hands of certain contemporary heretics, the Antidicomarianites and the Collyridians. The former group denied the perpetual virginity of Mary; the latter, erring in the opposite direction, maintained that divine worship should be given to her. To claim that Our Lady died was to give possible fuel to the former heresy (for it was to suggest that the body of Mary was subject to the corruption of the tomb, and thus minimize her prerogatives); to assert that she did not die was to encourage the latter.[63] Around the same time, Timothy of Jerusalem, affirmed that Mary did not die: "Wherefore the Virgin is immortal up to now, because He who dwelt in her, assumed her to the heavenly regions."[64]

St. Isidore of Seville († 636) appears to be the first to cast some doubt upon the fact of Mary's death: "Nowhere does one read of her death. Although, as some say, her sepulchre may be found in the valley of Josaphat."[65] Tusaredo, a Bishop in the Asturias province of Spain in the eighth century, wrote: "Of the glorious Mary, no history teaches that she suffered martyrdom or any other kind of death."[66] In the early ninth century, Theodore Abou-Kurra likened the death of Mary to the sleep of Adam in the Garden when God formed Eve from one of his ribs.[67] This, obviously, was not a true death.

---

[62] St. Epiphanius, *Adversus Octaginta Haereses* Book 3, Tome 2, Heresy 78, 11 and 24 in *PG* 42, 715-716 and 738.

[63] See G. M. Roschini, "Did Our Lady Die?" in *The Irish Ecclesiastical Record*, 80 (1953), 75-76.

[64] Timothy of Jerusalem, *Homily on Simeon* in *PG* 86, 246-247.

[65] St. Isidore of Seville, *De ortu et obitu Patrum*, 67 in *PL* 83, 150.

[66] Tusaredo, *Epistola ad Ascaricum*, II in *PL* 99, 1239-1240.

Most of the Fathers, however, reflecting on Mary's destiny and on her relationship with her divine Son, proposed that since Christ died, it would be difficult to maintain the contrary for His Mother. St. Augustine (354-430), who was not clear concerning the absence of original sin in Our Lady, stated baldly: "Mary, as a daughter of Adam died as a consequence of sin; Adam died because of sin, and the flesh of the Lord, born of Mary, died to destroy sin."[68] The Syriac Father, St Jacob of Sarug (d. 521), wrote that when the time came for Mary "to walk the way of all generations", that is the way of death, "the group of the Twelve Apostles" gathered to bury "the virginal body of the Blessed One."[69] St. Modestus of Jerusalem (d. 634), after a lengthy discussion of "the most blessed dormition of the most glorious Mother of God", ends his eulogy by exalting the miraculous intervention of Christ who "raised her from the tomb", to take her up with Him in glory.[70] St John Damascene (d. 704) asks the basic question: "For how could she, who brought life to all, be under the dominion of death? But she obeys the law of her own Son, and inherits this chastisement as a daughter of the first Adam, since her Son, who is the life, did not refuse it. As the Mother of the living God, she goes through death to Him."[71] St. Andrew of Crete (d. 720) also followed the line of those who affirmed, with very little argumentation, that Mary died because her Son died.[72]

---

[67] Theodore Abou-Kurra, *Opuscula*, op. 37 in *PG* 97, 1594.

[68] St. Augustine, *Enarratio in Psalmo 34*, 3 in *PL* 41, 501: "Maria ex Adam mortua propter peccatum, Adam mortuus propter peccatum, et caro Domini ex Maria mortua est propter delenda peccata."

[69] St. Jacob of Sarug, *Discourse on the burial of the Holy Mother of God*, 87-99 in *EM* 1493-1494.See also C. Vona, *Lateranum* 19 (1953), 188.

[70] St. Modestus of Jerusalem, *Encomium in dormitionem Deiparae semperque Virginis Mariae*, nn. 7 and 14 in *PG* 86 *bis*, 3293; 3311.

[71] St. John Damascene, *Homily 2 on the Dormition of the Blessed Virgin*, 2 in *PG* 96, 726. See also Idem, *Homily 1 on the Dormition of the Blessed Virgin*, 10 in *PG* 96, 714, where St. John Damascene asks: "Why is it that she who in giving birth surpassed all the limits of nature should now bend to its laws, and her immaculate body be subjected to death?" And he answers: "To be clothed in immortality, it is of course necessary that the mortal part be shed, since even the master of nature did not refuse the experience of death. Indeed, He died according to the flesh and by dying destroyed death; on corruption He bestowed incorruption and made death the source of resurrection."

[72] St. Andrew of Crete, *Oratio 12 in dormitione SS. Deiparae* in *PG* 97, 1051-1054.

Many Fathers attest the pious tradition that at least some of the Apostles were present at Our Lady's passing from this world. In the East, St. John Damascene wrote:

> When the Ark of God [Mary], departing from Mount Sion for the heavenly country, was borne on the shoulders of the Apostles, it was placed on the way in the tomb. First it was taken through the city, as a bride dazzling with spiritual radiance, and then carried to the sacred place of Gethsemane, angels overshadowing it with their wings, going before, accompanying, and following it, together with the whole assembly of the Church.[73]

In the West, St. Gregory of Tours (d.593) wrote:

> When finally the Blessed Virgin had fulfilled the course of this life, and was now to be called out of this world, all the Apostles were gathered together from each region to her house ... and behold the Lord Jesus came with His angels and, receiving her soul, entrusted it to the Archangel Michael and departed. At the break of day the Apostles lifted the body with the couch and laid it in the sepulchre, and they guarded it awaiting the coming of the Lord. And behold the Lord again stood by them, and commanded that the holy body be taken up and borne on a cloud into Paradise, where now, reunited with (her) soul and rejoicing with the elect, it enjoys the good things of eternity which shall never come to an end.[74]

Many of the great Scholastics taught that Mary died, because they were unable to see how she remained free from original sin. St. Thomas, since he could not see how Our Lady was conceived without original sin, maintained the she suffered the consequences, and in particular death.[75] In particular, St. Bonaventure wrote:

> If the Blessed Virgin was free from original sin, she was also exempt from the necessity of dying; therefore, either her death was an injustice or she died for the salvation of the human race. But the former supposition is blasphemous, implying that God is not just; and the latter, too, is a blasphemy against Christ for it implies that His Redemption is insufficient. Both are therefore erroneous and impossible. Therefore Our Blessed Lady was subject to original sin.[76]

---

[73] St. John Damascene, *Homily 2 on the Dormition of the Blessed Virgin*, 12 in *PG* 96, 738.

[74] St. Gregory of Tours, *De gloria beatorum martyrum*, 4 in *PL* 71, 708.

[75] See St. Thomas Aquinas, *Summa Theologiae* III, q.14, a.3.

[76] St. Bonaventure, *Commentarius in III Librum Sententiarum Petri Lombardi*,

Most interestingly this passage connects the question of Mary's death also with the role which she played in the Redemption. Even those authors who accepted the doctrine of the Immaculate Conception did not always deduce that Mary would have remained without death. Even Blessed John Duns Scotus, who was clear on the Immaculate Conception, did not hold that Mary would have been exempted from death. For Scotus, the sentence of death is so general, that neither Christ nor Mary are exceptions. The resurrection of the body is for him a victory over death, like that of Christ and his Mother.[77]

St. Alphonsus Liguori (1696-1787) held a nuanced position on Mary's death, pointing out that in one sense she should not have died, but in fact did die in order to be like her Son:

> Death being the punishment of sin, it would seem that the Divine Mother all holy, and exempt as she was from its slightest stain should also have been exempt from death, and from encountering the misfortunes to which the children of Adam, infected by the poison of sin, are subject. But God was pleased that Mary should in all things resemble Jesus; and as the Son died, it was becoming that the Mother should also die; because, moreover, He wished to give the just an example of the precious death prepared for them, He willed that even the most Blessed Virgin should die, but by a sweet and happy death.[78]

In the seventeenth century, there was renewed interest in the question of Mary's death. An Italian theologian Beverini proposed that Mary did not die.[79] After 1854, once Pope Blessed Pius IX had defined the Immaculate Conception the question of whether or not Our Blessed Lady died gradually became a subject of wide theological discussion. The impetus for further research out of which arose the present state of dispute was given by the writings of

distinction 3, question 2, in *S. Bonaventurae Opera Omnia* (Collegio San Bonaventura: Quaracchi, 1888), vol. III, p.66.

[77] See Bd. John Duns Scotus, *Fragmenta*, in K. Balić (ed.) *Theologiae Marianae elementa* (Sibenik: Kacik, 1933), 172.

[78] St. Alphonsus Liguori, "Discourse VII. Of the Assumption of the Blessed Virgin Mary" in *The Glories of Mary* (Rockford, Illinois: Tan, 1977), 371.

[79] B. Beverini, *De corporali morte Deiparae* (Roma: Academia Mariana, 1950). This work was republished in 1950, under the editorship of K. Balić.

Dominic Arnaldi (d.1895) of Genoa who proposed that Our Blessed Lady's complete freedom from sin demanded her immunity from the penalty of death.[80] Later in the twentieth century, the clearest proponents of the thesis that Mary did not die were Roschini and Gallus.[81] Others like Bonnefoy were clear proponents of Mary's death: "the death of the Most Holy Virgin may be considered as historically proved and explicitly revealed: as such (explicitly revealed) it may be the subject of a dogmatic definition: there is no reason why it should not be."[82]

Pope John Paul II has come closest to addressing the issue, and he inclined in favour of Mary's participation in death: "The fact that the Church proclaims Mary free from original sin by a unique divine privilege does not lead to the conclusion that she also received physical immortality. The Mother is not superior to the Son who underwent death, giving it a new meaning and changing it into a means of salvation."[83] The Pope went on to ask: "Could Mary of Nazareth have experienced the drama of death in her own flesh?" His response is that reflecting on Mary's destiny and her relationship with her divine Son, "it seems legitimate to answer in the affirmative: since Christ died, it would be difficult to maintain the contrary for his Mother.... Involved in Christ's redemptive work and associated in his saving sacrifice, Mary was able to share in His suffering and death for the sake of humanity's Redemption."[84] Clearly the Pope did not wish to close the question, but indicated the theological weight in favour of the position that Mary participated somehow in death's mystery.

There are two basic reasons in favour of the position that Our Blessed Mother actually died. First, that of conformity to Christ. The condition of the Mother should not be better than that of her divine Son. As the Mother of the passible and mortal Redeemer from whom

---

[80] D. Arnaldi, *Super transitu Beatae Mariae Virginis Deiparae expertis omni labe culpae originalis dubia proposita* (Genoa: Montaldum, 1879).

[81] G.M. Roschini, "Il problema della morte di Maria SS. dopo la Costituzione Dogmatica *Munificentissimus Deus*" in *Marianum* 13 (1951), 148-163; T. Gallus, *La Vergine Immortale* (Roma: 1949).

[82] J.F. Bonnefoy, "Définibilité de l'Assomption" in *Congrès Marial du Puy-en-Velay* (Paris: 1950), 241; cf. Idem, "La Bulle Dogmatique *Munificentissimus Deus* (1 Nov. 1950)" in *Ephemerides Mariologicae*1 (1951), 104-114.

[83] Pope John Paul II, *Discourse at General Audience* (25 June 1997), 3.

[84] *Ibid.*, 2 and 3.

He took His mortal flesh, Mary, too, had to be passible and mortal. This argument seems *post factum*, proposing to explain the fact of Mary's death once that death had been taken for granted. The Second Council of Orange is quite explicit in its teaching that those who hold that the penalty of death is transmitted to the body without the transmission of sin or the death of the soul to all the children of Adam, do an injustice to God.[85] Hence, where there is no sin there can be no mandatory death of the body in a child of Adam.

A second reason favouring Mary's death would involve voluntary acceptance on her part. Some theologians locate this within the framework of Mary's role of Co-redemptrix of the human race. They would maintain that Mary died, though she had a right to immortality. She, like her Son, freely accepted death in order that she might co-redeem the human race together with Him. Yet the objection can then be put that Mary should then have died on Calvary with Christ.

Contrary to the proposition that Mary died, one could say that it seems strange that she should have enjoyed any lesser privilege than Elijah or Enoch from the Old Testament, who seemingly did not die. Moreover, it could be argued that she enjoyed the first fruits of Christ's Resurrection and Ascension, in such a way that she did not die. Furthermore, one may apply to her the words of Jesus to His disciples: "For the Father loves the Son and shows Him everything He Himself does, and He will show Him even *greater things than these*, works that will astonish you. Thus, as the Father raises the dead and gives them life, so the Son gives life to anyone He chooses" (Jn. 5:20-21).

Since all theologians are agreed, at least after the definition of the doctrine of the Immaculate Conception, that Mary cannot have died as a penalty for sin, the issue remains as to what was the cause of death. It is clear that she cannot have simply died of illness, a consequence of old age. Neither would she have died of old age, as this is also connected with original sin. Also, a minority thesis, based on a misinterpretation of the prophecy of Simeon (Lk. 2:35), that she suffered martyrdom, has long since been rejected, among others by St. Ambrose: "Neither the letter [of Scripture] nor history, teach us that Mary departed this life after having been assassinated; whereby

---

[85] See Second Council of Orange, canon 2 in *DS* 372.

not the soul but the body was pierced by a material sword."[86] That leaves various other opinions. One is that she voluntarily gave up her privilege of immortality, in order to be more like her Son. Another line is that she died of sorrow in the aftermath of having seen her Son crucified.[87] Perhaps the soundest approach would be to say along with St. Francis de Sales that Mary's death was due to a transport of love.[88] He pointed out that as Christ's Mother lived her Son's life, she also died her Son's death:

> The virgin-mother, having collected in her spirit all the most beloved mysteries of the life and death of her Son by a most lively and continual memory of them, and withal, ever receiving directly the most ardent inspirations which her child, the sun of justice, has cast upon human beings in the highest noon of His charity; and besides, making on her part also, a perpetual movement of contemplation, at length the sacred fire of this divine love consumed her entirely as a holocaust of sweetness, so that she died thereof, the soul being wholly ravished and transported into the arms of the dilection of her Son.[89]

The saint also explained that this death was not violent, but rather her "death was more sweet than could be imagined, her Son sweetly drawing her after the odour of His perfumes, and she most lovingly flowing out after their sacred sweetness even into the bosom of her Son's goodness."[90]

Finally, it should be remarked that however one conceives of the end of Mary's life, namely whether Mary died or not, she was not subject to the *law of death*, which is the corruption of the body in the grave. If she died, then she was assumed into heaven before her sacred body saw corruption. For, so long as the bodies of the just remain in the dust of the earth, they are under the dominion of death, and they sigh for the ultimate redemption of their bodies.

---

[86] St. Ambrose, *Expositio Evangeliisecundum Lucam*, Book 2, chapter 2, 61 in *PL* 15, 1574: "Nec littera, nec historia docet ex hac vita Mariam corporalis necis passione migrasse; non enim anima, sed corpus materiali gladio transverberatur."

[87] This line was taken by St. Peter Damian, *De celebrandis vigiliis*, 1 in *PL* 145, 801.

[88] This was the line of Pope John Paul II, *Discourse at General Audience* (25 June 1997), 4.

[89] St. Francis de Sales, *Treatise on the Love of God*, book 7, chapter 13.

[90] St. Francis de Sales, *Treatise on the Love of God*, book 7, chapter 14. He added (13. 24) that "love at the cross gave her the supreme sorrows of death. So it was right that finally death should give her the sovereign pleasure of love."

MARY'S BODILY PARTICIPATION
IN THE REDEMPTION OF CHRIST:
THE JOHANNINE WITNESS

Kenneth J. Howell, Ph.D.

Catholic tradition has long recognized the participation of the faithful in extending the objective work of Christ's redemption in the world. The great spiritual writers of the past witness to the real communion (or *koinonia*) of the faithful in Christ's atonement such that their embodiment of Christ's merits allows them to become conduits of grace in this world. It is of the greatest importance, however, to recognize that this participation in redemption in no way substitutes for or supplants Christ's unique role as Redeemer and Mediator. Human cooperation in the economy of redemption is limited to the subjective application of Christ's objective sacrifice, that is, one person becomes the human instrument through whom the merits of Christ's grace reaches into the heart of another person.

However, one exception to this limitation of human participation stands out. The Blessed Virgin Mary's participation bridged the gap between the objective accomplishment of redemption and its subjective application. By the gift of her own body to Jesus, Mary uniquely united her own person to her Son so that she might share in His redemption in a unique manner. Bodily participation in Christ's redemption is not limited to Mary since the faithful can unite their bodies with Christ's passion through martyrdom or other less final corporal sufferings. Yet Mary's bodily participation did not begin from a personal appropriation of Christ's sacrifice, as is the case with others; rather the gift of her humanity to Jesus made possible our participatory appropriation. Thus, Mary's role as the *Theotokos* (*Deipara*) made possible the accomplishment of the objective redemption of Christ which culminated in His sacrificial self-offering on Calvary.

Our understanding of Mary's role, however, is severely truncated if we limit her bodily participation to the conception, gestation, and birth of Jesus in the stable of Bethlehem. Sacred Scripture offers a much wider and deeper understanding of Mary's role in the redemption. Two major witnesses are St. Luke and St. John, each of which discloses distinctive but complementary portrayals of Mary's lifelong union with Jesus' redemptive work.[1] It is especially the fourth gospel which portrays Mary's active involvement at key points of Jesus' public ministry: the wedding feast of Cana and the crucifixion. In this light, the Second Vatican Council gave an authoritative endorsement of understanding Mary's earthly life as a journey of faith in which she united herself with her Son's sacrifice. Its pronouncement reflects the long heritage, rooted in the patristic witness, of seeing in the Johannine account of the Passion Mary's consent to the immolation of Christ:

> The Blessed Virgin also advanced in her pilgrimage of faith, and faithfully persevered in her union with her Son unto the Cross, where she stood, in keeping with the divine plan, enduring with her only begotten Son the intensity of His suffering, associating herself with His sacrifice in her mother's heart, and lovingly consenting to the immolation of this victim who was born of her. Finally, she was given by the same Christ Jesus dying on the Cross as a mother to His disciple.[2]

---

[1] Here I will have to limit myself to certain aspects of the Johannine witness. For Luke's extended treatment of Mary's life in relation to Jesus see Luke 1:28 to 2:52. For insightful commentary on these passages see Stefano Manelli F.I. *All Generations Shall Call Me Blessed* (New Bedford, MA: Academy of the Immaculate, 1995).

[2] *Lumen Gentium*, 58. For more on Mary's cooperation in Christ's redemption see also *Lumen Gentium* 56 and 61. For an exposition of the Council's intention with regard to Marian cooperation see Mark Miravalle "Mary Co-Redemptrix: A Response to 7 Common Objections" in *Mary Coredemptrix Doctrinal Issues Today* (Goleta, CA: Queenship Publishing Co, 2002)

Following the lead of the Council, Pope John Paul II (in *Redemptoris Mater*) saw in Mary's presence at the cross a declaration of her universal motherhood:

> One can say that if Mary's motherhood of the human race had already been outlined, now it is clearly stated and established. It emerges from the definitive accomplishment of the Redeemer's Paschal Mystery. The Mother of Christ, who stands at the very center of this mystery—a mystery that embraces each individual and all humanity—is given as mother to every single individual and to all mankind.[3]

For John Paul II, Mary's maternal love at the cross came to "definitive maturity ...through her sharing in the redemptive love of her Son." He took the words "Woman, behold your son" as going to the very heart of the mystery of Mary because of "the unique place she occupies in the whole economy of salvation."[4] This maternal cooperation is even further enhanced when John Paul II's Theology of the Body is explored in connection with the Virgin Mary. In these sermons, John Paul II explored in a profound way the heart of masculinity and femininity which shapes human persons. In this chapter, I want to explore the relationship between John Paul II's exposition of femininity as applied to the Blessed Virgin Mary and the scriptural witness of her participation in Christ's atoning sacrifice on Calvary recorded in John 19:25-27.

The core of my contribution lies in showing the deep relevance of John 19:25-27 to Mariology, a relevance which arises from a careful analysis of authorial intent as latent in the literary structure of the pericope. Showing that a Mariological reading is not foreign to the author's intention seems necessary today in light of scholarly research on the fourth gospel which downplays the significance of Jesus' mother in this pericope. Recognizing that the author of the fourth gospel *intended* to comment on the mother of Jesus' role in redemption will confirm the historical founda-

---

[3] *Redemptoris Mater,* 23.
[4] *Ibid.*

tion of the Church's Mariological reading of this text. I then attempt to show how the Johannine witness to Mary's cooperation in redemption is deepened by placing these exegetical foundations within the context of John Paul II's Theology of the Body.

Before embarking on a literary analysis of John 19:25-27 and its contexts, a few highlights of the Mariological reading of this text in Patristic interpretation will help to reinforce the historical grounds of the magisterial teaching indicated above. In general, patristic preaching places great emphasis on Mary's maternal role which grows out of an even more deeply embedded tradition of Mary as the new Eve.[5] Consider, for example, St. Cyril of Alexandria's famous homily on Mary delivered at the Council of Ephesus (A.D. 431):

> We hail you, Mary, God bearer (*Theotokos*), revered treasure house of the whole world, an inextinguishable lamp, the crown of virginity, the scepter (*skeptron*) of orthodoxy, the indestructible temple, the

---

[5] For illustrative purposes, consider two witnesses from the second century: St. Justin Martyr and St. Irenaeus. In his *Dialogue with Trypho the Jew* (ca. A.D. 150), Justin explains that Christ destroyed the devil's work in the same way evil originally entered the world. Evil entered through Eve while she was still a virgin; so too salvation entered through Mary while she was still a virgin. In both cases each woman willingly participated in the act they performed. Neither was a unconscious instrument. Eve listened to the serpent and conceived death. Mary listened to the angel Gabriel and conceived life. Justin sees this clearly in Luke 1:38 when Mary said, "Let it be done to me according to your word." St. Irenaeus offers one of the clearest explanations of Mary's role as the New Eve, thereby showing how important this doctrine is for redemption. *Against Heresies* has as its central teaching the doctrine of recapitulation. This doctrine means that Christ embodied Adam and all his posterity in order to redeem mankind from sin. Basing his teaching on Paul's inspired doctrine of Christ as "the Last Adam" (cf. 1 Cor 15:45), Irenaeus viewed Jesus as reversing the effects of Adam's sin by bringing the life and righteousness that Adam lost (cf. Rom 5:17,18). Irenaeus saw the obvious implication. As Eve cooperated with Adam, the covenant head of humanity, so Mary cooperated with Jesus Christ, the covenant head of the new humanity. Thus Irenaeus says that Eve "by disobeying became the cause of death for herself and the whole human race, so also Mary ... was obedient and became the cause of salvation for herself and the whole human race." (3.22.4). Later the Bishop of Lyons says of these two virgins, "just as the human race was subject to death by a virgin, it was freed by a virgin, with the virginal disobedience balanced by virginal obedience." (5.19.1). For more on Mary as the New Eve among the Fathers see Luigi Gambero S.M. *Mary in the Fathers of the Church*. Trans. Thomas Buffer. (San Francisco: Ignatius Press, 1999). Some original Patristic texts employing the Eve-Mary parallelism are collected in M. J. Rouet de Journel S.J. *Enchiridion Patristicum* 11th edition. (Freiburg im Breisgau: Herder, 1937).

container of the uncontainable one, both mother and virgin. Because of you the holy gospels could say, "Blessed is he who comes in the name of the Lord."

Later in the same homily Cyril focuses on Mary as virgin-mother:

Who among men can speak of Mary's incomparable honor, this virginal mother? O what a wonder! The miracle overwhelms me with amazement. Who has ever heard of a builder being excluded from dwelling in a temple He Himself built? Who would invite mockery by asking his own servant to become His mother? Behold then the joy of the whole universe.[6]

Out of this general pattern of viewing Mary as the New Eve, whose role as virgin-mother blesses the world, the Fathers of the Church understood Mary's vocation as extending throughout the duration of her life.[7] As early as the third century, Origen of Alexandria discussed the uniqueness of John's gospel by offering a nuanced interpretation of Mary's presence at the cross:

We can be so bold to say that the gospels are the first fruits of all the Scriptures and that John's gospel is the first fruits of the gospels. No one except John was able to recline on Jesus' chest, nor did anyone receive from Jesus Mary who became his own mother too. So necessary is it to become another John that it is as if John were to be shown by Jesus to be another Jesus. Now since there is no son of Mary except Jesus — according to those who think of her rightly— Jesus says to His mother, "Behold your son." and not "Behold this is also your son." Equally he said, "this is the Jesus whom you bore." For everyone who has been perfected no longer lives by himself but rather Christ lives in him (cf. Gal 2:20). And since Christ lives in him, it is said to Mary about him, "Behold your son is Christ."[8]

---

[6] These two quotations come from Cyril of Alexandria *Homily 4* in *PG* 77 (cols 991, 995-996). All translations from the Scriptures and other ancient documents are my own. As in my discussion below, there are times when I have departed from most of the standard English translations.

[7] Raymond Brown speculates that Ambrose's Mariological-ecclesiological interpretation may be related to the earlier tradition of Mary as the New Eve. Raymond E. Brown *The Gospel According to John (xiii-xxi) The Anchor Bible. Vol.29A* (Garden City, NY: Doubleday & Co., 1966), 924.

[8] *PG* 14 (col. 32). My translation is from the text printed by A. E. Brooke *The Commentary of Origen on St. John's Gospel* vol. 1 (Cambridge: Cambridge University Press, 1896), 7. For a slightly different translation see Gambero, *Mary in the Fathers of the Church,* 80.

Origen's double equation (John = Jesus and John = believer) set the stage for a long history of reading this pericope as a balance between what Stefano Manelli called the "personal-private" and "representative-communal" interpretations.[9] The former, which has predominated in modern Protestant commentary, sees in this story only Jesus' personal concern for His mother as the consummate expression of His filial love. In this reading, the beloved disciple plays no other role than taking care of Mary in obedience to Jesus' last wishes. Endorsing this personal reading, Origen too sees the beloved disciple as unique since "no one except John was able to recline on Jesus' chest." However, clearly such a reading does not exclude a richer meaning in which the beloved disciple represents every Christian. By an artful concatenation of the Johannine account with Paul's theology of Christ's indwelling of the faithful, Origen is able to extend the significance of the account beyond one historical moment. For him, the words "behold your son" were deliberately chosen to indicate that Mary was to treat the beloved disciple as if he were Jesus Himself, and by extension to treat every disciple as if he were the beloved disciple.

This representative-communal reading of John 19:25-27 was not limited to the Greek-speaking Fathers. In the West, St. Ambrose of Milan draws upon another dimension of this text:

> You will be a son of thunder (i.e., like John) if you are a son of the Church. Let Christ say to you about the yoke of the cross, "Behold your mother." Let him say to the Church, "Behold your son." Then you will begin to be a son of the Church when you see Christ as victor on the cross. For whoever considers the cross a scandal, he is Judas, and not a son of the Church. Whoever considers the cross foolishness, he is a Greek (cf. 1 Cor. 1:20-25). But he is a son of the Church who considers the cross a triumph.[10]

In the way that Ambrose takes the words of John 19:25-27, Mary represents the Church while the beloved disciple represents the believer whom Ambrose exhorts to embrace the cross through the Church. While these identifications differ from Origen's because they are occasioned by different situations, they both share the appli-

---

[9] Manelli, *All Generations Shall Call Me Blessed,* 326.
[10] St. Ambrose of Milan, *Expositio Evangelii secundam Lucam* Bk. 7, sec.5; *PL* 15 (col. 700C).

cation of the words "behold your mother" to any Christian. These two examples illustrate the flexibility of interpretation of this text among the Fathers, but both are a type of representative-communal interpretation; neither Church Father limits this episode to the unique historical experience of the crucifixion.

Mary's Participation at the Cross

Now the question is whether this historical-interpretative (*auslegungsgeschichtlich*) openness in the interpretation of John 19:25-27—and the modern magisterial teaching based on it—can be justified exegetically. In other words, is the Church's tradition of balancing the personal and communal interpretations of John 19:25-27 consonant with the text or is it a dogmatic imposition on exegesis? On the surface, the relevance of the interpretation of John 19:25-27 to Mariology presupposes at least two levels of interpretation. The historical level (*sensus litteralis sive historicus*) grounds interpretation in the grammatical and historical context of the Passion narrative while a higher level reading *(sensus spiritualis)* seeks to find meanings beyond the historical event itself. The former reading views the text as a story only about the beloved disciple's duty to Jesus in taking care of Mary and is typically based on a historical appeal to original authorial intent.[11]

The representative-communal reading can take many forms, but its Mariological version is often thought to be based on dogmatic and/or pastoral concerns. Mariologists often appeal to the history of the Church's interpretation of this pericope as justification for the representative-communal interpretation because they recognize the authority of traditional readings for theology today. Many modern scholars of the fourth gospel, who often consciously set aside the Church's reading, tend to think that a Mariological

---

[11] A modern example of a rather traditional stripe is the Anglican Leon Morris, *The Gospel According to John The English Text with Introduction, Exposition, and Notes* (Grand Rapids, MI: Eerdmans Publishing Co., 1971), 810-812. He does not show any evidence of being aware of the possibility of a symbolic interpretation nor of Origen's contention that Jesus committed Mary to John because she had no other children. Haenchen sees no symbolic significance in the pericope, "there is nothing in the story that points to such a symbolic meaning for these figures." See Ernst Haenchen *John 2: A Commentary on the Gospel of John Chapters 7-21* (Philadelphia: Fortress Press, 1984), 193.

interpretation arises from theological dogma and is alien to the exegesis of the fourth gospel. For example, Fr. Raymond Brown, in one of the most extensive commentaries on John in the twentieth century, saw Marian doctrine based on this text as going "considerably beyond any provable intention of the evangelist."[12] Citing other Catholic exegetes (e.g., Tillmann, Wikenhauser), Brown viewed Mariological use of this text as an example of later theologizing. While he recognized the antiquity of seeing Mary as a symbol of the Church, Brown viewed the notion of Mary's spiritual motherhood based on this text as emerging in the ninth century in the East (George of Nicomedia) and the eleventh century in the West (Pope Gregory VII).[13] Rudolf Bultmann's highly influential commentary on John put forth a kind of symbolic-communal interpretation. For him, this pericope has no historical reality given its divergences from the synoptic tradition. The scene has a symbolic character. Jesus' mother represents Jewish Christianity while the beloved disciple represents Gentile Christianity. The meaning of the story is to exhort Gentile Christians, who have Jewish Christians as their mother, to make a place for them in their "house", that is, in the greater church community. The words from the cross ("behold your mother" and "behold your son") mean that the church needs to be united like what is said in John 17:20ff, "that they both may be one."[14]

I contend that a careful analysis of selected aspects of literary structure show that the authorial intent of the evangelist *includes* reading John 19:25-27 in a representative-communal manner with Mary at the center of that reading. Through an analysis of an expanding horizon of contexts, I wish to show that the tradition of Mariological reading is exegetically justified. The methodological concept "horizons of contexts" begins with the text itself and by noting its functions within its immediate environment (in the Passion narrative), and within the literary structure of the gospel as

---

[12] Raymond E. Brown, *The Gospel According to John (xiii-xxi) The Anchor Bible. Vol.29A.* (Garden City, NY: Doubleday & Co., 1966), 925.

[13] *Ibid.*

[14] Bultmann rejects the suggestion of Hirsch that Jesus' mother represents the church even though he affirms the Church is the mother of believers and the Bride of Christ. Rudolf Bultmann *Das Evangelium des Johannes* 10ed Goettingen: Vandenhoeck and Ruprecht, 1968), 521.

a whole, it shows that a representative-communal interpretation is consonant with the theology of the fourth gospel. I further contend that John intended a specific kind of representative-communal reading, one with Mary's maternal care at its heart. The pericope in question is deceptively simple and straightforward:

> Now there were standing by the cross of Jesus his mother, his mother's sister, Mary the wife of Clopas, and Mary Magdalene. So when Jesus saw his mother and the disciple whom he loved standing by, he said to his mother, "Woman, behold your son." Then he said to the disciple, "Behold your mother" And from that very hour the disciple received her for his own. (Jn.19:25-27).

An exchange is described here between Jesus, his mother, and the beloved disciple which is unique in the Passion narratives. The Synoptics have women standing at a distance (e.g., Mk 15: 40; Lk 23:49), and a declaration of faith made by the centurion (Mk 15:39), but they make no mention of any male disciple at the cross. Most modern exegetes agree that the author's specifying of four women was an intentional correspondence to the four soldiers who crucified Jesus.[15] Further, even those who see John's pericope as symbolic differ as to what Mary and the beloved disciple signify. By investigating certain aspects of this text and its contexts, I intend to show that the Church's Mariological reading is justified on the basis of the author's literary method.

1) Selected Aspects of John 19:25-27

One of the most intriguing questions of this text is why the author included a twofold exchange of "Woman, behold your son" and "behold your mother." One reason may be that the author is employing a revelatory formula which De Goedt detected elsewhere in the gospel. De Goedt suggested that in John's gospel there is often a pattern of "seeing, saying, and "behold" followed by the content of a revelation.[16] Such a pattern is consistent with

---

[15] Whether " His mother's sister" is "Mary the wife of Clopas" or is a separate person is unknown although it would not seem likely that Jesus' mother would have had a sister also named Mary. Even if there are three women, the presence of the beloved disciple would still make four witnesses, corresponding to the four soldiers.

[16] M. De Goedt "Un scheme de revelation dans le quatrieme Evangelie" *New Testament Studies* 8 (1961-62) 142-59.

this text and suggests that the two phrases are designed to unveil something profound to their recipients. The content of the revelation (i.e., "your son" and "your mother") indicates the unveiling of a new relationship which each recipient had to grasp. This revelatory formula underscores that Jesus intended to teach something to His mother and to the beloved disciple. Thus, it was not enough to have only one such statement for both Mary and the beloved disciple; both needed this new revelation in a manner appropriate to their respective positions.

The translation of the phrase *eis ta idia* at the end of verse 27 emphasizes this new relationship. The standard translation ("into his own home") is linguistically and contextually justified since it seems to reflect the beloved disciple's obedience to Jesus' implicit command to take care of His mother. The prepositional phrase *eis ta idia* could be an idiom with this meaning, in which case it would be equivalent to the more literal *eis ton oikon autou* ("into his house"). It has this meaning in John 16:32 and Acts 21:6; it is analogous to the use of prepositions in modern languages like German (*bei ihm*) and French (*chez lui*). The question is whether there is more intended than simple physical care. As noted above, some influential interpreters (e.g., Bultmann, Brown) see more than the mundane level of physical residence.[17] On the other hand, the root term *idios* carries a basic meaning of "one's own" with a connotation of personal possession. Thus, *eis ta idia* could mean something like "for his own" or "as his own" (cf. German *eigen*). In this case, much more than physical or residential care would be intended. Most commentators seem to see the need to choose between these or alternatives. I believe a more open view is possible.

I would argue that there is no need to choose between translating *eis ta idia* as "into his own home" or "into his care," or as above, "for his own" given that the evangelist often uses words on more than one level. In chapter 3, for example, John uses *anothen* on more than one level by drawing on the systematic ambiguity of the term *(double entendre)*. The experience of rebirth which Jesus enjoins on Nicodemus is simultaneously "again" and "from above."[18] On the lit-

---

[17] For example, Brown translates *eis ta idia* as "into his care."
[18] See below my discussion of *tetelestai* in John 19:30.

eral level (*sensus historicus*), the evangelist may well have meant for the beloved disciple (himself) to understand the words of verse 27 both in a physical manner (residence) but on a deeper level (*sensus spiritualis*), the Greek sentence *elaben ho mathetes auten eis ta idia* could be understood as a personal reception of Mary as his own mother.

Consider the systematic ambiguities involved. The aorist verb form *elaben* can mean "he took" or "he received."[19] In fact, the same verb clearly has the meaning of "receive" in John 1:11, 12 "He came unto His own (*eis ta idia*) and His own (*hoi idioi*) did not receive (*parelabon*) Him, but as many as received (*elabon*) Him, He gave them power to become the children of God." John's use of this verb and prepositional phrase in the Prologue argues, at a minimum, that the translation "he received her for his own" is reasonable. There is, however, a way to understanding the relation of John 1:11,12 to John 19:27 that goes beyond reasonable possibility. Below, I will offer evidence that John 19:27 intended to recall John 1:11,12 by using similar language due to the global purpose of the Prologue. In essence, the evangelist's Prologue (1:1-18) is a map for the rest of the gospel which he draws upon in later chapters. John 19:27 is a reference back to the Prologue to show what receiving Jesus means. The personal reception of Jesus spoken of in 1:11,12 finds a further development in 19:27 by an implicit command to receive Jesus' mother. Thus, this phrase (*elaben ho mathetes auten eis ta idia*) probably means "he received her for his own [mother]." Such a translation would certainly reinforce a representative function for the beloved disciple. And given the parallelism between Jesus' two commands ("behold, your son" and "behold your mother") the evangelist would certainly be emphasizing a symbolic function for both the disciple and Jesus' mother.

2) Structural Analysis of the Passion Narrative

The next step in analyzing John 19: 25-27 is to locate it in the wider context of the Passion narrative. Let us consider this fuller meaning of the pericope by observing a small grammatical

---

[19] It is not uncommon for a word in one language to have a range of meaning that is split up into two words by another language.

detail which signals John's intention to place this story into a wider context. Verse 24 and the beginning of verse 25 have the common Greek correlative pair *men ... de* ("on the one hand ... on the other hand")

> v. 24 So, *on the one hand*, the soldiers did these things (i.e., dividing Jesus' garments)
>
> v. 25 *But on the other*, there stood by the cross of Jesus his mother, and his mother's sister, Mary Clopas' wife, and Mary Magdalene.[20]

This syntactic structure simultaneously connects and contrasts the story of the women at the cross with the soldiers' ill-treatment of Jesus. The broadest level of contrast highlights the unloving treatment by the soldiers with the loving presence of the women at the cross. The pericope in verses 25-27 does not stand alone as a story to which the author is now turning. This connection suggests the need for a closer inspection of the dividing of Jesus' garments in verses 23-24:

> So the soldiers, when they crucified Jesus, took His garments and made them into four parts, one part for each soldier, and also a tunic. Now the tunic was seamless, whole from the top to bottom. So they said to one another, "Let's not tear it but cast lots for it to see whose it will be." This was to fulfill Scripture, "they divided my garments among themselves and they cast lots for my clothing." So, on the one hand, the soldiers did these things.

This account of the soldiers has two contrasting features: division and unity. If we compare John's account with the same mention in the Synoptics (see Mt 27:35; Mk 15:24; Lk 23:34), we discover John's version to be much more elaborate. The other gospel writers mention briefly the division of the garments by casting lots, with Mark giving the most explicit reference to Psalm 22:18. John, on the other hand, divides the story of the garments into two parts with each part linked to the quotation from Psalm 22:18. The dividing of Jesus' garments into four parts fulfills the words, "they divided my garments among themselves" while the casting of lots for the seamless tunic fulfills the words, "they cast lots for my clothing."

---

[20] It is worth reminding ourselves that the autographs of biblical books did not contain chapter and verse divisions. John is moving effortlessly from one story to another.

Why does John give this elaborate (twofold) description lacking in the other evangelists? The two separate actions on the part of the soldiers picture the themes of division and unity but both underscore the ignominious treatment of Jesus. Within the broader level contrast between the soldiers' treatment of Jesus and the treatment by the four women there is a parallelism of themes. In the story of verses 25-27 there is also division and unity. Jesus' death separates Him from His mother and the other bystanders; His words "behold your son" points away from Himself to His disciple. At the same time, the mother of Jesus is now united with the beloved disciple by Jesus Himself. The pain of the separation caused by death is balanced by the union of Jesus' mother with the beloved disciple.

Thus, the story of the soldiers' dividing Jesus' garments, connected syntactically with verses 25-27, serves to bring out the deeper meaning latent in the short pericope of the mother of Jesus and the disciple. Jesus' mother is portrayed as one who is simultaneously suffering separation from her Son, and being united as mother to the beloved disciple. Unlike the other women at the cross, whose pain is due to their Master's suffering, Mary's suffering arises from her Son being flesh of her flesh and bone of her bone. A disciple's suffering, however acute it may be, cannot compare with the maternal pain of Mary.

By expanding our horizons one more step, we see that the story also contains a pervasive sense of finality because it is bracketed by two decisive end moments. On the front end, Pilate's proclamation ("What I have written, I have written" 19:22) signals the conclusion of a debate between the Jews and the Roman Governor as to the proper reason for Jesus' crucifixion. On the other side of the story, Jesus ends his life with the final declaration, "it is finished" (*tetelestai*) in 19:30. Both declarations function on literal, historical and higher, symbolic levels. In the case of Pilate, the placard above Jesus proclaims Jesus' sentence and was the expected procedure for crucifixion where the condemnation was made public. Yet, beyond Pilate's intention the placard proclaims Jesus King of the Jews, the deeper meaning of which the Jews sensed. They urged Pilate to rephrase the sentence to say, "He said, I am the King of the Jews" (19:21). Against all human effort, the proclamation is made with one definitive stroke. At this higher symbolic level, Jesus is finally proclaimed to be what he truly is. In his final declaration in verse 30, Jesus too includes both the mundane, historical meaning that his life is over as well as the symbolic level in which the redemption he came to do is perfectly accomplished (cf. 4:34).[21] Within these brackets of finality, Jesus' actions on the cross also carry a sense of finality. The twofold act of giving (mother to son and son to mother) signals a definitive exchange which will have permanent value. The dramatic character of this exchange is heightened by the finality latent in its context and tends to strengthen the argument that the author intended a higher representative meaning, one in which both characters play an important role.

So the immediate context of the Passion narrative infuses our pericope with a sense of dramatic finality coupled with loving devotion. The pain of separation between Jesus and his mother is balanced by the new union she sustains with the community represented by the beloved disciple. This new relationship carries a sense of dramatic climax and permanence because it occurs in union with Jesus' redemption.

3) John 19:25-27 in the Literary Structure of the Gospel

The next step is to expand the context further by placing this pericope within the literary structure of the gospel as a whole. Due to limitations, I will focus on the most important structural feature outside the Passion narrative, the relation between Mary's appearance at the wedding feast of Cana (John 2:1-12) and her presence here at the cross. These are the only two loci where Mary appears in the fourth gospel; in neither pericope is she called by her proper name. She is always designated "the mother of Jesus." Together these two texts function as an *inclusio*.[22] An *inclusio* is a literary device which places a person, object, or word at the beginning and at the end of a unified

---

[21] John 4:34 "Jesus said, my food is to do the will of Him who sent Me and to finish His work." The same verb (*teleioo*) is used here and in 19:30.

[22] See, for example, Craig R. Koester, *Symbolism in the Fourth Gospel* (Minneapolis: Augsburg Press, 2003), 240.

literary unit. Often its presence implies that everything within the brackets is related to the *inclusio* element. The wedding of Cana in John 2:11-12 opens Jesus' public ministry while the crucifixion closes the same ministry. The *inclusio* structure suggests that Mary is to be seen as a crucial player in Jesus' ministry. At Cana, she intercedes with Jesus to ask for wine which symbolizes the joy of salvation. At Calvary, she stands silently in union with Jesus as He brings the work of salvation to its proper fulfillment. In both texts, John may be alluding to Genesis 3:15 with the use of the word "woman."[23] Jesus uses the word as an address to other women as well, but such usage does not mitigate its deeper significance with respect to Mary. The use of "woman" in John 19:26 recalls its use in John 2:4 and both Johannine texts seem to draw on Genesis 3:15 as "the woman" who would stand by her seed in crushing the head of the serpent. But the warfare predicted in Genesis 3:15 does not seem to fit the context of maternal love in John 19:26. How can the Genesis text be relevant to this pericope? The most obvious possibility is the New Eve analogy to be found among the early Church writers.[24] If this analogy does indeed date from apostolic times, John's usage may very well reflect that belief. It may be an allusion which is intended to suggest Mary as the woman who stands beside Jesus in his public work of redemption. The tone of warfare implied in the protoevangelium (Gen 3:15) is present in that all of Jesus' ministry in John aims at dispelling the darkness of the world by the light that He is (cf. 1:4-9). Mary then joins Him in His public work of redemptive victory.

Another cord binding together the wedding at Cana with the cross is the statement of John 2:4 ("My hour has not yet come") inasmuch as the theme of Jesus' hour is laced throughout the gospel. The expression "My or His hour" occurs seven times with a reference to the consummation of Jesus' mission.

2:4 My hour has not yet come.
7:30 His hour had not yet come.
8:20 No one seized Him because His hour had not yet come.
12:23 The hour has come for the Son of Man to be glorified.

---

[23] The use of "woman" in John 2:4 presents several exegetical issues which go beyond our purpose here.

[24] See examples in note 5.

12:27 Now My soul is troubled and what shall I say, Father, save
Me from this hour? Rather is was for this purpose that I came to
this hour.
13:1 Knowing that His hour had come to leave this world to the
Father, having loved His own etc.
17:1 Father, the hour has come. Glorify Your son that He may
glorify you.

In the first three instances (2:4; 7:30; 8:20) the arrival of the
hour is negated. Beginning in chapter twelve the tone changes
because the events narrated from then on are part of His "glorification", that is, His passion and death. One reason that John uses
the unusual term "glorify" with reference to Jesus' suffering is
because the Father will receive glory through the accomplishment
of redemption. The contrast between Jesus' miracle at Cana, when
it was not yet His hour, and the crucifixion, when His hour had
arrived, shows that Mary's presence is an important part in Jesus'
glorification on Calvary. What Jesus said to Mary at Cana is now
fulfilled; His crucifixion is His hour of glory in which the perfection of His redemptive work comes to a climax (cf. Jn 19:30). John
includes Mary in this *inclusio* structure to show that the mother of
Jesus accompanies her son in His fulfillment of the Father's will.

4) John 19: 25-27 and the Prologue of the Fourth Gospel

The patterns in the fourth gospel that I have outlined lead us
to one final step. The integrated structure of the Passion narrative
and the literary connections between that narrative and other parts
of the gospel lead back to one of the most important parts of the
entire gospel, the Prologue. Above I claimed that John 19:27 may
be a conscious reference back to 1:11,12 so that John intended us
to understand the personal reception of Mary as an extension of the
personal reception of Jesus stated in 1:12. Such a connection can
only be possible if the relation of the Prologue (1:1-18) to the rest
of the gospel is one of setting out a literary plan which John is pur-
suing in later chapters. The plausibility of seeing a connection
between 19:27 and 1:11,12 is reinforced by observing the larger
plan of the Prologue. Most interpreters have noticed how the

Prologue signals later themes within the gospel. While an extensive treatment of the structure and place of the Prologue is beyond our present purpose, I would like to point to one relevant example. The Prologue introduces the theme of light in 1: 4-9:

> In Him (it) was life
> And the Life was the Light of men
> And the Light shines in the darkness
> And the darkness did not overcome it
> He (it) was the True Light
> which enlightens every man
> Coming into the world

Light (*phos*) occurs twenty-one times in John. Only once does it *not* refer to Jesus (5:35 = John the Baptist). The other twenty times are not randomly distributed. There are a few specific contexts:

1. Prologue 1:4-9 5x
2. John 3:19-21 (Nicodemus) 5x
3. 8:12 "Light of the World" 2x 9:5 is an extension of 8:12 1x
4. 11:9,10 2x where "the light of the world" theme surfaces again.
5. 12:35,36 4x light is contrasted with darkness.
6. 12:46 1x where Jesus has come into the world as light.

It seems clear that John is introducing the theme of light in order to pursue his theological purpose of showing Jesus as the Light of the world. In the Prologue he stresses that this Logos-Light is the source of overcoming darkness and the sin that it implies.[25] The development of the light theme in later chapters explores different facets of how the Logos made flesh (*verbum factum caro*) is a light for the dark and sinful world. All of John's expositions of the light theme introduced in the Prologue reflect Jesus' central claim,

---

[25] The translation of *katalambano* in John 1:5 is best understood as "overcome" or "resist" although others are possible. Three have been suggested, 1) to understand in an intellectual sense, 2) to receive in a deeper sense, 3) to resist or overcome. All three meanings can find support in Greek literature, but in John 12:35 it clearly has the meaning of "overcome." It is possible that John was aware of the different meanings and was intentionally drawing on them to convey the inability of the darkness to comprehend and consequently to overcome the Light. As is the case with *anothen* ("again" or "from above") in John 3:3,7, where there is a *double entendre,* so John may be drawing on the different meanings of *katalambano*, to assert the complete contrast between Light and darkness and the complete inability of the darkness in the face of the overpowering force of the Logos as the Light.

"I am the light of the world" (8:12). As the light, Jesus both blinds certain individuals (cf. Jn 9:39-41) and reveals the truth. The theme of the Logos as light is one example of John's literary method of introducing and developing a key truth about the Logos and then showing how it is manifested in Jesus. And with this revelation is an implicit call to receive the light that is Jesus (Jn 8:12; 12:46).

The connection between the theme of light and 1:11,12 lies in the fact that the subject of the verb "he/it came" (*elthen*) in verse 11 is the "true light" in verse 9. At the same time, the subject of the verb is slightly ambiguous because it is also the *logos*. Verse 11 reads:

It [true light] came unto its [His] own, and his own did not receive Him.

It would have been smoother Greek if the neuter pronoun "it" (*auto*) were used instead of "Him" in the second half of verse 11 but there is a reason for the masculine (*auton*). The agreement in the masculine gender is with *logos*, not with the neuter noun *phos*. This suggests that the subject of the verb *elthen* may be vague with both the *logos* and *phos* being implicit subjects. Such vagueness would be consistent with the previous context where the light and the logos have been practically identified. Verses 11 and 12 are important in the structure of the Prologue because they signal a key theme in the rest of the gospel. Throughout John's gospel, some reject Jesus even though He came for them. Others receive Him and thereby become children of God. This division among Jesus' followers shows up in 2:23-25 where it says that "many believed on his name because they saw the signs He was doing, but Jesus did not believe (or commit himself) to them." This is an early signal in the gospel that John is teaching his readers how to distinguish true faith from its counterfeits. In the language of 1:11,12, John's gospel explores what it really means to receive Jesus. When He came for His own *(eis ta idia)*, He intended to be received so that He could bestow the status of children on His disciples. Given that 1:11,12 are suggestive about many episodes later in the gospel, it is entirely reasonable to conclude that the similar language of 19:27 is meant to evoke this original statement of the issue in 1:11,12. What I am suggesting is that the reading of 19:27 should be in the light of 1:11,12. The meaning of 19:27 is "the disciple received her for [or as] His own [i.e., mother]." This implies that the purpose of the pericope is to give an example of what it means to receive Jesus; it implies receiving Jesus' gift of His mother.

Nor has this personal reception gone unnoticed by the teachers of the Church. John Paul II, in his exposition of "the Marian dimension of the life of a disciple of Christ" says of John 19:27:

> Entrusting himself to Mary in a filial manner, the Christian, like the Apostle John, "welcomes" the Mother of Christ "into his own home" and brings her into everything that makes up his inner life, that is to say into his human and Christian "I": he "took her into his own home."[26]

and the footnote on this passage states:

> Clearly, in the Greek text the expression *eis ta idia* goes beyond the mere acceptance of Mary by the disciple in the sense of material lodging and hospitality in his house; it indicates rather a communion of life established between the two as a result of the words of the dying Christ: cf. St. Augustine *In Ioannis Evangelium tractatus* 119, 3: CCL 36, 659: "He took her into himself, not into his own property, for he possessed nothing of his own, but among his own duties, which he attended to with dedication."[27]

By looking carefully at John 19:27, we have seen that John Paul's insight is well justified. Neither John Paul nor the Greekless Augustine had analyzed the details and context of John 19:27 and yet their own filial piety led them to a well justified conclusion. The mother of Jesus is more than just one figure among many here.

Detailed attention to the expanding horizon of contexts has revealed a strongly representative-communal meaning in John 19:25-27, but there is not just one symbolic meaning. The figures of Jesus' mother and the beloved disciple are multivalent. They represent different realities when viewed through different prisms. Mary is a sign of Lady Zion or the Church who gives birth to other children (cf. Ambrose above). Or, we can take the beloved disciple as

---

[26] *Redemptoris Mater,* 45.
[27] *Ibid.*, footnote 130.

representing the Church and then see Mary as the mother of both Jesus and His fraternal disciples. This second perspective seems to be the primary symbolic arrangement since the language of 19:27 has all the marks of recalling and extending the meaning of 1:11,12 in the Prologue, but this semantic set does not in any way preclude different but complementary arrangements of the symbolic figures.

The contexts we have investigated point to a still deeper role for Mary in particular, one that connects her to Jesus' definitive accomplishment of salvation. This further step takes us beyond the limits of exegesis proper but it does not leave exegesis behind. The interpretation of John 19:25-27 itself points to these larger dogmatic concerns.

Mary's Bodily Cooperation in the Redemption

The analysis above suggests that John intended to place the mother of Jesus in a central position to tell the story of Jesus' crucifixion. When we ask what this structural analysis implies theologically, we are faced with the question as to how Mary's role in Jesus' Passion differs from the other attendants at the cross. Since John places four other people at the cross (three women, one man), it might be argued that there is little or no distinction between them. If we limit our consideration to the two most prominent attendants, it may still be claimed that Mary and the beloved disciple equally united themselves with the unique sacrificial death of Jesus. Nevertheless, a crucial and momentous distinction between these two attendants appears once we consider what their persons brought to the experience of the cross.

Like the other attendants at the cross, the beloved disciple acts as a witness to the authenticity of the crucifixion while Mary's maternal relationship to the Crucified implies much more. And it is here that we catch a glimpse of the bodily nature of her participation. Her cooperation is at once active and derivative, as the Dominican theologian Garrigou-Langrange summarized:

> Clearly, Mary is not the principal and perfective cause of the redemption. ... But she is really a secondary cause of salvation, dis-

positive, and subordinate to Jesus. She is said to be subordinated to Jesus not merely in the sense that she is inferior to Him, but also in the sense that she concurred in saving us by a grace which proceeded from His merits, and therefore acted in Him, with Him, and by Him. We must never forget that Jesus is the Universal Mediator. He redeemed Mary by preserving her from original sin. .... Mary's association with Jesus in the redemption is therefore not like that of the Apostles, but is something still more intimate. [28]

What was the nature of Mary's association as "something still more intimate?" Any positive or fuller answer to this question presupposes a panoply of truths derived from elsewhere in Scripture. Whether the evangelist was aware of this background because of his associations with the other apostles, with Luke, or with some community which understood it, we cannot say with certainty.[29] But we may pose the question of the connection of John 19:25-27 to other scriptural texts canonically. In other words, how does the teaching of this text presuppose other scriptural truths about Mary regardless of how much the author was aware of them?

The first essential truth has to do with Mary's vocation as the Mother of God. The Lucan treatment of Mary's role in the Incarnation places her participation front and center. In Luke 1:42-43 Elizabeth proclaims Mary as the "mother of my Lord" which is based on Luke's account of the Annunciation in which Mary is told of her future Son's divine origin (Lk 1:35). By its confirmation and definition of Mary as the *Theotokos* in the fifth century (A.D. 431 Ephesus and A.D. 451 Chalcedon), the historic Church was emphasizing the crucial importance of maternal mediation. Though Israel's history had many mediators, both men and women, Mary's mediation was of a completely different and higher order. Her vocation required the gift of her physical being, not in the sense of martyrdom, but *in order to* make redemption possible.

[28] Reginald Garrigou-Lagrange O.P. *The Mother of the Savior and Our Interior Life.* trans. Benard J. Kelly. (Rockford, IL: Tan Books and Publishers, 1993), 161-162.
[29] It is worth noting that all modern exegesis attempts to reconstruct background assumptions of the writer in an effort to explicate what the author was trying to say. Although such a historical investigation is an essential part of the exegetical task, we must always remember that little or no certainty can be had with respect to which set of background assumptions are the actual ones. The best an exegete can achieve is to use different sets of reconstructions to see which ones illuminate the text most clearly. Criteria for historical reconstruction are often very slippery.

Stefano Manelli has distinguished two aspects of maternal mediation — coredemption and mediation of grace — which have many relations between them.[30] By her consent to become the *Theotokos*, Mary became a mediatrix of grace because that grace was her Son, Jesus Christ. Because of this mediation, her participation in Jesus' redemptive work was unique. None other, no matter how great their subjective love, could participate in Jesus' redemption as Mary did. What took place on Calvary fulfills Jesus' conception, gestation, and birth. The intimate and inseparable union of the various parts of Jesus' life are taught in Luke and in John. This is one of the underlying theological reasons why John has tied together the wedding feast of Cana with Calvary by placing Mary in both pericopes. He wanted to show how Jesus' public ministry included Mary's presence as the unique giver of her body for redemption.

Mary also brought to Jesus' crucifixion another experience which was not shared by the other attendants. She could see her own presence at the cross as a fulfillment of the prophecy of Simeon in Luke 2:34-35. As she gazed upon her Son on the cross, she could see clearly that He was "a sign of contradiction" for Israel. And the human disgrace which attached to the mistreatment of her Son as a criminal would have caused a sword to pierce her soul (cf. Lk 2:35). From Jesus' infancy Mary knew that her own life would be marked by suffering because her Son's life was marked by the same. This experience of Jesus' crucifixion required her to call forth from her soul the spirit of offering which would have pervaded her whole being, body and soul. Manelli captured this well:

> The nails and the blood, the wounds and thorns which lacerated the divine body of Jesus form a single unity with the unspeakable sufferings of His Mother, the fiber of whose soul was devastated piece by piece by the sword prophesized by Simeon.... the mystery of the suffering of Mary forms a unity, a perfect synergy with the mystery of the suffering of Christ.[31]

My analysis of John 19:25-27 and its expanding horizon of contexts confirms Manelli's perceptive evaluation. John wrote this

[30] Stefano Maria Manelli F.I. "Mary Coredemptrix in Sacred Scripture" in *Mary: Coredemptrix, Mediatrix, Advocate Theological Foundations II* (ed) Mark A. Miravalle (Santa Barbara, CA: Queenship Publishing Co., 1995), 59-111.
[31] *Ibid.*, 94.

pericope to portray a twofold unity. One is the unity which Mary has with Jesus because she *alone* has given Him the body which hangs on the cross. A second unity binds Mary to all the beloved disciples of Jesus who will constitute His body the Church. Both types of unity are final, both are definitive, both are redemptive. Both of these unities point to an unsuspected third which the Theology of the Body explicates.

Mary's Participation and the Theology of the Body

Our appreciation of Mary's participation in Christ's redemption can be deepened from John Paul II's Theology of the Body. John Paul's reflections largely consist of expositions of the first two chapters of Genesis but they are not an exegesis in the ordinary modern sense. Rather, John Paul II saw in these chapters *the* primordial structures of human life and especially the complementarity of male and female in making up the image of God in man. In his reading, Genesis is not so much a reflection of one religious tradition among many; it recounts and explains the fundamental patterns of humanity.[32] One of the most relevant aspects of John Paul's interpretation for our purposes relates to the original unities which the late Pope sees in the pre-lapsarian state. Two dimensions of this unity are the internal unity of soul and body in each of the first human pair and the unity which they enjoyed between them.

Given the dogmatic status of the Immaculate Conception, we can now see how Mary could have had the strength to stand beside her Son and to offer Him up for the sins of the world. Her unity with Jesus' sacrifice grew out of the profound unity of body and soul which she possessed. Mary lived the Theology of the Body in an unparalleled way. Since she was conceived without the ravages of original sin, she could experience life in a manner similar to the experience of Adam and Eve prior to the Fall. She could have in

---

[32] In this respect, John Paul II stands in the line of a long tradition of hexaemeral interpretation which sees the creation narratives as revealing something fundamental in humanity. The Church Fathers did not see Genesis 1 & 2 as a perspective of the ancient Hebrews on their own ancestry or on humanity in general, as moderns tend to do. They read Genesis as teaching what was valid for all peoples and cultures because they believed in a fundamental human unity.

full what other human beings since the Fall experience only in part. For example, John Paul II explained that an analysis of Genesis chapter two shows how at the root of humanity lies the communion of persons. Without another human being to reveal our own humanity, we are left without any means of self-discovery. In the masculine-feminine dynamic there is an original structure for discovering the essence of humanity, an essence which consists of the image of God. In the context of her marriage, Mary had the structural prerequisites for understanding more of her femininity. To apply John Paul II's reflections on Adam and Eve to Mary and Joseph, we can say that both spouses learned their own distinctive personhood in carrying the divine image as they came to see more clearly their own femininity and masculinity.

Mary undoubtedly realized that her femininity involved a profound sense of receptivity inasmuch as the feminine body and psyche tend to reflect this aspect of the human person in a poignant way. John Paul II's analysis of femininity as receptivity goes a long way to explain Mary's words in her fiat, "Let it be done to me according to your word" (Lk 1:38). Long has this text been viewed as a paramount expression of humility by the Mother of God but in John Paul II's analysis it becomes a quintessential statement of feminine strength.

Mary's strength emerged naturally from her unparalleled unity of soul and body. As she experienced the sufferings of life, she could integrate these experiences of the fallen world into her own psyche in a manner that is infinitely more difficult for other human beings. Her internal unity of soul and body afforded her the necessary courage to stand beside her Son and to unite her own life with his.

The feminine-masculine dynamic is also applicable to her relationship with Jesus. This dynamic, while highest and strongest in marriage, nevertheless characterizes all male-female relations. One of the most insightful aspects of John Paul II's exposition of the image of God was to stress the "unity of the two" (male and female).[33] In the traditional formulation of the image of God there was mainly a focus on the individual by stressing that the divine

---

[33] John Paul II, *Mulieris Dignitatem,* 7.

image consists of having a rational soul. Without in any way denying this truth, John Paul II pointed out that all communion of
human persons, which is an essential element of the *imago Dei*,
has as its source the intra-trinitarian communion of persons in the
Godhead. This has important implications for understanding the
unity between Mary and Jesus.

In the original creation, the image of God consisted in the
"unity of the two" as well as in each one individually. This iconic
unity was marred by the entrance of sin and its effects, but it still
exists in all male-female relations because these have inherently
within them at least the potential for a communion of persons.
Such unity exists in mother-son relations as well and, in the case
of Mary and Jesus, this unity is not frustrated by the presence of
sin, either original or actual. So, the unity between the divine Son
of God and His mother must have been far higher, far deeper and
far more divine than in other human relationships. According to
St. Paul's teaching in several texts, one of the purposes of Jesus'
redemption was to restore this original image of God in humanity.
In 2 Corinthians 4:4 and Colossians 1:15 Christ is specifically
called the "image of God." Later in Colossians 3:10 Paul speaks
of interior renewal of the faithful as "putting on the new (man)
which being renewed for perfect knowledge according to the
image of the One who created him."

In a similar vein, Paul speaks of the purpose of predestination in Romans 8:29 as "being conformed to the image of His (i.e.,
God's) Son so that He might be the firstborn among many
brethren." These texts strongly suggest that conversion and renewal of the human person include a restoration of the *imago Dei*. If
this "unity of the two" was part of that image, then part of its
restoration was to reestablish the unity. That restoration of unity,
like every other aspect of the image, could only be accomplished
by the God-Man. However, the loss of that unity between male
and female had to be healed by male and female together, and so
Mary's union of herself, body and soul, with Christ helped to
restore that "unity of the two." Mary's participation in Christ's

redemption was conscious, active, and complete. John 19:25-27 implies that her union with the faithful of Christ's body will also be conscious, active, and complete.

Mary's Participation and Ours

At the beginning of this essay, I noted that there is both continuity and discontinuity between Mary's participation in Christ's redemption and ours. In Mary's cooperation with Christ she has played a singular and unique role. This participation extended throughout her life with her body and soul. We have seen in the famous pericope of John 19:25-27 a unique role for Mary. Even when the text might superficially suggest that Mary was just one other attendant at the crucifixion, a contextual reading leads beyond this superficial impression to the conclusion that John has placed Mary at the cross to show her intimate and complete union with her Son. None other can take Mary's place. Just as we can never stand in Jesus' place, so we cannot stand in Mary's either.

Still, the faithful can and must participate in Christ's salvation through evangelization, prayer, and sacraments. And it is especially in this latter respect that we see Mary's continued importance in the subjective application of Christ's salvific work. Mary's bodily participation in the accomplishment of redemption is extended in and through time to the application of Christ's merits in the lives of the faithful. Supreme among the means of this application is the Eucharistic Body of Christ, as John Paul II so rightly perceived:

> The piety of the Christian people has always very rightly sensed a profound link between devotion to the Blessed Virgin and the worship of the Eucharist: this is a fact that can be seen in the liturgy of both the West and the East, in traditions of the Religious Families, in modern movements of spirituality, including those for youth, and in the pastoral practice of the Marian Shrines. Mary guides the faithful to the Eucharist.[34]

John Paul II's insights are more than pious sentiments. He saw clearly that what Mary did on earth, she continues to do in heaven. She guided people to Jesus (cf. Jn 2:4) and offered her

---

[34] *Redemptoris Mater,* 44.

own body to make redemption possible. In offering His body on the cross, Jesus sanctified the faithful (cf. Heb. 10:5-10), that same body which He had assumed from His mother. In the Eucharist, He is still sanctifying the faithful by giving the same body which he took from the Virgin. In guiding "the faithful to the Eucharist" Mary is still offering her Son, now not on the altar of the cross, but on the altar of heaven in which every earthly altar participates. It is this same body born of the Virgin that allows the faithful to stand by the cross and to offer up themselves in adoration and sacrifice for the salvation of the world.

THE ANTHROPOLOGY
OF FATHER JOSEPH KENTENICH
AND THE IMAGE OF MARY

Sr. M. Isabell Naumann, I.S.S.M., S.T.D.

Before launching into the anthropology of Joseph Kentenich it is important to outline briefly his theological concern. This will provide a backdrop onto which to view his anthropology.[1]

Joseph Kentenich's Theological Concern

Joseph Kentenich's place in modern and contemporary theology is not that of an academic or professional theologian. He never claimed to be an academic theologian. Moreover, endowed with a unique charism, he was foremost the founder of a marian-apostolic movement of renewal within the Catholic Church.[2] This fact has to be taken into consideration in order to interpret and appropriately place his theology and spirituality. His theological and pedagogical treatises, conferences and *pastoral* experiential applications were focused on the great aim: to help form and educate a new Christian personality in a new Christian community.

---

[1] The following text presents the slightly revised and abridged part of Chapter I of my study *Cum Maria ad altare: Toward an Integration of Mariology and Ecclesiology; The Interrelation between Mary and the Church in the Works of Father J. Kentenich* (STD Diss., 1999), 25-54.

[2] Father Joseph Kentenich (1885-1968) is the founder of the International Schoenstatt Movement, an ecclesial movement within the Catholic Church. See Monnerjahn, E., *Joseph Kentenich: A Life for the Church* (Cape Town, SA: Schoenstatt Publications, 1985) and *Häftling Nr. 29392: Der Gründer des Schönstattwerkes als Gefangener der Gestapo 1941-45* (Vallendar: Schönstatt Verlag, 1972); W. Mahlmeister, "Apostolische Bewegung," in *Schönstatt-Lexikon: Fakten–Ideen–Leben*, eds. H. Brantzen et al. (Vallendar-Schönstatt: Patris Verlag, 1996), 8.

His theological reflection concerning the transcendence and immanence of God is represented in his conviction and belief in *the God of life*, who in unfathomable love creates, nourishes, sustains, and leads to life,[3] and who seeks to unite the human person to Himself in an everlasting covenant of love.[4] This covenant relationship is for Kentenich the foundation and meaning of the entire history of salvation and the theological basis for the new type of *relation* offered by God in Christ as exemplified in the new type of community formed by the Church. For the believer "the history of salvation is unveiled as a distinct covenantal history."[5] Its reality is reflected in many images in Sacred Scripture. Within this universal salvific covenant history, Kentenich placed Schoenstatt's unique covenant of love with Mary as "an original, concrete form of the covenant that God had established with the human person in paradise and which God wants to bring to realization through the history of salvation as well as through world history."[6] Out of this perspective, Kentenich aimed at a Christian dynamism which in an organism of *bindings* reflects a movement of life and grace. In a masterly way he brought about a synthesis between the richness of the deposit of faith and the spiritual tradition within the Church, and the existential actuality of contemporary humanity. His theological reflection in this sense may not be seen as a popularization of traditional ideas within the Christian heritage nor as an actualized nominalism or pragmatism.[7] His own personal, empirical evidence and that of his pastoral activity enabled him, as an independent thinker, to bring about a spiritual movement with an immanent, inner coher-

---

[3] Joseph Kentenich, *Aus dem Glauben leben: Predigten in Milwaukee*, 17 Vols (Vallendar-Schönstatt: Patris Verlag, 1969-1994), Vols 1-2 ed. G. Roos; Vol 3 G. Roos, G. M. Ritter; Vols 4-17 G. M. Ritter, Vol 15: 79; Kentenich, *Bundestagung* (TMs, December 26-29, 1950), 85; Kentenich, *Brasilienterziat*, Santa Maria, Brazil, 1952, 3 Vols (TMs, Offset 1971) II, 211.

[4] H. King, *Marianische Bundesspiritualität: Ein Kentenich Lesebuch*, Schönstatt-Studien 8 (Vallendar-Schönstatt: Patris Verlag, 1994), 234.

[5] Joseph Kentenich, *Das Lebensgeheimnis Schönstatts*, 1952, 2 Vols (Vallendar-Schönstatt: Schönstatt Verlag 1971), II, 26.

[6] *Ibid.*, II, 25.

[7] Joseph Kentenich, *Schoenstatt Founding Documents* (Waukesha,WI/USA: Schoenstatt Sisters of Mary, 1993), 99.

[8] Unkel, *Theorie und Praxis des Vorsehungsglaubens nach Pater Joseph Kentenich,* 2 Vols (Vallendar-Schönstatt: Patris Verlag, 1980), II/1, 19-20; B. Schneider, "Pater Joseph Kentenich als religiöser Erzieher," *Regnum* 12, 1

ence.[8] Joseph Kentenich's theological concern in his pastoral activity may be seen in the tradition of the early Church Fathers and their pastoral activity, as Pope Paul VI noted:

[the Church Fathers] felt the need to adapt the Gospel message to contemporary thought and to nourish first themselves and the people of God with the food of the true faith. The result was that for them catechesis, theology, Sacred Scripture, liturgy, spiritual and pastoral life were all joined together into a vital unity. Their work spoke not only to the intellect but to the whole human person, embracing intellect, will and emotion. They further possessed a richly abundant treasure of the Christian spirit, derived from their personal holiness; in their school of faith they were not content simply with intellectual elucidation, but were also intent upon the mystical sense.[9]

Such a theological enquiry is of significance for the Church in the postconciliar period due to the fact that:

renewal requires a theology that is no less pastoral than scientific; that maintains close contact with biblical sources; that is christocentric. It requires a theology that looks upon the human person within the context of salvation history that is consistently faithful to the Word of God and devoted to the Magisterium of the Church, yet, at the same time, is attentive to all the voices, all the needs, and all the authentic values of our time.[10]

The originality of his theological reflection within the parameters of a religious and wholistic education and pastoral activity shows a universal dimension that is viably marked by a profound creative sense for historical relevance and historicity. Kentenich not only draws on theology and metaphysics, philosophy and psychology, but also on anthropology and sociology.[11] In

---

(1977): 22-32. L. Penners, *Eine Paedagogik des Katholischen:* Studien zur Denkform P. Joseph Kentenichs, Schönstatt Studien 5 (Vallendar-Schoenstatt: Patris Verlag, 1983), 24; O. Amberger, *Modelle subjektiver Glaubenserkenntnis bei John Henry Newman und Josepf Kentenich: Darstellung und vergleichende Diskussion,* Schönstatt Studien 9 (Vallendar-Schönstatt: Patris Verlag, 1994), 16-18, 146-147.

[9] Pope Paul VI, "Talk given to members of the Augustinianum Patristic Institute," May 4, 1970, in *Fidelity and Relevance: Thoughts for an upsurge in efforts toward sanctification and the apostolate,* 95.

[10] *Ibid.,* 95-96.

[11] B. Schneider, "Pater Joseph Kentenich als religiöser Erzieher," *Regnum* 12, 1 (1977): 22-32, 23.

his response to an innate dynamism within faith itself, he draws on all these elements and branches of science which allow him to illumine one or another aspect of the mysteries of faith.[12]

Aspects of the Anthropological Foundation of Joseph Kentenich's Theology

Joseph Kentenich's anthropology is essentially *theological*, for the image of the human person is determined by the image of God. For him one cannot speak of one without speaking of the other; therefore this part will include the following themes: the human person, created in the image and likeness of God, as *representatio Christi*, as a relational being and the human person's place in history. Secondly, founded on these observations, relevant elements of Kentenich's Mariological thought will follow, showing Mary as the *causa exemplaris* of the redeemed person.

The first and fundamental element of Kentenich's Marian charism is the molding of a *new person* in a *new community*.[13] The characteristics of this interrelatedness, the "openness and surrender," in the reciprocal "personal giving of oneself and the being taken into the you in a bond of love between the personal I and the you," points to the essential life within the mystery of the Trinity.[14] The Trinitarian mystery is for Kentenich the ultimate ideal of this *new community*, of which he speaks as

a *perfect community* based on *perfect personalities*, both of which are born by the elemental fundamental power of love, the *new person* is a personality who is independent, inspired, inwardly responsible and inwardly free, who is joyful, ready to make decisions, who distances himself equally from rigid enslavement to form, and arbitrariness that results from being completely unattached. Hence

[12] Congregation for the Doctrine of Faith, *Instruction on the Ecclesial Vocation of the Theologian*, May 24, 1990, *AAS* 82 (1990), 1550-1570.

[13] Kentenich, *Brasilienterziat*, II, 229-230; M. Bleyle, *Erziehung aus dem Geiste Schönstatts* (Vallendar-Schönstatt: Schönstatt-Verlag, 1970), 67-69; M. E. Frömbgen, *Neuer Mensch in neuer Gemeinschaft: Zur Geschichte und Systematik der pädagogischen Konzeption Schönstatts* (Vallendar: Schönstatt-Verlag, 1973); H. Schlosser, "Zum Begriff der 'neuen Gemeinschaft' in Schönstatt," *Regnum* 5,2 (1970): 49-56 and *Der neue Mensch–die neue Gesellschaftsordnung,* mit Originaltexten von P. J. Kentenich im zweiten Teil (Schönstatt-Vallendar: Schönstatt-Verlag, 1971), 63-124.

[14] Joseph Kentenich, *[North] Amerika Bericht*, 2 Vols (TMs, 1948) II, 41.

such personalities do not claim absolute autonomy. Since they take their bearings from the ideal of the Triune God, life in all its phases of development follows the ontological laws of the Triune God, thus they combine autonomy with heteronomy.[15]

This concept of the ultimate ideal of the *new person* establishing the *new community* as a reflection of the *Trinitarian community* is founded on Joseph Kentenich's anthropology,[16] which takes as starting point the biblical-theological perspective of the concrete human person, created in the image and likeness of God [Gen 1:26-27; 5:1, 9:6],[17] and called into a union of love with God.[18]

The Human Person–Created in the Image and Likeness of God

This reality of creation is embedded in christology and soteriology because Christ, through His incarnation and redeeming deed, unites Himself with each person and confirms in this union the original unity between the creator and the human person.[19] In the mystery of the incarnation and the redemption the human person becomes redeemed by being newly created;[20] thus Kentenich

---

[15] Joseph Kentenich, *What is my philosophy of education?*, 1958/59/[61], Engl. trans. M. Cole (Cape Town, SA, 1990), 9-10.

[16] The following considerations are predominantly based on J. Kentenich, *Kindsein vor Gott*, eds. G. M. Boll, L. Penners (Vallendar-Schönstatt: Patris Verlag: 1979), 99-105 and J. Kentenich, *Oktoberbrief 1949*, Buenos Aires, Argentina, ed. M. E. Frömbgen (Vallendar-Schönstatt: Schönstatt Verlag, 1970), 42-60. J. Kentenich provides no comprehensive and systematic anthropology in his works. See J. P. Catoggio, *Das Theologische Menschenbild by P. Joseph Kentenich* (Licentiate Thesis, Münster/Germany, 1982, 271 pages), 8.

[17] Kentenich, *Oktoberbrief 1949*, 43; B.-M. Erhard, *Frau-Gott-Mann: Die zweigeschlechtliche Welt–Abbildung des dreipersönlichen Gottes, Eine Studie* (Vallendar-Schönstatt: Patris Verlag, 1988), 39.

[18] Kentenich, *Das Lebensgeheimnis Schönstatts*, II, 33. For the following anthropological considerations I am indebted to the works of Catoggio, *Das Theologische Menschenbild by P. Joseph Kentenich* and H. Czarkowski, *Psychologie als Organismuslehre:* Joseph Kentenich und die moderne Psychologie unter besonderer Berücksichtigung der Tiefenpsychologie, Schönstatt-Studien 1(Vallendar-Schönstatt: Patris Verlag, 1973).

[19] Pope John Paul II, *Redemptor Hominis*, March 15, 1979, AAS 71 (1979), 257-324, 1.

[20] Kentenich speaks, in affiliation with the apostle Paul [2 Cor 5:17-18], of the *nova creatura in Christus*. J. Kentenich, *Nova Creatura in Jesu at Maria, 1941-1942* [Coblence Prison], (TMs, Schönstatt: Schönstätter Marienschwestern, 1986, 181 pages), 41, 150-151 [passim]; J. Kentenich, *Der erlöste Mensch, Priesterexerzitien* (TMs, 1936, 112 pages), 71-72, 79-80; J. Kentenich, *Marianische Werkzeugsfröm-*

differentiates between the natural and the supernatural image and likeness, the latter being Christologically and pneumatologically founded: "The natural likeness allows us to see the human person as a divine masterpiece in the order of creation. The supernatural image points to the splendour of the order of grace as it has taken concrete shape in the redemption through Christ and in the sanctification and unification through the Holy Spirit."[21]

The trinitarian relatedness is given by the fact that the human person is "a work of the Trinity"[22]—"it is the Triune God who issues in my soul the life of grace. The Father through the Son in the Holy Spirit bestows upon me the supernatural, divine organism"[23]—and bears the image of the Trinity. Given the reference to Genesis 1:26, "the human person is not mainly the work but also the image of the [Eternal] Father, the Son and the Holy Spirit. He is the work, and natural as well as supernatural image of the most blessed Trinity: of the divine creative power of the Father, of the wisdom of the Son and of the love of the Holy Spirit."[24]

As shown above Kentenich speaks—in accord with traditional Christian anthropology—of a natural and supernatural dimension in the human person.[25] While the natural dimension is creation-theologically founded [Gen 2:7],[26] the supernatural one is Christologically-soteriologically constituted.[27] Both dimensions have a static and a dynamic element. In a retreat for priests in 1937,

---

migkeit, 1944 (Vallendar-Schönstatt, Schönstatt Verlag: 1974), 159-160; J. Kentenich, *Aus dem Glauben leben: Predigten in Milwaukee*, Vol 4: 72, Vol 5: 12-15; J. Kentenich, *Maria, Mutter und Erzieherin: Eine angewandte Mariologie*, ed. M. E. Froembgen (Vallendar-Schönstatt: Schönstatt-Verlag, 1973), 351.

[21] Kentenich, *Oktoberbrief 1949*, 44-58; J. Kentenich, *Marianische Werkzeugsfrömmigkeit*, 44-50; 158-163; 179-187; J. Kentenich, *Maria, Mutter und Erzieherin: Eine angewandte Mariologie*, 338-381.

[22] Kentenich, *Oktoberbrief 1949*, 43.

[23] Joseph Kentenich, *Wachstum im Höheren Gebetsleben*, Priestertagung, 20-22 Januar 1941, eds., Schönstattpatres/ Anbetung (Vallendar-Schönstatt: Patris Verlag, 1977), 128.

[24] Kentenich, *Oktoberbrief 1949*, 43-44.

[25] Kentenich, *Wachstum im Höheren Gebetsleben*, 20-21; M. Bleyle, *Erziehung aus dem Geiste Schönstatts*, 24-30; H. Schlosser, *Der neue Mensch–die neue Gesellschaftsordnung*, mit Originaltexten von P. J. Kentenich im zweiten Teil 24-30.

[26] Kentenich, *Oktoberbrief 1949*, 44.

[27] *Ibid.*, 49.

Kentenich speaks of these two aspects. The *static* element focuses on the fundamental question of Christian anthropology: "What and who is the human person?" and refers to the original ontological substance of the human person as a complex and finite being, characterized by instability and the search for the ultimate, a sublime being of contrary potentialities. The second, the *dynamic* element, centers on the developmental potential of the person that he will be.[28] Regarding the *static* element[29] he delineates the human person as a complex being comprised of various substances and polarities, thus referring to the human person as "God's greatest venture."[30] Basic to this view is the scholastic understanding of the human person as a microcosm which partakes at the various levels of being, the vegetative, sensitive, and spiritual life.[31]

> The human person is according to his ontological structure an *animal oeconomicum, hedonicum, vitale*. That means: the person is cohering to material values, the economical goods, the sensorial enjoyments and the natural vitalities like health, spontaneity and vigor. One calls the human person rightly an *animal philosophicum [metaphysicum], ethicum, aestheticum et religiosum*. That means: he is committed to spiritual values, to truth, good, beauty and the holy. In the natural order the person is bound to all these values.[32]

---

[28] Kentenich, *Kindsein vor Gott*, 99-105.

[29] Kentenich's terminology seems to derive from P. Wust, *Ungewißheit und Wagnis* (München: Kösel-Verlag, 1955).

[30] Kentenich, *Oktoberbrief 1949*, 45.

[31] J. Niehaus, *New Vision and Life: The Founding of Schoenstatt* (Waukesha, Wis/USA: Schoenstatt Fathers/Budd & Thomson, 1986), 37-51.

[32] Kentenich, *Oktoberbrief 1949*, 45, 83, 144; Kentenich, J., *Marianische Werkzeugsfrömmigkeit*, 158. Within the context of the above, J. Kentenich, speaks of the influence of the milieu, and illustrates the changes from the Middle Ages to modernity: "Each kind of receptivity for values—like the goods themselves [for which we are receptive]—allows many variations which are essentially codetermined by the circumstances of life and nature, and especially by the milieu. Every typical attitude towards the material, rational and religious goods can create an original, individual and communal type of human person and thus shape and determine the image of the human person of [a particular] time. Medieval man was extraordinarily theocentric in orientation. The Renaissance man who followed him was primarily self-centered. The aspect which he presents depends on which individual values are stressed or monopolize the whole field—in one era it is the hedonistic man, in another the economic or vitalistic man, in another the intellectualistic or aesthetic or ethical man. It is in this way that he determines the shape of the time which he dominates." Kentenich, *Oktoberbrief 1949,* 45.

In regard to the *static* element, Kentenich further compares the limitations, the inner tension and instability of human nature with an *oscillating pendulum*.[33] This characteristic of the human person becomes increasingly apparent in the context of modern times, where the person endeavors to find security and inner harmony in all possible spheres except in the direction toward the *ultimate*. This instability and insecurity in human nature imparts the third characteristic: the human person as a *seeker*.[34] Although modern consciousness finds it arduous to come to terms with *ultimates* and *absolutes*, basically the person is always following his innate urge *to seek the absolute*,[35] to seek the good, ultimately God.[36]

---

[33] "The human person is a pendulum being or a creature of suspense . . . in his being, attitudes, and life. Why do we find ourselves so often in a state of suspense? Because it corresponds to our nature, because we are beings at the border [of irrational, rational, and spiritual]. How often do we not experience that one day the irrational side of man seeks to assert itself, the next day the rational side fights for supremacy, while the day after the child of God in us seeks to triumph. Even in regard to our human or Christian existence we are in a continual state of oscillation. This expression describes well our modern experience of life and will be more pertinent in time to come. Where is this oscillating creature's place of rest? Where can modern man, who expreriences his human condition so deeply, come to rest? Those who live in bourgeois circumstances are inclined to think that the proper kind of rest is that of a table, with its four legs on the ground. But this is not so. If man swings to and fro like a pendulum, the security and rest proper to him can only be found above: held in the hand of God the Father. This is the only place where we find rest–the only rest toward which we may aspire." Kentenich, *Kindsein vor Gott*, 100-101, 277. Wust writes: "Nur der Mensch ist einerseits eingebettet in den Strom der natürlichen Kausalität oder der blinden Notwendigkeit, andererseits aber auch freigesetzt für ein eigenes Sinn- und Zielstreben." P. Wust, *Ungewißheit und Wagnis*, 98.

[34] Kentenich, *Kindsein vor Gott*, 101-102. Wust speaks of the human person as a "metaphysisches Sucherwesen," "*insecuritas humana*" and "*insecuritas*-Not," P. Wust, *Ungewißheit und Wagnis*, 48, 32, 175, 265.

[35] Theology speaks here of the *potentia oboedientialis*. Kentenich, *Maria, Mutter und Erzieherin: Eine angewandte Mariologie*, 361-362, 417.

[36] Kentenich, *Kindsein vor Gott*, 101-102. "This longing for God, the Eternal, the Infinite, is undyingly connected and bound up with our human nature, although, as long as we are pilgrims here on earth, it can never be fully satisfied. This is why the sickness of the human person, also of modern man, is this unfulfilled urge to God. Man is homesick for God." Kentenich, *Aus dem Glauben leben: Predigten in Milwaukee*, Vol 10: 136-137.

In contrast to the answers of collectivistic,[37] vitalistic[38] and economic[39] present-day anthropological ideologies, Kentenich presents the Christian answer to the human search for meaning and inner harmony. At the core of the personality where, through the innermost unity with God, the bipolar tension within the person can be mastered—"fullness of being and emptiness of being, richness of value and poverty of value, dignity and unworthiness."[40] "Everyone senses what strength and power abides in a personality who from the core of his personality is able to endure in ever growing measure over decades the eminent tension mentioned . . . and who is able to unite them into a higher ordered entity with an impenetrable closedness and steadiness in an organic interplay of all powers of body and soul and all faculties of nature and grace."[41] Kentenich explains the harmonious connection between nature and grace, their unity, as follows:

> They do not exist side-by-side or in hierarchical order, like two floors of a house or two separate rooms. Nor do they pass over into each other in such a way that one can speak of a mixture in the

---

[37] Kentenich describes the collectivistic person as a person "whose core has been broken away from the total constellation of his inner self, who knows only acts and impressions but not the permanent attitudes of soul from which vibrant life should rush forth like from a spring. He only places one act after another upon command, acts which lack connection with the root of his soul and with each other, which fail to affect or complement each other. He has simply lost his 'soul,' and is therefore personified discontinuity–not knowing a *unitas multiplex*, but only a *multiplicitas sine unitate* and thus representing the most perfect depersonalization." Kentenich, *Oktoberbrief 1949*, 144-145, 72-77.

[38] For Kentenich this is characteristic of philosophical existentialism. "What [modern man] calls strength of character or personal acceptance of one's 'set-adrift-ness' is compulsion to the n-th degree, is rigid and becoming-rigid compensation, an uninhibited take-over of repressive tendencies of the soul, is obstinancy and stubbornness, is an act of despair in human nature and its higher meaning [*Sinnbezogenheit*]; [it] is, so to speak, existence for death, not existence for life and fullness of life." Kentenich, *Oktoberbrief 1949*, 145, 77-78.

[39] The *homo oeconomicus* knows only one category of values, "that which is attainable and measurable with the senses; [he] does not feel any tension with the different values of the higher order; [it is the person] who worships only one god to which he is unreservedly enslaved: money and possessions." Kentenich, *Oktoberbrief 1949*, 145, 72-77.

[40] Kentenich, *Oktoberbrief 1949*, 144.

[41] *Ibid.*

truest sense of the word. One is rather inclined to say that they are united within each other to form a harmonious active principle without, on that account, losing their identity.[42]

Further, the human person is also sublime in carrying the most adverse potentialities: the *mysterium caritatis*[43] and the *mysterium iniquitatis*. These two tendencies: toward the positive, good, and the tendency toward the negative and destructibility, are part of human nature;[44] and it is here where we have the most appropriate manifestation of human *freedom*.[45]

The Human Person–Called to Freedom

Freedom is an integral attribute of the human person as an image of God: "And God created man in His own image, in the image of God He created him. . . ." (Gen 1:27a). "The infinite God is *free*, He is a personal God, not an indistinct it, no *fatum;* likewise God's image is also as a free personality thought of and created by [God], the archetype."[46] In another place Kentenich says: "Obviously the drive for freedom is one of the most fundamental archetypal drives in human nature. We are images of God. God is the absolute free being. Otherwise, as God's images, we could not be so powerfully electrified by the urge of freedom."[47] He calls "the freedom of the human will" the "greatest miracle in the natural order,"[48] for "the human person is not in everything a slave of

---

[42] Kentenich, *What is my philosophy of education?*, See in this context H. de Lubac, *Surnaturel* (Paris: Aubier, 1946).

[43] P. Wust, *Die Dialektik des Geistes* (Augsburg: Verlag Beno Filser, 1928), 102.

[44] Kentenich, *Kindsein vor Gott*, 102.

[45] Thus Wojtyla writes: "It is in the structure of man's becoming, through his actions, morally good or bad, that freedom manifests itself most appropriately. Here, however, freedom is not only a moment; it also forms a real and inherent component of the structure, indeed, a component that is decisive for the entire structure of moral becoming: freedom constitutes the root factor of man's becoming good or bad by his actions; it is the root factor of the becoming as such of human morality." K. Wojtyla, *The Acting Person.* Analecta Husserliana. The Yearbook of Phenomenological Reseach, Vol X, trans. by A. Potocki (Dordrecht/Holland: D. Reidel Publishing Company, 1979), 99. See also Wust, *Ungewißheit und Wagnis*, 55 and *Die Dialektik des Geistes*, 654-656.

[46] Kentenich, *Marianische Werkzeugsfrömmigkeit*, 159-160.

[47] Kentenich, *Kampf um die wahre Freiheit* (MTs, 250 pages), 15.

[48] Kentenich, *Nova Creatura in Jesu at Maria, 1941-1942* [Coblence Prison], (TMs, Schönstatt: Schönstätter Marienschwestern, 1986, 181 pages), 126.

the blind rhythm of causality in natural happenings. He can swim against the current . . . and can start a new succession of causation, because he has a free will. The human person . . . can freely decide and, against all obstacles, carry through the freely made decision. This [free] ability to decide is the essential core of freedom."[49]

Philosophically speaking, Kentenich differentiates between two dimensions of the free will, the *ability to decide* and the *ability to carry out a decision;*[50] both dimensions he sees increasingly lacking in the collectivistic mentality of contemporary humanity.[51] The human person "appears more and more unable to make–in the full awareness of his own weaknesses–serious decisions . . . Rather, he wants to be carried or driven along without personal responsibility and effort."[52] "As far as the person is still supernaturally oriented . . . he has not the courage nor the strength, in dependence on God and as his animated instrument, to take effectually his fate in his own hands and master it."[53]

Theologically, this ability to decide freely "enables the person to make God's scale of value, in and with Christ in all its details, from within, his own . . . it is the true greatness of a free human being to surrender oneself in and with Christ to the loving will of the eternal Father . . ."[54] For Kentenich the gift of freedom and the education toward authentic freedom, that is, the inner freedom of the children of God, are so significant that he never tired of pointing out these essentials of every human person and the community as constituents for any spirituality. "Education of the person toward a free decision for God and the divine" must always be the primary task.[55] Hence, for Kentenich the question regarding freedom is not so much *freedom*

---

[49] *Ibid.*

[50] Kentenich, *Kampf um die wahre Freiheit*, 15; Joseph Kentenich, *Daß neue Menschen werden: Eine pädagogische Religionspsychologie*, 1951, ed. M. E. Frömbgen (Vallendar-Schönstatt: Schönstatt Verlag, 1971), 117-118.

[51] Kentenich, *Brasilienterziat*, II, 198-199, 201.

[52] Kentenich, *Oktoberbrief 1949*, 150.

[53] *Ibid.*

[54] Kentenich, *Nova Creatura in Jesu at Maria*, 126.

[55] Joseph Kentenich, *Marianische Werkzeugsfrömmigkeit*, 1944 (Vallendar-Schönstatt, Schönstatt Verlag: 1974), 47.

from as *freedom for*,[56] which is essentially connected with *magnanimitas*[57] and love.[58] In a conference for priests in 1946 he said:

> The battle for freedom is diverse. Outer and inner freedom, political and economical freedom, social freedom, national freedom, etc., are expressions which echo deeply in the soul because the yoke of slavery is still pressing us. The more powerful the yoke of slavery, the more elemental is the drive into the opposite [direction]: to political freedom, economical, national, pedagogical freedom. These are all outer forms of freedom . . . beyond these there is also an inner freedom, a freedom of the heart, which means: a being free from all that is non- and anti-divine, in order to become free for the divine. On the one hand is the battle for liberation; on the other hand is the battle to conquer, that is, to become free from all non- and anti-divine in our nature, so that we can free our vital powers in order to belong totally to God. This inner freedom is also the prerequisite, source, and measure of outer freedom.[59]

This true inner freedom can only come from God; consequently Kentenich cited repeatedly the word of St. Irenaeus, "*augmentum ad Deum*"[60]—the human person growing toward God, who "has addressed Him personally . . . and has deeply imprinted upon him His [own] features. [God] placed him as personal you, as personal partner in love, before him with the commission to lovingly entrust himself to God in a free personal decision."[61]

In Mary, Kentenich saw this truly free personality who is founded in God and incarnated in the divine order. "She makes us aware that God also respects and protects our freedom [and] that God will not redeem and sanctify the world without our cooperation."[62]

---

[56] Kentenich, *Kampf um die wahre Freiheit*, 14.

[57] Kentenich, *Priesterexerzitien*, 376-377; Kentenich, *Marianische Werkzeugsfrömmigkeit*, 139; I. Nei, "Magnanimitas: Zu einem Zentralbegriff der Schönstätter Spiritualität," *Regnum* 1, 2 (1966): 65-74.

[58] Kentenich, *Marianische Werkzeugsfrömmigkeit*, 36-37.

[59] Kentenich, *Kampf um die wahre Freiheit*, 9, 143.

[60] St. Irenaeus, *Adv. haer.* 4, c. 11. n. 2., *PG* 7: 1002; Kentenich, *Marianische Werkzeugsfrömmigkeit*, 160; Kentenich, *Maria, Mutter und Erzieherin: Eine angewandte Mariologie*, 423.

[61] Kentenich, *Maria, Mutter und Erzieherin: Eine angewandte Mariologie*, 424; Kentenich, *Marianische Werkzeugsfrömmigkeit*, 182-183.

[62] Kentenich, *Maria, Mutter und Erzieherin: Eine angewandte Mariologie*, 154; Kentenich, *Schoenstatt Founding Documents*, 11-22; Kentenich, J., *Marianische Werkzeugsfrömmigkeit*, 66-67, 181-182.

"Therefore, the more the person grows into the freedom of God, the more he matures into the true freedom of the children of God [and] the more human society becomes a perfect community that is built on the foundation of perfect personalities. The more both are born not only by the laws of truth and justice but also by the elemental power of love, the more perfect will be the human person and society."[63]

The Human Person–A Relational Being

Essential to Kentenich's anthropological considerations is also the relational, social dimension of the human person as a being in relation, and of dialogue.[64] It is the natural dimension of the human likeness to God, where the human person is a being whose inner nature is able to say "I" and "You."[65] The person can exist apart and alone, autonomous and independent. At the same time the person is also orientated toward the "You" and therefore toward community, self-surrender and giving of self.

---

[63] Kentenich, *Marianische Werkzeugsfrömmigkeit*, 280-281.

[64] In affiliation to Gabriel Marcel, Kentenich writes of the essence of the human person in the perspective of a positive Christian existential personalism. Kentenich, *Maria, Mutter und Erzieherin: Eine angewandte Mariologie*, 338-381. See G. Marcel, *Homo Viator: Prolégomènes a une Métaphysique de L'Espérance* (Paris: Aubier, 1944), 15-91, 233-256, 297-358; M. Müller, *Die Verheissung des Herzens: Zur Theologie des Ewigen im Menschen* (Freiburg: Herder, 1953). Regarding a *Christian personalism*, Kentenich writes: "Przywara counts us among the representatives of a Christian personalism; Urs von Balthasar does the same in an academic talk at the University of Fribourg [Switzerland]. This can have a twofold meaning depending on whether the counterpart they mean is impersonalism or solidarism [solidarity]. *In any case, our 'personalism' stands up to oppose each and every 'impersonalism' and includes solidarism as an essential element.* We gladly let ourselves be called 'personalists' when it expresses our attitude toward impersonalism. …" Kentenich, *[North] Amerika Bericht*, II, 56-57, 58-73. "As much as we regard the word 'personalism'—in contrast to the impersonalism—as a title of honor, we likewise reject it if it is understood to exclude solidarism or would restrict its existence. That becomes obvious to everyone who understands correctly—as mentioned above—the inner relationship between the pedagogy of ideals, pedagogy of attachments, and movement pedagogy… we not only speak of the personal ideal but also of the community ideal which takes fully into account the social drive of the human person." Kentenich, *[North] Amerika Bericht*, II, 74. See further O. Amberger, *Modelle subjektiver Glaubenserkenntnis bei John Henry Newman und Josepf Kentenich*, 147-148.

[65] M. Bleyle, *Erziehung aus dem Geiste Schönstatts,* 117-150; Kentenich, *Maria, Mutter und Erzieherin: Eine angewandte Mariologie*, 340-341.

As a natural reflection of God, man is the being whose inner nature can and will and must say "I" and "You." We are beings who do and must exist apart and alone, inimitable in being, task, and vocation, autonomous and independent, standing on our own two feet in inner freedom and responsibility for our actions. If this is not so, we must degenerate and become stunted and lose our identity. At the same time, we are beings engaged in the struggle to preserve and make something of ourselves because and to the extent that I say "I" and because and to the extent that I stand on my own two feet. As Duns Scotus explains, it is the nature of our being that we are subject to and dependent on ourselves: *persona est ad se.*[66] Because of the innate disposition of our nature, however, we also need the personal "You " and therefore community, self-surrender, and giving of self, or, as Bonaventure[67] puts it: We are inclined to the other—*persona est ad alium.*[68]

The establishment of true community and the exchange between the personal "I" and the personal "You" is only possible when the personal "I" has developed its full originality and is able to offer itself unconditionally to the "You," to surrender to the "You" in a spirit of openness and total giving which in return is reciprocal, thus leading one's personal autonomy to its full development and full maturity.

The light of the intellect shows us that whatever the person gains and stands for in his solitude and individuality, this he offers as a part of the gift of self to the personal 'You'—through the instinctive and inborn inclination to community. It shows that true community, the communion and fusion and exchange of hearts between the personal 'I' and the personal 'You' is only possible when the personal 'You' develops its full originality and selflessly offers [this wealth] to the 'You.' And that the surrender to the 'You'—in its spirit of unbounded openness and total giving—has a reciprocal effect on self, leading one's personal autonomy to its full development and full maturity. In the absence of this dynamic, community becomes a mass, that is, leads to the loss of inner identity for some and the self-glorification and self-adulation or tyrannical cravings and conduct for others.[69]

---

[66] Duns Scotus, *Ox* 1d.159. un.n.3 [x 280a].
[67] Bonaventure, *Sent.* Id.9a-9. 2 Solut. 3/I 183b.
[68] Kentenich, *Maria, Mutter und Erzieherin: Eine angewandte Mariologie*, 339-340.
[69] *Ibid.*, 340.

This interchange is essential and cannot be replaced by anything else; it is integral to the human individual and human nature:

> The 'I' can only become interiorly mature and perfected, resilient and creative through self-surrender to a personal 'You,' that is, through the passive process of being given a home in the heart of the other and the active process of spiritually giving a home in one's own heart to the other. These personal bonds between the 'I' and the 'You' are so essential that they cannot be replaced by anything else. They are simply part and parcel of the integral character of the human individual.[70]

No matter how fruitful and enriching such an exchange is,[71] ultimately

> there will be the sense of something missing in this surrender to another human being, an unfilled space in need of fulfilment—a space which goes far beyond all created things, a space, a supernatural space, God. Even when the soul finds a home in human arms and a human heart, its ultimate search is for an image and reflection of the arms and heart of God. If it does not find [this reflection], the soul becomes weary, wounded and infirm. It will become homesick and rapidly shrivel up.[72]

The human self reaches into the supernatural sphere and that is finally the divine personal "You."[73] Because of our broken nature there will always exist a constant tension between the abiding-in-self and the abiding-in-others; there will always be a search for a legitimate and appropriate balance of this tension.[74] The supernatural dimension of the human likeness to God gives a mysterious participation in the divine nature through grace; it is a taking into the inner trinitarian life of God.[75]

---

[70] *Ibid.*, 340-341.
[71] *Ibid.*, 343.
[72] *Ibid.*
[73] *Ibid.*, 352-353.
[74] *Ibid.*, 350.
[75] *Ibid.*; Kentenich, J., *Mutter und Erzieherin: Eine angewandte Mariologie*, 349, 352; M. J. Scheeben, *Die Herrlichkeiten der göttlichen Gnade,* ed. A. M. Weiss (Freiburg: Herder, 1920), 56.

The Human Person–*Representatio Christi*

Next to the static aspect, Kentenich speaks of a dynamic aspect of Christian anthropology, referring to the innate potentiality to become in a most perfect way what the person is. Here one has to speak of the significance of Christ in our life, because He has freed mankind from sin and death, and in membership with Him the human person is taken into the passover event of His suffering, dying and rising from the dead.[76] Through these events transformation of the person becomes possible, and the divine image and likeness can again emerge in its full potential. Redemption however is a pure gift—utterly beyond human powers. In our human freedom, we have to cooperate with the divine gift and recognize and embrace the primary significance of Christ in our lives.[77] Thus Kentenich says, "The idea of being human is to become a child,"[78] and the meaning of this becoming a child is the representation of Christ in us,[79] as found in the words of St Paul: "Not I live but Christ lives in me [Gal 2: 20]."[80] Man must proclaim to the world "the great mystery of God and Christ: Christ in us and we in Christ."[81] "The God-man, the incarnate Child of God [Christ], should take *gestalt* and form in our lives."[82] Hence, "to be in Christ means according to him [Paul]: to suffer with Christ, to die with Him, to be buried with Him, to rise with Him, to live with Him, to be transfigured with Him, to reign with Him . . . to be incorporated in Him and to be configurated to Him."[83]

Kentenich makes an explicit distinction between a moral unity, as for example in love, and the unity with Christ which is an ontological community of life. Referring to Scheeben,[84] he says: "It is a *unio quasi physica* . . . that is a mysterious, ontological two-in-oneness between me and Christ. *Vidisti fratrem tuum, vidisti*

---

[76] Kentenich, *Das Katholische Menschenbild*, 46-47.

[77] Kentenich, *Marianische Werkzeugsfrömmigkeit*, 162-163.

[78] Kentenich, *Kindsein vor Gott*, 103.

[79] *Ibid.*, 103-105.

[80] Kentenich, *Nova Creatura in Jesu at Maria*, 148-149.

[81] *Ibid.*, 150.

[82] Kentenich, *Kindsein vor Gott*, 104.

[83] Kentenich, *Nova Creatura in Jesu at Maria*, 151.

[84] E.g., M. J. Scheeben, *Nature and Grace*, trans. by C. Vollert (St. Louis: B. Herder Book Co., 1954), 304-338.

Christum. I repeat how St. Augustine emphasized it. We belong not only to Christ . . . I *am* Christ. To be a Christian means to be Christ. Thus we have to see one another."[85] Through the essential membership in Christ, as mentioned above, the human person as the grace-endowed person becomes a true *child of God* and a *sanctuary of the Trinity*:

> [Only] faith shows und unveils to us the human person in his entire greatness and God-related splendor. Is the human person without grace . . . merely a creature, a servant of God, so he will become through grace and through the rebirth [in Christ] . . . God's child with all the splendor of a child, with the right of a child, with the duty of a child. The person becomes God's friend . . . bride of God . . . member and brother of Jesus Christ [1 Cor 12:12-14; Mt 25:40]. He becomes "temple of the Holy Spirit," a dwelling of the Triune God, a sanctuary of the Trinity, which is dedicated to the Triune God and in which the Trinity abides. Indeed, he becomes an image of the Triune God and is in a mysterious way united with God not only in a community of like-mindedness but in an unspeakable community of life.[86]

The realization of the divine idea of the human person is individual and communal—both aspects are important for Joseph Kentenich—because the gradual development of becoming the human person finds its purpose and meaning in the transformation in Christ, and in the membership in the organism of the kingdom of God. Hence, the Christian image of the human person comprises the *becoming human* and *being transformed in Christ*, both considered as one whole in the order of nature and the order of grace; the God-signed image of the community is given in becoming a member and being incorporated into the Kingdom of God.[87]

The Human Person–Agent in History

Within the above-mentioned Christological, soteriological, pneumatological and ultimately trinitarian reality in Christian anthropology, Kentenich points also to the historical dimension, for from a theistic understanding, "the meaning of world history is the

---

[85] Kentenich, *Rom Vorträge,* 4 Vols (TMs, 1965-66) II, 208-211.
[86] Kentenich, *Maria, Mutter und Erzieherin: Eine angewandte Mariologie*, 349-350.
[87] Kentenich, *Oktoberbrief 1949*, 44.

systematic, gradual unfolding of the divine idea of the human person . . . [this idea] itself and its realization is divine according to its origin, content and aim."[88]

In this context I would like to draw attention to Kentenich's understanding of *history*. For him, all history is *salvation history* with the Christ-event as its core, and unification of the actual salvific deed [*Heilstat*] becomes salvifically significant [*Heilsbedeutung*] in the mediation of salvific experience [*Heilserfahrung*].[89] Thus, "the meaning of history is preparation for, continuation, rounding off and completion of Christ's life, with the aim of perfect, loving union with the Father.[90] The time before Christ was the preparation for His coming . . . The time after Christ is the mysterious repetition of the individual stages of his life, both in certain individuals and in whole generations."[91]

The different facets of the Christ-event that come to the foreground are at times

the childlike Savior who governs the individual and the times and sets His stamp on both; at other times it is the militant Christ. When this happens, the chill of Good Friday and the jubilation of Easter are tangibly repeated. When the first people left paradise to go into exile with the longing for this lost paradise in their hearts, Christ associated Himself with them with the protogospel in hand, and never again left them or their descendants. As *logos spermaticos*[92] He follows the pagans, and under a mysterious veil he accompanies Christians. Here He prepares for Advent or Christmas, even if only very few people come to adore Him, even if very few are prepared to offer Him gold, frankincense and myrrh. Elsewhere He *re* -lives his life in Nazareth. He does this wherever Christian families allow Him to enter. In the priests and laity He goes through the world preaching and healing.[93]

---

[88] *Ibid.*, 42.

[89] *Ibid.*, 49-51; Kentenich, J., *Address at the Dedication of the Shrine of the Union*, Pentecost, May 14, 1967 (TMs, Engl. trans. and ed., Waukesha, WI: Schoenstatt Sisters of Mary, 28 pages), 13.

[90] Kentenich also speaks of the meaning of world history as "the return home to God...." Kentenich, *Das Katholische Menschenbild*, 45.

[91] Kentenich, *Oktoberbrief 1949*, 49-50.

[92] See Justin Martyr's teaching on the *Logos spermaticos*, in which he speaks of mankind before the Christian revelation as having received the seed of the Logos and thus was fitted for a partial perception of the truth that later would be fully revealed in Christ. J. Martyr, *2 apol.*, 10 n. 1-5 also 6; *1 apol.*, 46.

[93] Kentenich, *Oktoberbrief 1949*, 50.

Christ is and remains a sign of contradiction in history:

> Everywhere His words and actions force people to decide for or
> against Him. . . . In a mysterious way He relives Holy Week with
> and in everyone who, like Paul, make up in their bodies for what is
> still lacking to the sufferings of Christ [Col 1:24], who remain
> silent when the crowds call out insistently to the Pilates of their
> times: "Crucify Him!," who do not break down when Judas betrays
> them and sells them for thirty pieces of silver. Day by day He cel-
> ebrates Easter, even if He finds very few believing witnesses to His
> resurrection and glorious victory. He sends the Holy Spirit to all
> who persevere in prayer and the breaking of the bread.[94]

To all tragedy in the events in time and world and in every
life "Christ is the solution. . . . One speaks of tragedy when human
weakness is confronted with stronger, higher powers, and breaks
down in such a way that rich blessing flows from defeat. In our
case theology tells us: in Christ the *mysterium iniquitatis* is transformed into the *mysterium gratiae*."[95] Hence, the objective
Christological meaning of world history becomes subjectively relevant for each individual believer: "What influence should I grant
to Christ? I should use every event as a new chance to decide for
Christ, and the most difficult happenings should inspire me to
come to a new, freely chosen and freely willed decision for Christ.
. . . The meaning of world events, and of my life and striving, is
that all the events of my life should cause me to surrender myself
to the Lord once more."[96] Thus, it is in history where God leads
and directs all happenings so that they serve the realization of the
divine idea of the human person in all details. World history can
be called the "exquisite commentary of the divine idea of the
human person."[97]

The anthropological perspective, which considers the human
person as a being created in the image of God enabling him to
respond to himself and to a "you" and to the ultimate "You" of
God, always becomes effective in the concrete historical situation
of the person. It is not an abstract person but always the concrete

[94] *Ibid.*, 50-51.
[95] *Ibid.*, 51.
[96] Kentenich, *Das Katholische Menschenbild*, 48.
[97] Kentenich, *Oktoberbrief 1949*, 42-43.

human person in the actual concrete framework of history to whom God's *saving* action is manifested.

In this concrete human and salvation-historical context, the individual person is called to respond to God's offer creatively as God's partner in the covenant. The Old Testament and the New Testament give us vivid examples of this reality of God's covenant with His people from the primitive beginning, as described in the Old Testament, until its fulfilment in the person of Jesus Christ. This covenant which is a *covenant of love*, is the basic form of the whole of salvation history.[98] As such, it is intended to lead to the most perfect unity of love between God and His people.[99] God, who speaks in love to the human person, is waiting for the response of love from the human person. Kentenich emphasizes that each person in his distinctness and dignity is uniquely addressed by God and able to give a unique answer to God.

Through the unique response to God, the person in concrete history becomes the bearer of a mission. As such, the person is directly called and sent by God in the concrete situation of that particular person with the task to effectively meet the reality of the new covenant established in Christ, that is, to respond to God as a new creation, as a new person. In the words of Paul, through baptism the old person has died and the new person has emerged. The person is mysteriously taken into the inner trinitarian life of God and thus becomes a partner of the Trinity.[100] This partnership, which is essentially a genuine childhood before God, enables the person in the loving obedience of faith to grow and to mature into the ultimate freedom of the children of God. It is this fully-integrated Christian personality, the *new person*, who is able to establish and maintain communal relationships in the building up of the *new community*.[101] Yet, the realization of Kentenich's aim to help to form the *new person* in the *new community*, that is, the true believer in the ecclesial *commu-*

---

[98] Kentenich, *Das Lebensgeheimnis Schönstatts*, II, 45.

[99] *Ibid.*, II, 33.

[100] *Ibid.*, II, 57.

[101] "According to St. Augustine, love is, seen from the perspective of the soul, an *inscriptio cordis in cor* [*Letter to Pauline of Nola*, PL 33: 122], a fusion of hearts. As a result, perfect love must be seen as an *inscriptio perfecta, perpetua, mutua*–a perfect, perpetual, and mutual fusion of hearts. It is not something isolated, but has a living, personal being at its focus which, as an image of God, ultimately awakens and nurtures the warmth of love and leads and transmits it back to the

nio, is necessarily bound up with the image and task of Mary, the Mother of God.

Mary the *causa exemplaris* of the Christian personality

For Joseph Kentenich, Mary is the *causa exemplaris* of this integrated Christian personality, the fully redeemed person in Christ, who in union with Christ is "the most perfect resemblance of Christ."[102] Thus, in Mary he perceived the "Catholic image of the human person;"[103] in other words, she stands before us as the "through and through divinized, Christianized, noble,[104] high-minded, animated, moral-ethical,[105] realistic [*wirklichkeitsnahe* and *wirklichkeitsgeladene*],[106] God-dependent and God-bound person, who is directed toward and capable of human complementation.[107] Further, within the ecclesial community, Mary, as the truly free person,[108] is the *new person* in Christ, who wants to educate the faithful toward the true freedom of the children of God.[109] From this perspective, Marian teaching and devotion are essential to Christian faith. It was integral to Kentenich's charism to present, in a timely and relevant manner, the person of Mary and her task in salvation history, fruitful and relevant for *the Church on the new shore*.[110]

---

heart of God. However, it does that by leading the immediate human object of noble love with itself into God and God's love. That is so true that the *visio beata* not only consists of the mysterious spiritual intimacy between soul and God, but also between one soul and another, between human partners." Kentenich, *Das Lebensgeheimnis Schönstatts*, II, 129-130. See also Joseph Kentenich, "Heroische Naivität im Kontext der Zeitenwende (1949)," *Regnum* 8,1 (1973): 19-28.

[102] Kentenich, *Das Katholische Menschenbild*, 120.

[103] *Ibid.*

[104] *Ibid.*, 20.

[105] *Ibid.*, 31.

[106] *Ibid.*, 32, 48-49.

[107] *Ibid.*, 34.

[108] "The Mother of God was wholly detached from herself and totally given to God. She is the perfect model of freedom. We admire in her the splendor of her inner freedom: without sin, without original sin, without concupiscence, spotless, without any blame. . . . She did not have to fight in order to gain this freedom [i.e., it was given to her]. Yet there is also another kind of freedom: a freedom *for* God that means to be free to the things of above, a growing into God. This freedom *for* God did cost the Mother of God uncountable battles. It required of her the heroism of faith and surrender, the death-leap of faith and of the heart." Kentenich, *Kampf um die wahre Freiheit* (MTs, 250 pages, 1946), 249.

[109] Kentenich, *Kampf um die wahre Freiheit*, 249-250.

[110] Kentenich, *Kirche im Aufbruch ans Neue Ufer: Texte aus Kursen und Schriften*

Mary and Salvation-History

It is foreign to Kentenich's theological thinking to consider Mary and Marian devotion as an isolated tract of theology; rather, he has integrated them into the whole context of theology. It is Mary's position in God's economy of salvation which is for him the point of departure for everything in regard to Marian teaching and education. Thus, theologically established in salvation-historical reality, he explains the anthropological relevance as follows:

> The main reason for love for Mary is and remains her position in the plan of salvation. This is first of all independent of the value which it has in life, independent of individual needs and wishes of people, it is independent of age and gender, it is not speculative of—at least not immediately—its influence in regard to education and knowledge or certain healing. Although God has in His wisdom and mercy cared that His ordained order is not only an opportunity or an acknowledgment of God's supremacy and the reason for our personal response of love, it is also meant as a means for personal perfection, enrichment and happiness. This last aspect may therefore be only a secondary reason; it may not be in the foreground; otherwise, God-willed order would be turned upside down. It is true, for example, that the Blessed Mother can be for man an ideal animating complementation and for woman an eminent ideal of womanhood, and generally speaking she can be for the human person the high ideal of noble and aristocratic humanism. One can see her also under this aspect and show and portray her thus and one may proclaim the love for her as an educational power of great value, but one cannot remain there. Lastly, all these positive consequences should only be the result and not the purpose and aim of Marian devotion; they should be a *ut consecutivum* and not a *ut finale*.[111]

Here it is significant to notice that for Kentenich the acceptance or nonacceptance of Marian devotion or Marian theology is neither an arbitrary decision, nor is it based on psychological or purely anthropological reasons or merely a means in pastoral ministry. It can commence from these areas but it may never be the foundation of Marian theology and Marian devotion. The foundation is and must remain the order of being as exemplified in salva-

---

v. Pater J. Kentenich, Festgabe der Schweizer Schönstattfamilie zum 50. Jahrestag der Gründung Schönstatts, ed. A. Ziegler, G. Roos (Manuscript, 264 pages), 109; B. Pereira, "Marianische Sendung," *Regnum* 4 (1949), 52-58.
[111] Kentenich, *Das Lebensgeheimnis Schönstatts*, II, 100-101; I, 152.

tion history.[112] According to this order the Mother of God has a God-willed objective place in the divine economy of salvation. Pope John Paul II stated in *Redemptoris Mater* that she [Mary] inaugurated the redemption by her "Yes."[113]

Inherent in Mary's place in the order of salvation is the divine idea of Mary as the official helpmate and associate of Christ in the entire work of redemption.[114] This description of Mary's vocation and mission has become the constituent idea of Joseph Kentenich's Marian teaching.[115] From this central idea, Mary's life and activity can be viewed in such a way that the fundamental truth of Christ as the sole Mediator and Redeemer is not diminished, because Mary is and remains in *total dependence on Christ*–thinking of her as the fully redeemed person under the aspect of her Immaculate Conception, sharing in the natural and supernatural fullness of life–and at the same time she is *totally orientated toward Christ* in her activity as Mother of the Church in educating and leading the faithful toward Christ.[116]

---

[112] Basic and fundamental to Kentenich's thinking is the principle: *ordo essendi est ordo agendi*. Essential to such thinking is a metaphysical religious fundamental characteristic in which ultimately all aspects of perception are directed toward God's designs, intentions and wishes. The fundamental orientation on the order of being has to be the determining factor for all human action. See St. Thomas Aquinas, *Summa Theologica* 1a IIae 90-94; Kentenich, *What is my philosophy of education?*, 8-11.

[113] Pope John Paul II, *Redemptoris Mater*, March 25, 1987, AAS 79 (1987), 361-433.

[114] Here the parallel of Adam-Christ and Eve-Mary comes in perspective. Constitutive to the unity between Christ and Mary is the *predestinatio muta, perpetua, perfecta, absoluta*. Kentenich, *Texte zum 31. Mai 1949*, 64, 92. The above descriptive formula—sometimes with variations—refers to the "personal character" of Mary, which designs all the essentials of Mary's mission, task and position in the work of redemption. Kentenich, *Texte zum 31. Mai 1949*, 35-63. See also Kentenich, *Octoberwoche 1950*, 278. The notion of "personal character" derives from M. Scheeben's considerations regarding the distinguishing mark of Mary's person. M. J. Scheeben, *Mariology*, trans. by T. L. M. J. Geukers, 2 Vols (St. Louis: B. Herder Book Co.: 1947), Vol I, 187-217. "Personal character" can also be perceived in terms of "paradigm," in the way Bearsley defines "Marian paradigm" as a central thematic idea which is "rich and powerful enough to provide a vantage point from which to view all the other great truths about Mary." P. Bearsley, "Mary, the perfect disciple: A paradigm for Mariology," *Theological Studies* 41 (1980): 461-504.

[115] See Peter Wolf, *Maria—ihre Sendung nach Josef Kentenich*. (Vallendar: Schönstatt—Verlag, 1999).

[116] Kentenich, *Maria, Mutter und Erzieherin: Eine angewandte Mariologie*, 120.

As the permanent helpmate of Christ, Mary has a supratemporal mission and a temporal mission: supratemporal as the permanent companion of Christ, covering all epochs of salvation history, and temporally her activity becomes specifically relevant in the concrete historical context of each particular epoch. Mary, as the Christ-*formed* woman, wants, as the Christ-*forming* woman, to form Christ in us.[117] Thus Mary's activity is not intended to diminish the activity of the Holy Spirit, but to open up the person for the Holy Spirit, so that the Holy Spirit can form Christ in each person who calls out: Abba, dear Father.[118] Ultimately Joseph Kentenich's Marian theology is not only Christological and pneumatological but trinitarian.[119]

Mary, the Prototype of the Redeemed Person in Christ

Mary's cooperation in the work of Christ in salvation history is exemplary for Joseph Kentenich in view of the cooperation between God and the human person, because in Mary we have the most perfect case of free action, of free response to God and his covenant. Here the active cooperation of the Mother of God fulfills the law *Deus operatur per causas secundas liberas*.[120] In the divine economy of salvation Mary is central to the incarnation and redemption. This centrality of Mary's place at the side of Christ is basic to Kentenich's concept of *Marian modality*,[121] which is indicative of two relational characteristics: receptivity and response

---

[117] Kentenich, *Das Katholische Menschenbild*, 120-121.

[118] Kentenich, *Octoberwoche 1950*, 270.

[119] Kentenich, *Das Lebensgeheimnis Schönstatts*, I, 99-100.

[120] "What is true in regard to secondary causes, is per eminentiam true of the Mother of God." Kentenich, *Victoria Patris, Vorträge in Oberkirch*, 2 Vols (TMs, 1967) II, 57. The scholastic theological term *causae secundae* upholds that God acts through secondary or instrumental causes. From the mid-twenties on, J. Kentenich uses the term *causa secunda*. The main impetus for the use of the term comes from Przywara, who in a study from 1923 presents Augustine as a representative of the *causa prima* and Thomas Aquinas as a representative of the *causa secunda*. See E. Przywara, *Gottgeheimnis der Welt,* Drei Vorträge über die geistige Krisis der Gegenwart (München: Theatiner-Verlag, 1923); P. Vautier, "Die Theologie Scheebens und die Zweitursachenlehre Pater J. Kentenichs, *Regnum* 10 (1975): 67-79.

[121] Kentenich took this terminus from E. Zeitler, Die Herz-Mariä-Weltweihe: Dogmatisch-zeitgeschichtliche Schau (Kaldenkirchen: Steyler Verlagsbuchhandlung, 1954), 18. See also Kentenich, *Marianische Erziehung,* Pädagogische Ta-

toward God and the divine.[122] Mary in her person personified and exemplified this receptivity and total response of creation and of humanity toward God. Hence Kentenich could say, "The Mother of God stands before us as the personified openness for the divine,"[123] or in Mary, "the motherly principle is built into salvation."[124]

In the perspective of *Marian modality*, the actuality of Mary's participation and cooperation in the mystery of Christ becomes exemplary for the ecclesial community and for the individual person before God. It signifies in the most eminent way and in its ultimate ideal, the creaturely participation and cooperation with the creator in history, that is, the free response of the human person to God's love in a union of love. Mary's cooperation not only exemplifies the fundamental human attitude before God but also represents that attitude in its *lasting* effectiveness. Kentenich speaks therefore of this Marian dimension and Marian devotion [*Marienverehrung*] not only as a *Formprinzip* but as a *Formalprinzip*, which shows significant pertinence in Marian education:

> Marian devotion is in all of our conduct in some way present [and] active: *tota in toto*. My entire spiritual life, my entire ethical and moral life and conduct ... has a Marian hue. Therefore, long before this [issue] entered modern discussion, we stand, and we stood, with the conviction that the whole order of salvation has a Marian modality.[125]

gung 1934, ed. F. Lüttgen (Vallendar-Schönstatt. Patris Verlag: 1971), 15; P. Vautier, *Maria, die Erzieherin*: Darstellung und Untersuchung der marianischen Lehre P. Joseph Kentenichs (1885-1968), Schönstatt-Studien 3 (Vallendar-Schönstatt: Patris Verlag, 1981), 129-130.

[122] See in this context *Wort* und *Antwort*, in H. U. von Balthasar, *Theo-Drama: Theological Dramatic Theory* (San Francisco: Ignatius Press, 1992) III, 283-292.

[123] Kentenich, *Daß neue Menschen werden: Eine pädagogische Religionspsychologie*, 251.

[124] Kentenich, *Texte zum 31. Mai 1949*, 59; Kentenich, *Marianische Werkzeugsfrömmigkeit*, 57, 104, 137, 168; Kentenich, *Mutter und Erzieherin: Eine angewandte Mariologie*, 237.

[125] Joseph Kentenich, *Vorträge 1963*, Vol.2, 102-112, cited in H. King, *Marianische Bundesspiritualität: Ein Kentenich Lesebuch*, 284-285. Kentenich also noted the following: "If the Mother of God has this position [in the history of salvation], then we must also take care . . . that it is translated practically into everyday life. *Tota in toto*. This is what we understand when we say that for us, from the beginning, Marian devotion has been not only a form principle

In conclusion it can be said that Mary's position in the order of salvation demonstrates a twofold relevance for a Christian anthropology. The *incarnational relevance* is shown by Mary's being taken into the mystery of the incarnation where she witnesses to the *concreteness of Christ's incarnation* against rationalistic and idealogical tendencies.[126] Also, Mary is, in her election and through her active cooperation with God's will, the *prototype of the human person and the ecclesial community*. Taken into loving union with God, Mary becomes a sign of God's saving action. This saving action engenders in a person a transparency of God's self, thereby enabling that person to see all of creation as transparent toward God.[127]

[*Formprinzip*] but an informing principle [*Formalprinzip*]." Kentenich as cited in H. King, *Marianische Bundesspiritualität: Ein Kentenich Lesebuch*, 284-85. See also Kentenich, *Octoberwoche 1950*, 258.

[126] Kentenich, *Daß neue Menschen werden: Eine pädagogische Religionspsychologie*, 95-97; Kentenich, *Das Lebensgeheimnis Schönstatts*, II, 99-100. "Any pragmatic piety—including the Marian variety—is the opposite extreme of *idea*-listic piety. The one focuses onesidedly only on ideas, while the other focuses only or almost only on the existential value of religion. It is therefore constantly in danger of becoming psychologistic or naturalistic or pedagogistic. It loses the ultimate anchor and moral force which it should have in a sound order of being and the effective power of attachments to persons. It is therefore, without really noticing it, in danger of falling prey to the very idealism we just described." Kentenich, *Das Lebensgeheimnis Schönstatts*, II, 151-52; Kentenich, *Marianische Erziehung* 186-87.

[127] Kentenich, *Marianische Werkzeugsfrömmigkeit*, 65.

A SPEYRIAN THEOLOGY OF THE BODY

Michele M. Schumacher, S.T.D.*

Common to many of the contemporary theologies of the body inspired by Pope John Paul II is the phenomenological movement from the experience of the body in a relationship of love—especially filial-maternal or sexual, but not exclusively—to an appreciation for the gifted significance of personhood: the experience of oneself as loved—and thus lovable—and the experience of actually loving another in return, whereby is also experienced the meaning of one's own freedom and agency and thus one's divine likeness. In the words of John Paul II, the human body has a "nuptial attribute," whereby is meant the "capacity of expressing love, that love in which the person becomes a gift and—by means of this gift—fulfills the meaning of his being and existence."[1] While this may be understood as a typically human trait, the body also has a properly theological significance. Precisely as a "sacrament" of the person, it is "capable of making visible what is invisible: the spiritual and the divine. It was created to transfer into the visible reality of the world the mystery hidden from eternity in God [our redemption in Christ], and thus to be its sign."[2] In this way, John Paul II argues for a bi-directional movement of analysis—based upon a mutual clarification—between the mystery of redemption and the body-person with his

* With gratitude to the National Swiss Scientific Foundation for their generous support of my research on this subject.
[1] John Paul II, *The Theology of the Body: Human Love in the Divine Plan* (Boston: Pauline Books & Media, 1997), 63.
[2] *Ibid.*, 77.

or her conjugal significance.[3] The biblical analogy of marriage thus illuminates the mystery of redemption, and this mystery in turn "defines and determines the adequate manner of understanding the analogy."[4]

Complementary, but different, is the Trinitarian, mystical approach of the Swiss mystic and physician Adrienne von Speyr (1902-1967), whose own theology of the sexes (*Theologie der Geschlechter*)[5] was dictated several decades prior to the General Audiences of Pope John Paul II that serve as the context for his catechetical teaching on the body. Not unlike John Paul II, Adrienne recognizes the human body, precisely in its nudity, as "a being formed for love."[6] Hence the corporality of our first ancestors is portrayed by Adrienne as expressing the unity of their persons.[7] This unity was not an end in itself, however; for she describes the ecstatic experience of the sexual union as one of surpassing one's own finitude, so as to be introduced into the infinite realm.[8] It is thus not surprising that Adrienne uses the same experience to describe, by way of analogy, the incomprehensible mystery of Trinitarian love.[9] Beyond the analogical similarity between these two very different personal unions—that of human persons in a physical, punctual relationship of sexual love and that of the divine persons in a spiritual, eternal communion of love—she notes "a

---

[3] "The 'first Adam'—man, male and female—created in the state of original innocence and called in this state to conjugal union (in this sense we are speaking of the sacrament of creation) was a sign of the eternal mystery. So the 'second Adam,' Christ, united with the Church through the sacrament of redemption by an indissoluble bond, analogous to the indissoluble covenant of spouses, is a definitive sign of the same eternal mystery. Therefore, in speaking about the eternal mystery being actuated, we are speaking also about the fact that it becomes visible with the visibility of the sign." (*Ibid.*, 338).

[4] *Ibid.*, 332.

[5] *Theologie der Geschlechter* (Einsiedeln: Johannesverlag, 1969). Although the volume was published two years after her death, it is composed of dictations that were given between December 1946 and January 1947.

[6] *Ibid.*, 147.

[7] *Ibid.*, 159.

[8] *Ibid.*, 147.

[9] *Ibid.*, 143: "So there results from our experience of the body in love a step to the incomprehensible mystery of the Trinity." Adrienne also compares the original unity of Adam and Eve in their nakedness to the unity of the divine persons. See *Ibid.*, 159.

certain unity between the mystery of the body and the mystery of God," whereby "the former is contained in the latter."[10]

Here the progression of thought moves from the experience of the body as an instrument of communion to the knowledge of God as a Trinity of persons, but this movement is itself preceded by the primordial "movement" of the Trinity "to" the body. The human body was created, Adrienne teaches, by the Father for the Son and the Spirit. The Son, in turn, incorporates us into His body as members by means of the Eucharistic mysteries, which He establishes in obedience to the Father and with the help of the Spirit who bears Him. As for the Spirit, He takes residence in the body, as in a temple built by the Father and sanctified by the Son through the latter's Incarnation and Cross. From this Trinitarian perspective, the human body is revelatory of Trinitarian love, especially within the context of the Eucharistic mysteries: "The Spirit effects the Eucharistic existence of the body of Christ in the Church, as He already accomplished the Incarnation in the womb of Mary." For this reason, as we shall see, she (Mary) is "the image and womb of the Church, to whom the Son surrenders Himself in a spousal manner in the Eucharistic mystery."[11]

As is particularly evident in these passages, it is God's surrender—from the Trinity to the Incarnation, from the Incarnation to the Eucharist, and from the Eucharist to the Church—that explains and determines the meaning of the human body as the instrument "of a much more comprehensive surrender."[12] Combining, in some sense, the experiential approach, characteristic of phenomenology, with a properly theological approach proceeding from the data of revelation, Adrienne's mystical perspective invites her reader to so live the sacramental mysteries of the Christian faith that he or she might experience his or her own body as an instrument of obedience and thus also as an essential means of participating in the bridal mission of the Church, who in turn shares the filial mission of Christ: a mission, as we shall see, to be the Father's Eucharist for the world.

---

[10] *The World of Prayer* (San Francisco: Ignatius Press, 1985), 190.
[11] *Der erste Korintherbrief* (*The First Letter to the Corinthians*) (Einsiedeln: Johannesverlag, 1956), 188.
[12] *Theologie der Geschlechter*, 106.

In an effort to expose this unique perspective of the body in Adrienne's theology, this essay will attempt to systematize its mystical content which must be, as it were, reconstructed from the various elements, rich in insight, that are scattered throughout her more than sixty volumes. Concentrating largely—but not exclusively—upon her volume dedicated to the theology of the sexes, her volume on objective mysticism,[13] her various biblical commentaries,[14] and her volumes on Mary,[15] I will give voice to Adrienne, who—as I have already demonstrated in a previous work[16]— expresses the faith of the Church with a certain Christian transparency. To this end, I will lead my reader through an examination in *Part I* of the meaning of the Incarnation as a Trinitarian act of love: the Father's love for the Son and the Son's love for the Father in and through their common Spirit. This conception of the Incarnation dominates, as we will see in *Part II*, her theological vision that I will present in terms of a corporal-spiritual unity. Because the Trinitarian love of God, which explains the Incarnation and Eucharist, is also the fundamental and final reference for Adrienne's theological perspective, I will argue in *Part III* that the supernatural mysteries are used to clarify natural, bodily

---

[13] *Das Wort und die Mystik, Teil II: Objektive Mystik* (Einsiedeln: Johannesverlag, 1970).

[14] *Die Schöpfung* (*Creation*) (Einsiedeln: Johannesverlag, 1972); Das Hohelied (*Song of Songs*) (Einsiedeln: Johannesverlag, 1972); *Markus* (*Mark*) (Einsiedeln: Johannesverlag, 1971); *John I: The Word Becomes Flesh* (San Francisco: Ignatius Press, 1994); *Johannes II: The Discourses of Controversy* (San Francisco: Ignatius Press, 1993); *John III: The Farewell Discourses* (San Francisco: Ignatius Press, 1987); *John IV: The Birth of the Church* (San Francisco: Ignatius Press, 1991); *The Letter to the Colossians* (San Francisco: Ignatius Press, 1998); *The Letter to the Ephesians* (San Francisco:Ignatius Press, 1996); *The Victory of Love: A Meditation on Romans 8* (San Francisco: Ignatius Press, 1990); *Der erste Korintherbrief* (*The First Letter to the Corinthians*) (Einsiedeln: Johannesverlag, 1956); *Die Johannesbriefe* (*The Letters of John*) (Einsiedeln: Johannesverlag, 1961); *Die Apokalpye* (*The Apocalypse*) (Einsiedeln: Johannesverlag, 1976); *Isaias* (*Isaiah*) (Einsiedeln: Johannesverlag, 1958); *Achtzehn Psalmen* (*Eighteen Psalms*) (Einsiedeln: Johannesverlag, 1957); *Dienst der Freude* (Service of Joy: commentary on Philippians) (Einsiedeln: Johannesverlag, 1951)

[15] *Handmaid of the Lord* (San Francisco: Ignatius Press, 1985); *Maria in der Erlösung* (Einsiedeln: Johannesverlag, 1979).

[16] See Michele Schumacher, "Die existenzielle theologie Adriennes von Speyr," *Internationale katholische Zeitschrift: Communio*, 32 (November-December 2003): 601-614.

realities within her theology. Hence, the mystery of our redemption as the one-flesh union of Christ and His Church will also be presented in *Part IV* as a Eucharistic mystery grounded in the eternal Trinitarian exchange of love. *Part V* will focus upon the goal of the Eucharistic exchange as the incorporation of believers in the life, mission and thus also the humanity of Christ. Finally, by way of conclusion in *Part VI*, I will present the Virgin Mary as the first "cell" of the Church and thus also as an archetypical member of Christ's body.

I. At the Heart of a Theology of the Body: The Incarnation as a Revelation of Trinitarian Love

In this effort to systematize Adrienne's very rich theology of the body, we shall begin with what I esteem to be the heart of the whole. Any authentically Christian theology of the body will, more specifically I insist, be rooted in the divine Incarnation and as such will be concerned with the most fundamental of all questions derived from Trinitarian faith: *Cur Deus homo?* The response as formulated in the Nicene Creed—*propter nos hominis et propter nostram salutem*—is certainly not to be denied by one who held so tightly to that faith as did Adrienne von Speyr. Indeed, the entire human nature of Christ is, in Adrienne's words, "earmarked for the redemption."[17] From the moment of His conception in the Virgin's womb until His descent among the dead, the body of Christ "is burdened with the task of redeeming the world."[18] In this sense, the redemption was already established in the Incarnation. "Already at that moment His blood was the blood of redemption. (…) He assumed it solely in order to be able to shed it, in order to give it to us as a gift."[19] Indeed, the Son willingly accepts this body as proof of His willingness to redeem the world as an act of love for the Father,[20] and throughout His earthly life He regards it—in "even the smallest actions"—as an instrument given by the Father for this end.[21] "He was ready to

---

[17] *Ephesians*, 36.
[18] *Colossians,* 36. "The Incarnation of the Son is inseperably connected to the Cross." (*Die Schöpfung*, 39). "He came so as to redeem by dying." (*Marc*, 636)
[19] *Ephesians,* 35.
[20] *Ibid.*, 156.
[21] *Ibid.*, 36-37. Christ's readiness to fulfil the Father's will in the body given him by the Father is evident not only in the extraordinary signs that He works, but even

assume it but also to give it up again for the salvation of the world."[22] In actually giving His flesh and blood as food and drink in the Upper Room, the Lord hastens the coming of the Passion; for His Eucharistic existence, whereby He "lives in other bodies, bodies of sinners, delivers Him utterly up to sinners, making it possible for Him to be injured, mocked, spat upon, crucified by all sinners."[23] As the "fulfilment of His perfect surrender to the Father,"[24] the Lord's surrender to sinners is the means whereby He admits them—and the whole reality of sin—into "what is most central and intimate to Him," namely his relationship with the Father.[25] Hence, the suffering humanity of Christ can never be separated, in Adrienne's theology, from His divinity: It is not a "foreign body" that suffers here, but the Son's own body "fully integrated with His divine-human spirit."[26]

It follows from the foregoing that His is "no indifferent flesh and blood", whose sanctification is determined "by right use or some blessing." Rather, it is "holy flesh and blood essentially and from all eternity."[27] Indeed, the designation of the Lord as redeemer in the flesh precedes the world's creation and even the question of whether or not Adam will fall, which is to say that the Son might have become man "only to recapitulate the whole creation in Himself, to raze completely the boundaries between heaven and earth, to establish full unification between God and man, to introduce us into the vision of the Father through Himself, not as redeemer, but as consummator."[28] Beyond all speculation about what might have been, however,

---

in the very ordinary actions of daily human life, such as eating and drinking. Precisely in respecting the human needs of this body, Adrienne recognizes "how much He is in communion with the Father, how much He does His will and observes the laws that He gave to nature in creating it." (*Objektive Mystik*, 535).

[22] *Ephesians,* 156.

[23] *Passion from within* (San Francisco: Ignatius Press, 1998), 45. Hence every eucharistic communion is realized, Adrienne argues, "in the shadow of the Cross," which awaits the Lord as he departs from the Upper Room. See *Ibid.,* 41.

[24] *Objektive Mystik,* 53.

[25] "Everything in them that is directed against God is now directed against his body." (*Passion from within*, 41).

[26] *Theologie der Geschlechter,* 100-101.

[27] *Ephesians,* 36.

[28] *Ibid.,* 28. This would be accomplished "by placing us at the point where the vision from the world to the Father and from the Father to the world is one in himself." (*Ibid.*)

Adrienne argues that the Son's mission is timeless: It is fulfilled before it has begun.[29]

More fundamental a motive for the Son's Incarnation than man's redemption is, however, in the speyrian perspective, His love for the Father and the Spirit, which is revealed to us precisely in and through His incarnate existence.[30] The Son, Adrienne argues, comes to atone for sin, which He experiences as an insult directed against the Father and the Spirit, and to assure the Father, expressly as a man, that His creation really is good.[31] More positively expressed, He becomes man so as to be the Father's Son on earth "as other men are His children." The desire to do so belongs, Adrienne explains, to the particularity of His divine person—to the fact that He is the Son— and it reveals this particularity.[32]

Of one will with the Father from all eternity, the Son accomplishes on earth what the Father had in mind for Adam in creating him,[33] and He does so precisely in the form of one of the Father's creatures.[34] The decision to create the world (and man in the world) is an act of the Father's love for the Son who, in turn, has adored the Father from all eternity and who recognizes in the creation of man still another form in which to adore the Father.[35] By assuming a human body and offering it "no longer as a finite, but as an infinite response of love to God",[36] the Son accomplishes man's likeness to God, with which he is invested at creation (cf. Genesis 1:26) and invites him to share in this (His own) response—His eternal

---

[29] *The Word Becomes Flesh,* 145.

[30] "So the motives of Christ's love for us lie in heaven: in the Father and the Spirit. The whole Incarnation lies within the context of these motives. He will become man for the Father and for the Spirit. And in becoming man, He reveals to us *this* love in an appropriate form, comprehensible to us." (*Objektive Mystik,* 110)

[31] *Ibid.* Cf. *World of Prayer,* 80 and *Objektive Mystik,* 261.

[32] *Objektive Mystik,* 82. Adrienne continues (*ibid.*): The Incarnation of the Son is *the* paradigm for the grounding [Begründetheit] of the [divine] appropriations overall."

[33] *Ephesians,* 36. "It is as if He [Christ] saw Himself in Adam, since Adam is the first image of God in the yet sinless world, the fulfilment of the work of creation." (*Die Schöpfung,* 38)

[34] *Johannesbriefe,* 191.

[35] *Objektive Mystik,* 522.

[36] *Ibid.,* 523.

[37] The Son is unique in understanding the profundity of love from which creation

Eucharist—arising out of Trinitarian love.[37] Our redemption is not, Adrienne insists, merely "the content of an article of faith or of a celestial agreement between Father and Son, but one that the Son lives through and accomplishes" precisely as man: that is, in the flesh.[38] Indeed, it belongs to His mission "to feel each one's failure in his body" and to surmount them with His love for the Father.[39] Adrienne notes in Pilate's words, "Behold the man!" (Jn 19:5), that without knowing it, he is referring to "*the* man, the archetype of man, man as God has always conceived of him."[40] "Adam destroys the image of God, and the Lord restores this image on the Cross."[41] It is not surprising, then, that Adrienne recognizes a profound unity between the work of creation and that of redemption as symbolized in the vision of the Cross present in her mystical vision of creation. It is the Cross, Adrienne discerns, which actually determines the divisions between day and night, earth and land, and which likewise rules over the division, within man himself, between body and soul.[42] Similarly, the darkness that descends upon earth at the moment of Christ's death is likened by Adrienne to the original darkness preceding creation: a heavenly sign of the dawning of a (the first) new day, "the intersection of that which is to be separated, but also of that which is already separated."[43]

---

stems, Adrienne argues, and in becoming man, He is unique in responding to this extravagant love of the Father from within this creation: in the Eucharist. Both the Eucharist and Creation have their origin in the "eternal, flowing grace of God". (*Objektive Mystic*, 522). This does not preclude that the Son responds to the Father's love in the form of a question—which Adrienne describes as including all of man's questions to God—in the dark night of "abandonment" on the Cross. (See *Isais*, 224). The trinitarian meaning of the Eucharist is developed at length in what follows.

[38] *Colossians*, 26.

[39] *Passion from within*, 41. "In him lies the strength to overcome their failure; the effort comes from his innermost center." (*Ibid.*)

[40] *The Birth of the Church*, 78.

[41] *Die Schöpfung*, 39. "When Adam is sinless, the Son sees Himself in him, but when Adam falls, he distances the Son from himself. On the Cross, he once again takes up this image of Adam into Himself." (*Ibid.*)

[42] *Ibid*. See also *Die Schöpfung,* 31-37.

[43] "When the Son dies on the Cross, the earth is obscure, and this sudden darkness is a sign of the beginning of day, which is picked up and hidden and now again visible in the Apocalypse as a sign of what was and what is to come, as the intersection of that which is to be divided and that which is already divided." (*Die Apokalypse*, 385)

The Son is present at the world's creation not merely in the foreshadowing of the Cross, however, for the image of God, restored to Adam by Christ also has its origin in Him. The birth of Christ presupposes the world's creation, but the latter is incomprehensible to the man who has not "experienced" Christ's birth.[44] Indeed, the world and man are created with regard to a fulfilment: the Son, who will become man.[45] And the Son brings all things to fulfilment in Himself "by impressing upon them His stamp and character."[46] "The Father is the original image (*Urbild*), man the created image (*Abbild*), the Son the prototype (*Vorbild*) for the Father in the creation of men."[47] It is not surprising, then, that the Father's eternal act of begetting the Son is, in some sense, the origin of His creative act of bringing forth the world and man in the world.[48]

As prototype, the Lord is in no way static, however; for already at Creation and always-ever since, He is and remains "the one who comes": the one who comes eternally to take our life into His eternal life. He comes forever and always, for if he were to be considered as having arrived, His coming would have certain boundaries and would thus cease to be eternal.[49] As the Incarnation is implicit in the act of creation, the Eucharist is implicit in the Incarnation. "The Son's life can be in us," Adrienne reasons,

[44] *Achtzehn Psalmen*, 16.

[45] *Objective Mystik*, 50. Similarly, Adrienne argues that the divine love "provides for the Son in advance and associates all things with Him and makes everything ready for Him. In this caring love the things themselves also attain their destined purpose, which can only be a purpose of love: every promise implicit in them comes to fulfilment in the Son, and the manifestation of the Son should become such a comprehensive, overwhelming revelation that heaven and earth will be filled with in, in order that the Father may recognize in heaven and earth that which is the Son's, and the Son may comprehend the Father's creation to be nothing other than that which was created for him and which therefore together with Him, who is the Way to the Father, is under way to the Father." (*Colossians*, 31-32).

[46] *Ephesians*, 48.

[47] *Objective Mystik*, 522. The Son is "the Immensity, unto which God created His world. Say rather: modelled his world after Him, since the Son's breadth, His divine essence is *before all things,* taking up and sustaining everything." (*Colossians,* 33)

[48] *Ibid.,* 525. "The Father is the Creator of the world, because the act of creation corresponds to the act of begetting. *As* He begets the Son, *so* does He create the world. What one [divine] Person does corresponds respectively to the Trinitarian will." (*Ibid.*, 80)

[49] *Die Apokalypse*, 823.

"because our life has the privilege of being in Him."[50] Life thus takes on a still richer meaning than that of being created by the Father; it also means, for the Christian, being "newly created through the Son."[51] It is not, therefore, as if the Father simply leads fallen man back to the point from which he departed. Rather, he "unites him more profoundly with Himself in His Son": the first Adam is included in the Second Adam's return to the Father.[52] The Son "destroys in Himself the old Adam (...), yet he destroys only after having taken up into Himself the thing to be destroyed. He destroys it by dying Himself and by letting what He has assumed die together with Him." With His resurrection, on the other hand, the world is "recreated" in the Son: "in His love made flesh," which in turn—precisely as Eucharist—is presented as "the substance of the vivification of the new man."[53]

> God created Adam just once; but He begets the Son, who becomes flesh and blood, in every Holy Mass. Adam, who was created at the beginning, sinned. God now creates the Son over and again in time, just as he perpetually begets Him in eternity as the Son, who most certainly will never sin and whose sinlessness he communicates to us in the Eucharist.[54]

To summarize then, not only the creation of the world, but also the Incarnation of the Son of God and even the sanctification of believers in Christ are foreseen from all eternity, Adrienne teaches, for "the purpose of giving pleasure to the triune God".[55] Indeed, the whole mystery of the Lord's terrestrial life stands, within Adrienne's theology, as testimony of the Son's love for the Father and His (the Father's) creation as well as to the Father's love for the

---

[50] *Colossians,* 33. Thanks to Christ's Eucharist, not only does man live in God, without separation from Him, as did Adam in paradise; God also lives in man, Adrienne teaches. (*Objektive Mystik*, 524-525).

[51] "Life now means not only created through the Father, but also newly created through the Son. Life arises as much from the birth of the Son as from Creation." (*Dienst der Freude*, 35).

[52] *Objektive Mystik*, 261. Because the Son's eternal return to the Father is already implied in His eternal generation by the Father—which, as we have seen, includes the Father's act of creation—man's own return to the Father through the Son is also implied in the creative act.

[53] *Ephesians,* 104-105.

[54] *The Holy Mass* (San Francisco: Ignatius Press, 1999), 83.

[55] *Ephesians,* 31.

Son and this same creation: "testimony of a love within the Deity that in circulating has drawn into itself that creation which was created because the Son *is*."[56]

As determinative of all creation, Trinitarian love is not only at the heart of the question most central to Adrienne's theology of the body—the question of why God took on a human body—but also of her incarnational perspective, which in turn is essential to her theology of the body, as we shall see in what follows.

II. Adrienne's Incarnational Perspective: A Corporal-Spiritual Unity

In light of the foregoing exposition of the Incarnation as revelatory of the Trinitarian exchange of love, it is not surprising that Adrienne's theology should be characterized by a realism "that goes into specific details," all in remaining "dominated by a vision of the higher order," as Hans Urs von Balthasar appropriately describes it.[57] Concretely this means not only that the order of creation is incorporated, within Adrienne's vision, into the Christological and ecclesial order of redemption, but also that the latter has precedence over the former. It is with this precedence in mind that one should regard Adrienne's many anthropomorphisms: her common manner of approaching the divine by means of the human, or more correctly, of speaking of the divine in human terms. As shall become increasingly evident, Adrienne often addresses the Trinity in terms analogical to human relations. This approach—so significant to her theology of the body—should be understood within her general intention of recognizing the human (and even nature itself) as pointing to the divine, as originating in and as orientated toward the divine: as existing "in Him [in whom] we live and move and have our being" (cf. Acts 17:28). Through Christ, in fact, the whole multitude of creation is "incorporated in the revelation of Trinitarian life,"[58] Adrienne notes. "It is not about 'God in all things,' but about 'all things towards God, towards

---

[56] *Colossians*, 30; cf. *Ephesians*, 29. God created the world, Adrienne teaches, so that it might participate in His divinity, so that our "being-here" might be the beginning of a "being by God." (*Der erste Korintherbrief,* 378).

[57] Hans Urs von Balthasar, *Our Task: A Report and a Plan* (San Francisco: Ignatius Press, 1994), 67. As Adrienne's confessor, spiritual director and editor of all her works, Balthasar is particularly well-suited to describe Adrienne's approach.

[58] *Der erste Korintherbrief,* 376.

Christ; all things as signposts'."[59] Consequently creation should not be considered a merely "natural" matter. "Behind it lies the free, powerful will of God to reveal Himself."[60] In the supernatural intention of God to reveal Himself, on the other hand, lies the origin of the natural: the creature is willed as the receiver and bearer of God's self-revelation. It is therefore impossible in any divine revelation, Adrienne argues, to clearly distinguish nature from super-nature.[61]

As a case in point, Adrienne maintains that the subjective (human) differences between the so-called feminine and masculine manners of experiencing and addressing God reflect actual objective differences within the Trinity: not necessarily differences directly attributable to the divine persons (such that any one divine person would be identified as masculine or feminine, for example), but differences manifesting the multitude and richness of "opposition" within the Trinity: the infinite possibilities of surrender and reception among the divine persons, which she recognizes as characterizing their love.[62] Hence the Trinity is, from Adrienne's perspective, the foundation and well-spring for all that we, as human persons, know and experience as difference.[63] All in admitting that there is no becoming or development in God, Adrienne recognizes within the Trinitarian communion of persons the archetype for the differences—Adrienne uses the term "tension," or "opposition"—that make love possible.[64]

---

[59] *Der Mensch vor Gott* (*Man before God*) (Einsiedeln: Johannesverlag, 1966), 59. See also Balthasar's contribution in *Adrienne von Speyr und ihre spirituelle Theologie*, 130-131.

[60] *Objektive Mystik,* 31. "It is as if God created human nature in order to have a natural witness of His super-nature, a receptor for the storehouse of His grace." (*Ibid.,* 34)

[61] *Ibid.,* 31-32. When, for example, Balthasar complains that her task of dictating the commentary on the Gospel of St. John was supernaturally empowered whereas his own noting by shorthand was achieved by completely natural means, Adrienne objected: "Please don't say that. The supernatural and the natural intermingle in every prayer, in all meditation. Even the one who has never had a vision cannot claim, especially in religious matters, that the interpretation comes from him. After all, he knows how dependent he is on grace, especially in interpretation, in transmission." (Balthasar, *Our Task,* 89)

[62] *Theologie der Geschlechter*, 143.

[63] *Ibid.,* 115-116.

[64] See, for example, *Die Apokalypse,* 64. "Eternity," Adrienne continues, "is not a simple state, a pure presence. It is much more like a birth, a result, a created happening."

While one might consequently fear a profaning of the sacred, Adrienne herself mourns the absence of what had been the sanctifying of the profane. She observes, more specifically, that modern man has lost the sense of wonder arising from the recognition of the created order as revelatory of the uncreated. Accustom, instead, to seeing things with a sort of habitual reference to the past—as if to admit that there is nothing new under the sun—man has lost the sense of creation itself: the orientation of all things in the future, in hope: *in the Son to the Father*.[65] Adrienne thus challenges us to regard all of human life as "access to the life of God in heaven,"[66] and in so doing to recognize a very clear unity between the natural and the supernatural, between nature and grace:

> The whole means: 'heaven and earth', or 'God and creature', because to speak of the earth and its relations without also considering God's heaven from which the earth stems, towards which it moves, and which is always open there above it, is to understand nothing, and certainly nothing Christian. The whole means: 'Trinity-Christ-Mary-Church-the Christian'; the chain is unbreakable; one can know nothing of the last link without knowledge of the second to the last and so on up to the mystery of Trinitarian love.[67]

In that which concerns Adrienne's theology of the body, this unity of the natural (and thus corporal) and the spiritual (divine and human) is particularly evident. Far from being "hostile" to sexuality, Christianity, Adrienne argues, imbues it with a new meaning: a meaning rooted, as we shall see, in the unity between Christ and His Church, which in turn is anchored in the eternal unity of the three divine persons.[68] This Trinitarian perspective

---

[65] Der *Mensch vor Gott*, 59.

[66] *Der erste Korintherbrief,* 377. Our "being here" is, Adrienne argues, the beginning of our "being by God" (*Ibid.,* 378).

[67] Balthasar's introduction to Adrienne's *Das Buch von Gehorsam* (*Book of Obedience*) (Einsiedeln: Johannesverlag, 1966), 7-8. "The unity of Adrienne's works," argues Balthasar, "lies in the fact that every human perspective needs to be traced to and grounded in an ecclesial perspective, every ecclesial perspective within a christological one and every christological perspective within a trinitarian one." (*The World of Prayer*, 9-10). Similarly: "Every individual in the chain belongs to the order that is God and that He even now begets as He did so before the beginning of time." (*Das Wort und die Mystik I: Subjektive Mystik* [*The Word and Mysticism: Subjective Mysticism*] [Einsiedeln: Johannesverlag, 1970], 30).

[68] *Der erste Korintherbrief,* 319-320; see also *Ibid.,* 315.

ought not to be confused, however, with some sort of spiritualization that denies or ignores the concrete, bodily dimension of Christianity. If the concrete were not essential to Christianity, if the Lord were not truly flesh but "merely the product of an idea," then Mary might have been only spiritually pregnant, Adrienne reasons; but the reality of the incarnation requires that she "feel his weight in her body and, after His birth, in her arms."[69] Indeed, the Son wills this authentically human—that is, corporal and spiritual—bond with His mother so as to be united to her as human children are united to their parents.[70] Not surprisingly, then, Adrienne cites the Marian doctrines as evidence that the truth cannot be measured according to degree of spiritualization.[71] Furthermore, she reasons that if only the spiritual dimension of Christ's mission—preaching, instruction and admonishment—was important, then the mission of the prophets would have been sufficient. As it is, however, the Incarnation is a sort of testimony to the importance of "the bodily presence of God's fullness on earth," even to the extent that Christ's flesh "contains the whole mystery. It is the sign, the sacrament that connects men with the fullness of God."[72] It follows from all of this that corporality is "absolutely necessary for the explaining, understanding and grasping of Christianity."[73]

This very firm conviction caused Adrienne to mourn what she esteemed in the Church of her time "an artificial de-corporalization," opposed to the divine intention of imbuing the flesh with the Spirit's truth.[74] As a case in point, Adrienne points out the significance of Christ's nakedness on the Cross. "The loincloth was the beginning of the Church's not-wanting-to-see." We should be conscious, she continues, that it is the Church—and not the Lord—who covered up His nakedness. The Church may do so with good reason, Adrienne admits, "but she has too often forgotten that the Lord's

---

[69] *Maria in der Erlösung*, 35.

[70] *Ibid.*, 15.

[71] Hans Urs von Balthasar, *First Glance at Adrienne von Speyr* (San Francisco: Ignatius Press, 1981), 247.

[72] *Colossians*, 83. Within the context of her commentary on Colossians, Adrienne argues that if the fullness of God resides in Christ in bodily form, then Christ's body obviously has an important part to play in this fullness.

[73] *Maria in der Erlösung,* 35.

[74] See *Ibid.*, 36.

nakedness exists."[75] Even more drastic for Adrienne are the abstractions that she witnessed in her Protestant upbringing: "Protestants miss the ultimate seriousness of the Incarnation, the becoming flesh. That is why everything often remains so theoretical, speculative."[76] In contrast, Adrienne recognizes as highly significant the corporal dimension of the Catholic Church. Having assumed flesh as an act of love for the Father, the Lord is henceforth "so committed to it, it binds Him so closely to the Father that He gives this *body* to the *Church*."[77] As the incarnate Lord is completely and simultaneously spirit and flesh, so too is His Eucharist, Adrienne teaches. Hence His command to eat His flesh is "wholly unambiguous," allowing for no misunderstanding.[78] Because, moreover, the Church that administers this very real body of the Lord becomes herself the body of the Lord, it follows that the Church "is not an idea; she is perfectly concrete."[79] Indeed, the function assumed by the fleshly body of Christ—namely, "to embody His spirit for us, to render it present, to make us aware of it, to communicate it"—is continued by his Church after Him. She "shows us and presents the Lord to us," especially in the Eucharist.[80] So too, the individual Christian in the Church: each one, in virtue of his own corporality, embodies in some sense the teaching of Christ, which might otherwise remain abstract, giving it a "fleshly-concrete" existence.[81] The point is well-mentioned by Adrienne, given the concrete unity between her life and teaching, between the subjective and objective dimensions of her faith. Hers is a faith that is concretized in both word and action, a faith which—as we shall see—is expressed in her theology by a certain regard 'from above'.

III. The Speyrian Method: The Spiritual Reveals the Meaning of the Corporal

The things of this world, to summarize Adrienne's incarnational perspective, cannot "be valued in a stepwise progression from

---

[75] *Theologie der Geschlechter*, 11.
[76] Quoted by Hans Urs von Balthasar, *First Glance at Adrienne von Speyr*, 247.
[77] *Colossians*, 34.
[78] *The Word Becomes Flesh*, 65.
[79] *Colossians*, 34.
[80] *Ephesians*, 73.
[81] *Der erste Korintherbrief,* 376-377.

the corporal to the spiritual; common to all of them is that they are directed to the Son and have in Him their continued being."[82] The Son, in turn, is orientated, as we have seen, to the Father. Despite therefore the great significance of corporality within the speyrian perspective, the "higher" (more obviously spiritual) mysteries dominate—in the sense of directing—the natural (corporal) ones. The whole relation between the sexes in the time spanning the Old and New Covenants is, for example as Adrienne sees it, directed towards redemption: "Men enable women to become fecund so that, at last, the Word might become flesh and the Church might issue from the Word-made-flesh."[83] And, prior to the Old Covenant, Adrienne argues that this goal even sheds light upon the creation of the sexes, which is to say that the full meaning of sexuality—like all that is human—lies in Christ. It is not so much that Christ assumes the original meaning of sexual relations by associating the human "other"—woman—with Him in His redemptive mission as that He thereby creates this meaning. This He does as the eternal Son of the Father who bears His (the Father's) image even in the incarnate nature whereby He is born of woman. To be sure, He *does* assume the original meaning of sexuality implicit in the Father's creation[84]— by willing to be born of a woman and nourished at her breast, for example—just as He assumes everything that is human: as an act of love for the Father and with respect for the Father's creative intentions. That He does so follows necessarily from the reality of His incarnation. He assumes this meaning, however, only after having first *established* this meaning within His eternal, divine will and with respect to His 'coming' incarnation. Adrienne, to explain, recognizes Christ as giving a new "fullness" to the relation of man and woman: a fullness which is "altogether heavenly," without being any-the-less bound up with human sexuality.[85] Neither man nor woman can, without the other, represent the whole of humanity, Adrienne argues. And, in that which concerns Christ, he is man, not woman. "As the new Adam he needs the new Eve, for he wants, as a whole person [that is, to say, in the man-woman unity], to

---

[82] *Colossians*, 33.

[83] *Theologie der Geschlechter,* 155.

[84] See, for example, supra, notes 6, 7 and 71.

[85] *Der erste Korintherbrief,* 324. The particular reference here is to 1 Corinthians 11:12 and the fact of man coming forth from woman, i.e. from woman's womb.

redeem the whole human being."[86] Hence, He desires not only to trace Himself "back" to Adam, but also Mary back to Eve.

> Not only should man be redeeming and redeemer, but woman also [should be] the originally redeemed [ursprünglich Erlöste] and there-by co-redeeming [Miterlösende]. And as Adam and Eve sinned toge-ther, so also, on another level, must the Son and Mother redeem toge-ther; they plant the work of redemption where the Fall occurred. Eve brought man into sin, and Christ draws Mary into the redemption.[87]

Given, as we have seen, the place of the Cross in Adrienne's visions of Creation, it is not surprising that Mary—precisely as "co-redeemer" and thus also as "pre-redeemed"—is somehow present at—that is, preceding—the world's creation.[88] Adrienne admits "of course," that Mary is not actually present on the first day of creation, but she "co-creates" in the work of "correcting" creation, that is to say, in the rectification of Eve.[89] The "first-born of Redemption,"[90] she realizes "the idea of the accomplished human being" that God had in mind in creating the first woman.[91] Eve willingly distanced herself from this idea, but it is effectively realized in Mary.[92] She is "the true creation, as it goes forth from the Creator's hands and as it returns to God without distancing itself, without dispersing its unity." As such, she is not simply a natural creature, but one enjoy-ing "a new impulse" of grace through her "corporal and spiritual tie" with the Son.[93] By means of this authentically human tie, the Son acknowledges and affirms in her graced humanity "the essence of human nature as the Father willed it."[94] Hence, she is "actually not

---

[86] *Handmaid of the Lord*, 37.

[87] *Maria in der Erlösung*, 33.

[88] "She has her place in the event of the world's creation, namely in reason of her quality of 'co-redeemer.' The idea of 'co-redemption' is 'older' than that of pre-redemption. The latter is a consequence of the former, a means to the end." (*Maria in der Erlösung*, 9). Adrienne explains that Mary "is conceived and creat-ed as much from the Cross as to the Cross." (*Ibid.*)

[89] *Ibid.*, 33.

[90] *Cross, Word and Sacrament,* 34.

[91] *Maria in der Erlösung*, 10.

[92] See *Ibid.*, 21.

[93] *Ibid.*, 15. Cf. p. 22: "The whole is a mystery of the pregnancy and of fruitfulness in which divine grace can no longer be separated from the human, graced mediation."

[94] *Ibid.*, 15. "As the Creator accomplished His work, He saw that it was good. And it would be perverse to believe that the Son finds in His Mother only that which

the second, but the first Eve," the one "who did not fall," who looks on as the second Eve falls.[95] Adrienne thus insists upon a certain priority of Mary over Eve: "Christ is not only the won-back Adam; He is God. Mary is not only the reintegration of Eve, she is the Mother of God."[96]

Faithful to this inspiration of regarding the Christ-Mary bond as preceding, within the divine intention, the bond between Adam and Eve, Adrienne recognizes the former relationship as embodying not simply the meaning of sexuality in general—the 'original' meaning of sexuality as it was intended by the Creator—but also "all the later relationships between man and woman in the Church." It is "the first bond between man and woman" so as to be "decisive for all later bonds."[97] It is thus not surprising that Adrienne's theology of the body draws its inspiration here. In contrast to the popular tendency of explaining the spiritual fruitfulness of virginity in terms of the corporal fruitfulness of marriage, for example, Adrienne takes as her starting point the "pre-eminent" fecundity of the virginal, consecrated life so as to justify the fecundity and the sacramental significance of marriage. It is, more specifically, the mystery of the spousal relationship between Christ and Mary-Church[98] and that of the maternal-filial relationship also between Mary and Christ and later between Mary and John that found and explain the original, created meaning of sexual relations and thus also of marriage. The latter relation, in turn, is a sort of revelation of—based upon a participation in—the former relations.[99] Within this perspective, sacramental marriage is "primarily a supernatural thing" such that the corporal dimension is integrated within the larger realm of the supernatural and the spiritual fruitfulness of the sacrament is considered greater than bodily fruitful-

God entrusted to her as a special grace. He finds in her the good of the human which, without resistance, serves His unity and befits his human form, nourishes it, makes it altogether possible." (*Ibid.*, 19)

[95] *Ibid.*, 10.

[96] *Ibid.*, 33.

[97] *Handmaid of the Lord*, 85.

[98] The identification of Mary with the Church will become evident in the final section of this essay. For the present it is important to recognize a concrete female figure beside Christ, contributing to (participating in) His redemptive mission.

[99] Adrienne argues, for example, that in giving Himself corporally to the Church in the Eucharist, the Lord, simultaneously elevates the man's "surrender" (*Hingabe*) to his wife within the marital act. See *Theologie der Geschlechtern*, 132.

ness.[100] On the other hand, even in the consecrated life, "the celibacy of man and woman enhance one another in pairs" according to
the likeness of "the first virginal couple, Christ and His Mother."[101]
Regardless of whether one realizes one's paired-sexuality within
the vocation to marriage or within the vocation to the consecrated
life, however, the ultimate source of fecundity resulting thereby is
always the Trinitarian love of God: As the Son lives constantly
from the Father and to the Father, the Church lives essentially from
the Son and to the Son, Adrienne explains.[102] And, as if to clarify
that this "as" implies a continuation between the one relationship
and the other rather than a simple analogy between the two,
Adrienne explains that the Son's fruitfulness in the Church stems
from the Father, rather than Himself, whereby it also reveals the
Father. As such, it is, Adrienne insists, necessarily virginal.[103] It
follows for Adrienne that the "law" governing both the religious
and married states of life is that of remaining within the "circula-
tion" of Trinitarian love—from God to God.[104]

Given the importance of the Trinity in Adrienne's conceptu-
alization of sexual relations, it is not surprising that even sexual inter-

---

[100] *Ibid.,* 117. The primacy of spiritual love is first apparent, after the fall,
Adrienne argues, when the Spirit descends upon Mary to make of her the Mother
of God. (*Objektive Mystik,* 534). In that which concerns the fecundity of sacramental marriage, Adrienne argues, that one must know "the world of grace" in
order to appropriately correspond with one's body.

[101] *The Farewell Discourses,* 266. Adrienne explains that "because the priest is
celibate, the nun can be so, and vice versa. Far from alienating themselves
through virginity, they rather enhance each other as a couple that corresponds to
the first virgin couple, Christ and his Mother." (*Ibid.*)

[102] *Hoheleid,* 50-51.

[103] *Birth of the Church,* 125. "If He were not [virginal], then there would be
moments at which He would reveal and mirror Himself rather than the Father."
(*Ibid.*) The connection between the one relationship and the other is the Eucharist,
Adrienne explains, with the result that whoever rejects the Eucharist "is without
access to the Trinitarian fellowship." (*The World of Prayer,* 72)

[104] Ultimately Adrienne argues that there can be no "third" state of life, because
unlike marriage and the consecrated life, it could not procure the fruit arising
from sexual difference, which in turn lies within the mystery of Trinitarian love
and divine fecundity. (See *Theologie der Geschlechter,* 116). "It is not the virginal
disciple alone nor the virginal Mother alone who embodies, for the future of the
Church, the form of virginal life," Adrienne argues. "Instead, at the beginning of
this way of life stands a virginal couple." They are "founders of a new lineage;
that of his priests and monastic people." (*Birth of the Church,* 130)

course is explained by her in Trinitarian terms. At the root of the analogy, for example, between sexual intercourse and Eucharistic communion,[105] is the fact—she teaches—that sexual relations were "eucharistically conceived" by the Creator. To clarify, Adrienne argues
that the Eucharist models the "giving and receiving and giving back
of the body as the concretisation of love—the 'I' finding itself in the
'Thou'—and as 'apostolic' fruitfulness in the child."[106] Still more fundamental, however, the Eucharist is a sort of "descriptive summary of
the whole being-there [Dasein] of the incarnate God," whereby it is
also a description of "the Triune God's manner of being-there
[Daseinsweise]: namely, so to be, that this being—in its very foundation—is the always-there of the ever-now-occurring ascent of
Trinitarian love."[107] Because it is the Son who founds the Eucharist,
He is characterized, Adrienne reasons, even within the Trinity, by an
eternal "Eucharistic attitude," which is at the origin of His "Eucharistic surrender". This surrender is, more precisely, his filial "response" to the Father's begetting act.[108] Beyond this filial surrender
revealed in the Son's bodily gift of Himself in the Eucharist, Adrienne
presents a "Trinitarian Eucharist of the divine Persons," whereby she
means "their going-into-one-another," which in turn "presupposes
their mutual, fully accomplished [self-] disclosure."[109] This disclosure
is, more precisely, an archetypical "surrender,"[110] whereby "each is
everything to each": the Father's essence belongs to the Son, whose
essence belongs to the Spirit, etc. In this way, the divine persons—all
in being vis-à-vis one another—are "fully in one another."[111] Hence
the mystery of Christ's union with the Church through His
Eucharistic surrender is effected "within the mystery of His being

---

[105] "The sperm comes from the inner depths [dem Innersten] of the man and flows
forth into the woman, so as to make way, seeking into her own inner depth. This
is a great mystery, comparable to [eucharistic] communion." (Theologie der
Geschlechter, 113; see also pp. 127 and 132; The Holy Mass, 69; Das Hoheleid,
43-44; etc.) The same image of sexual intercourse is used by Adrienne to explain
the mystery of mysticism in the Church. See Subjektive Mystik, 22.

[106] Objektive Mystik, 534. See ibid., 113 for the original meaning of love at the
time of creation in precisely these terms.

[107] Ibid., 101.

[108] Ibid., 525.

[109] Ibid., 524.

[110] Adrienne uses the word Hingabe, which simultaneously denotes surrender and
devotion.

[111] Objektive Mystik, 524.

one with the Father and the Holy Spirit."[112] In the final analysis, "the Adam-Eve reciprocity, which was itself an image of Trinitarian love, is fulfilled in the Christ-Church [Christ-Mary] reciprocity in the Eucharistic mystery, whereby the divine Archetype prevails over the created image."[113]

IV. The Eucharist: Man's Inclusion in Trinitarian Love

All that has been mentioned in the foregoing might be summed up in what Adrienne refers to as "the greatest mystery in Christianity," namely, that Christ is one flesh with His Church. This mystery, which he effects within "the mystery of His being one with the Father and the Holy Spirit," is in turn that to which the whole mystery of redemption is ordered: "[T]he Lord was always at work on it [the establishing of this mystery] through all the years of His activity, through His whole Passion and His return to heaven."[114] "He, the Incarnate One, is the Bridegroom who does not leave His Bride when He returns to heaven."[115] This relational perspective of redemption is presumably in contrast with a mystical doctrine, presenting Christ as a salvific reality in Himself: in Him is "married" the divine person and the human nature.[116] This mystical marriage is, however, presented within the Church tradition as ordered to that "other" marriage of Christ and the Church whereby the substantial grace of the hypostatic union—the union of the two natures in Christ—might also be understood as "capital" grace: that grace which belongs to Christ as Head of the Church and thus the source, or well-spring, of all grace given to mankind.

Similarly within the theology of Adrienne, the presentation of Christ as a substantial Eucharist is that whereby He is also the source of our Eucharistic communion in Him. He is the Sacrament in per-

---

[112] *Ephesians*, 241.

[113] *Objektive Mystik,* 534.

[114] *Ephesians*, 240, 241.

[115] *The Mystery of Death* (San Francisco: Ignatius Press, 1988), 73.

[116] Hence, for example, the Augustinian portrayal of Christ coming forth from the womb of the Virgin as from a bridal chamber: "Verbum enim sponsus, et sponsa caro humana; et utrumque unus Filius Die, et idem filius hominis : ubi factus est caput Ecclesiae, ille uterus virginis Mariae thalamus ejus, inde processit tanquam sponsus de thalamo suo..." (Augustine, *In Joannis Evangelium*, VIII, 2, 4 ; *Homélies sur l'Evangile de Saint Jean*, Bibliothèque Augustinienne, 71 [Paris : Desclée de Brouwer, 1969], 474, 476)

son, from whence originate the sacraments of the Church. The "locus" or "embodiment of the sacraments," He is—in virtue of the incarnation—"the predetermined connecting link between heaven and earth" with the result that: "Everything that He does contains the sign of His connecting being; (…) He connects, because He is Himself connection. He is connection so as to mediate; He possesses so as to give." Hence He is also the source of the sacraments proper: "He binds us through every sacramental reception."[117] As Adrienne remarks, the whole Gospel is situated between two movements of divine surrender: "In the Incarnation lies the promise of the Eucharist, and the Eucharist is a confirmation (or verification) of the Incarnation."[118]

> The Son does not merely perform the work of redemption. He is as the beloved of the Father, the redemption in person; He contains it as He contains His blood, in order to communicate it to the world by shedding it and, by this shedding of Himself, to give the world the holiness that is the holiness of God Himself.[119]

As if to comment upon this image, Adrienne makes use of still another: the distinction between Christ's body and blood in the Eucharist.

> When He speaks of the body, attention is focused chiefly on the personality of the incarnate Lord; when He appears in the blood, He does so in service of the Covenant that He brings. The body is, as it were, personal, whereas the blood is the depersonalized dimension of His mission. (…) The body is the Incarnation, whereas the blood is the reality of the Incarnation being poured out. The body is the one sent, whereas the blood is the sending that flows from the substance of the one sent into the Church He founded.[120]

This distinction in turn points to the paternal and filial qualities of the Eucharist. The Incarnation is, Adrienne teaches, "the Father's Eucharist," with the result that the Son's Eucharist is a sort of earthly reflection of the same: "In giving His body eucharistically, He does on earth the same as the Father in heaven when He gave His

---

[117] *Markus*, 447. See also *Colossians*, 83.
[118] *Objektive Mystik*, 529. The Incarnation is "a foreshadowing of the Eucharist" (*Colossians*, 33)
[119] *Ephesians,* 35. Holiness, she adds (*ibid.,* 29), is participation in God's life. "*Holy* means: living His life." (*Ibid., 28*)
[120] *The Holy Mass,* 66.

Word as seed to the Mother."[121] As the Father eternally begets the Son, the Son eternally begets the Church through His Eucharist. To be sure, the Father also begets the Church, Adrienne teaches, but this He does *through the Son*. It is His will—as an expression of His love for the Son—"that the Church bear the Son's character (…) So He will beget the church in no other way except through the Son."[122] Adrienne similarly describes the Lord as the origin of the Church in two complementary manners: as the one who begets, that is, "as the original truth of Christian doctrine," and "as the one eucharistically distributed." These two forms—"the spirit-form as Word" and "the body-form as Eucharist"—are, however, "the double expression of one reality: that He is the incarnate Word of the Father."[123]

In the theology of Adrienne—strongly influenced by St. John, as is here evident—Christ is *the Father's gift* of eternal life to the world, precisely *in virtue of His own self-gift* to the Father for the accomplishment of His (the Father's) will. In virtue of the same— that is, in obedience to the Father's will—He is given without limit to the Church and the world alike. In the Lord's bodily surrender of Himself to the Father for the world and to the world for the Father, Adrienne discerns both the receptive and generous aspects of His absolutely vulnerable—that is to say, unreserved, unlimited—self- gift. With regard to the first aspect, He gives Himself as a sort of receptacle for sin, whereby as we have seen, he not only "feel[s] our failures in His flesh,"[124] but also "gathers up all sin and makes it vis- ible in the absolute injury to the body."[125] With regard to the second aspect, He gives Himself in such a way as to *live in other bodies*, namely, the bodies of sinners, whereby He is subject to them and delivered to death. This entire degradation of the Lord is, however, orientated to our enrichment. Redemption is not conceived by Ad-

---

[121] *Objektive Mystik*, 529.

[122] *Passion from within*, 43. Similarly: "If the Father is perennially in the act of generating the Son, the Lord is perennially generating His Church. He generates her in a sort of dependence upon the Father's generation." (*Ephesians*, 240). Adrienne recognizes in the Lord's final words, "Into Thy hands, Father, I give My spirit," the expression of His being "the image and symbol of generation." (*The Word Becomes Flesh*, 91).

[123] *The Passion from within*, 45.

[124] *Ibid.*, 41.

[125] *Ibid.*, 45.

rienne as a sort of destruction of human nature with the goal of creating "a second natural life." It is, rather, the creation of the old human nature anew.

> The Father made creatures come forth from nothing; the Son does not have to annihilate them in Himself in order to recreate them in Himself out of nothing. He destroys in Himself the old Adam, the wall of separation and sin, yet He destroys only after having taken up into Himself the thing to be destroyed. He destroys it by dying Himself and by letting what He has assumed die together with Him. He includes the act of destruction to enable resurrection with Him out of the nothing of death. (…) The Son has recreated the world, in Himself, in His love made flesh, which He offers in order to give to the destruction of sin and division the meaning of love.[126]

The Lord has, in other words, actually taken up our bodies with His to be "co-crucified," with the result that they have henceforth the quality of "being for Him, living for Him and dying for Him."[127] This means that redemption from a speyrian perspective is, to summarize, nothing less than our inclusion—body and soul—in the Lord's own "accomplished corporality" by means of His resurrection, Church and Eucharist.[128] The body of Christ is given so radically as to become *our* body, with the result that we become *His*. "Being flesh and spirit simultaneously, He reaches our spirit through our bodies and spiritually soaks our bodies through and through, so that what is spirit in us and what is *His* spirit in us may return to the Father."[129] The Lord has, by His passion and death, not only made "room for us in Himself," He has also made "Himself to be this room."[130] There nonetheless remains our real participation, which is to say that the "corporeality of the Cross" and "the whole loving life of the Son of Man require a corporeal sharing of believers therein."[131] To be sure,

---

[126] *Ephesians*, 104.
[127] *Der erste Korintherbrief*, 179.
[128] *Ibid.*, 185. cf. *Colossians*, 33.
[129] *The Word Becomes Flesh*, 117. (Emphasis mine) "He lived on earth the perfect unity of spirit and flesh," Adrienne explains, "in order afterward to transmit this unity to us in a living way in the Eucharist." (*Ephesians*, 102)
[130] *Colossians*, 37.
[131] *Ibid.*, 26. Although Christ has already redeemed the world, the process of redemption still has need of us, Adrienne explains, that is to say, of the suffering and pain which bind us to the Lord's Cross. See *Victory of Love*, 70.

the Christian's body serves the reception of Holy Communion so that it might work in His soul; and the more "available" the human being is for this reception, "that much more intimately and completely can the Eucharistic Lord work within Him."[132] Hence, the final consequence of the Incarnation—as expressed in His cry of fulfilment, "It is consummated"—is the same as the first: that the Son might have a center of action within us.[133] It is this mystery which I will address in what follows.

V. The Eucharist of Believers: A Participation in Christ's Mission

Redemption—to repeat what I have expressed above—means being in Christ, and for Adrienne "this *in Him* is as essential, as personal and as corporeal as one can possibly understand it to be."[134] At stake here is our participation in Christ's humanity, precisely as members of His body.[135] Having created the Church without members, as it were, he grants us the possibility of being incorporated into His body (precisely as members), and through us, He continues to exercise new functions in the Church and in her service.[136] This incorporation—not unlike the service that follows therefrom—is realized through the sacraments, especially the Eucharist which, far more than realizing the continuation of the Lord's terrestrial body, actually effects the inclusion of our body in His.[137] In transforming Himself into a new state, the Lord seeks ultimately to transforms us, drawing us, as it were, into Himself.[138] The Lord's being, received by us in the Eucharist, effects our "becoming,"[139] which is to say that the unity of

---

[132] *Theologie der Geschlechter*, 113.

[133] *Victory of Love*, 24.

[134] *Colossians*, 26. Indeed, as if to insist upon the corporality of our salvation, Adrienne remarks: "Whatever he did for us: whether he was being born, in order to take upon himself the burden of our guilt, or whether he was dying on the Cross under this burden, he did it as much with his flesh as with his spirit." (*Ephesians*, 103)

[135] "Hope," Adrienne explains, "does not want to cover up the road the Son has trod [i.e. "of suffering, pain and groaning"], but to reveal it in order to give participation in it. Man's body and spirit are capable of participation." (*Victory of Love*, 70)

[136] *Ephesians*, 237.

[137] *Colossians*, 33.

[138] "At first He transforms as if from the inside out, by letting Himself become eucharistic, by shifting his center into the host. But because He can do that, He can also do the opposite: transform from the outside in, drawing things into His center." (*Ephesians*, 48)

[139] *Colossians*, 71; cf. *Objektive Mystik*, 106 and *Ephesians*, 30.

our lives and of our very persons ought no longer to be in ourselves but in Him.[140] In precisely this way, we share in the Son's own movement to the Father. "For He *is* this movement and this life, and thus He is this movement and this life also in those who believe in Him, love Him, and hope in Him."[141] The Eucharistic communion of believers is, therefore, "not only a communion with the Body of Christ, but also with His whole life."[142] We are all really "co-beings" with the Eucharistic Lord, Adrienne explains, "in whom God so allows his Trinitarian being to occur in the world that He squanders Himself on [us] all."[143] Adrienne thus observes a development in the Gospel of John from the presentation of Christ as having all life in Himself to that of believers having all life through him and in Him by way, most especially, of the sacraments.[144] "What he has established in them through his presence is transformed immediately into His presence in them."[145] Receiving Him is, in this sense, "identical with being received by Him."[146] "For it is not only He who communicates His Body and His Blood to us, who lives now in us, but we live in Him."[147]

Despite the obvious emphasis here upon the Lord's action, Adrienne insists that the Eucharist, like all the sacraments, is not intended uniquely as an "*opus operatum*," happening to us in the absence of our knowledge and will.[148] Indeed, the Incarnation, Church and sacraments have definitively assured man's communication with God, Adrienne teaches, not only by presenting the Trinity in terms comprehensible to the human spirit, but also by enabling us— through the Son's active presence *in us*—to comprehend the Lord's grace and to give answer.[149] Hence, the Spirit of Christ serves a double function in the sacrament of the Eucharist: He gives this special form to the Son's body and He gives to believers the certainty of faith

---

[140] *Ibid.*, 72; cf. *Ephesians*, 48.

[141] *Discourses of Controversy*, 66; cf. *Ibid.*, 71.

[142] *Ibid.*, 35. It "contains and mediates also a participation in the whole course of His life." (*Ibid.*)

[143] *Objektive Mystik,* 101.

[144] Hence the Eucharist, for example, is presented as the Lord's "own substance without which we could not live." (*Ephesians*, 105)

[145] *Discourses of Controversy*, 66.

[146] *Colossians*, 71.

[147] *Discourses of Controversy*, 70.

[148] *The Cross: Word and Sacrament* (San Francisco: Ignatius Press, 1983), 10.

[149] *Ephesians*, 22-23 ; cf. *Isaias*, 222-224.

and hope. "The Son says, 'This is My body; it will work in you when you receive it.' But between the Son's word and its accomplishment, there remains a sort of margin in believers, which is filled by the Spirit."[150] In virtue of the Spirit's action and the believer's coopera- tion, the Eucharistic Lord presumes a certain mutuality of love: He not only obliges Himself in our regard, "He obligates us, too, in His own regard."[151] This means, first of all, that the Christian has "the duty of finding his salvation in the body of the Son Himself, in His blood shed on the Cross, in His entire humanity."[152] Adrienne recog- nizes, for example, the importance of all the figures gathered around the Cross in her vision of the Passion, and she notes that the more the Lord's own "self-surrender is accepted, the more His life is taken from Him."[153] This acceptance of the Lord as redeemer, in turn, implies an on-going reception of the Eucharistic Lord, which in each communion is a *growth towards Christ*: "we take what He gives us and give what He wishes to take from us."[154] This He does not only by making more room in us for Himself—expanding, as it were, our assent (Amen) so as to prepare us in each Communion for the next— but also by making use of us, once we have received Him, to give of Himself to others. Indeed, He gives Himself so radically that "in doing so He is given by us."[155]

Like all the sacraments, which connect believers with the Cross of Christ, the Eucharist "both [shares] and give[s] a share in the Son's mission."[156] From the moment He is received, the Eucha- ristic Lord brings about in the communicant a movement *to the Lord*: not only an acceptance in faith of His Incarnation and life, but also of "everything He wants to do in us… a surrender, a taking on of new tasks."[157] Because—to employ still another image—the Eucharist is "infinite distribution and communication," as Adrienne expresses it, the received Host does not remain within the confines of the com- municant. Bearing "visibly on His person that distinguishing some-

---

[150] *Objektive Mystik*, 528.
[151] *Discourses of Controversy*, 70.
[152] *Colossians*, 26.
[153] *The Cross, Word and Sacrament*, 10.
[154] *Discourses of Controversy*, 73.
[155] *The Word becomes Flesh*, 83.
[156] *The Cross, Word and Sacrament*, 11.
[157] *Victory of Love*, 23. See also *Discourses of Controversy*, 64.

thing which the soldiers saw on the body of Christ," He is marked for "the wordless apostolate": "the outflowing of love as such, which simply communicates itself."[158] Whoever receives the Eucharist must, therefore—Adrienne reasons—mediate this grace through fidelity to what is received. He ought to sin neither in his body, nor in his speech; for in doing so "the word of Christ, the word that is Christ loses its Eucharistic content." From the moment that one receives the Lord on his tongue, the Word of God "has a claim" over the communicant's word. "As Word of God's love, He has a claim on my word of love of neighbour."[159]

Similar is the Christian's relation to his body following his reception of the Lord's body in communion. Being thus united with the Lord in one body, he is really enabled to so give of himself and of each of his bodily members that God's will is realized *in his body*.[160] Almost ironically, Adrienne sees in man's essential unity with a body whose nature is demanding, burdensome, and capable of suffering as preparatory for his supernatural end. The often very painful experiences of meeting up against the limit of our own corporality train us as "God-seekers," that is to say, as those who long to surpass the constraints of this world so as to enter into infinity.[161] To be sure, Adrienne acknowledges from her own objective experience as a physician and her subjective experience of bodily suffering, including her mystical share in the stigmata of Christ, that the human body is naturally opposed to sacrifice: It is, as it were, "installed in its function and does not want to be disturbed." It is not, however, for the body to determine the boundaries of its own instrumental utility, Adrienne argues. As "the instrument of a fundamental unbounded obedience," the Christian's body—like that of Christ—should be radically in the service of God, who determines how they are to be used.[162] Indeed, the body of the 'accomplished' Christian is characterized by

---

[158] *The Birth of the Church*, 140. On the Eucharist's power to surpass the confines of the individual to "be all to all," see *Objektive Mystik*, 500.

[159] *Passion from within*, 46. "The Spirit lies in the Word-Seed, but how diffusive can only first be clarified when the Church receives the spirit of the mission and thus is ready to receive God's seed." (*Theologie der Geschlechter*, 135)

[160] *Der erste Korintherbrief*, 389.

[161] *Ibid.*, 178. Cf. *Victory of Love*, 70.

[162] *Theologie der Geschlechter*, 183. Man has been given a body, Adrienne argues,

Adrienne as governed by Christ's own Spirit.[163] To the extent that this is the case, his body is holy.[164] When, on the other hand, we disobey and misuse our bodies, it is not only our own, but also the Lord's body that is dishonoured.[165]

This example of the Christian's body bringing dishonour to Christ's body only really makes sense when the whole Christian—body and soul—is understood as a member of the one body of Christ: when he or she is given, surrendered to Christ in a manner likened unto—but also receptive of—his own sacrificial surrender to the Church and to each individual member of the Church; when, that is to say, he or she is authentically united to Christ so as to form one body with Him. Hence the Eucharist is fittingly presented by Adrienne—in reference to and by way of commentary of the rich sexual imagery in *The Song of Songs*—as the fruitful encounter of the Lord's sacrificial surrender of Himself to the Church and the Church's own reception of this sacrifice within herself.[166] "As a woman should allow herself to be marked by the man's act, so also the Church through the Lord's Eucharist."[167] As the sexual analogy so fittingly demonstrates, the body's significance is only really discovered when it is given to another through an act of surrender.[168] So too, what sense would there be in the Church having a tabernacle, Adrienne asks, "if the Lord were not there?"[169] In the marital embrace, a man "awakens" his wife's body "to love" with the result that she does not real-

---

so as to carry out God's intentions. (See *Ephesians*, 234). Hence our care for our bodies ought also to be measured according to their "enlistment in service." (*Ibid.*, 236).

[163] *Der erste Korintherbrief,* 186.

[164] "The holiness of every human body is measured by whether it is assigned a space within the Lord's mission of love, even if it is a mission of suffering, sickness, and death." (*Ephesians*, 36).

[165] *Der erste Korintherbrief,* 185: "We, along with our body-members, *are* His body and therefore we truly dishonor His body when we misuse ours."

[166] "The Lord leads His Church to the place where He gives Himself for her and where the thanks of the Church in her reception of the sacrifice and the thanks of the Lord in the sacrificial surrender are fused in a unity, in the Eucharist." (*Das Hohelied*, 43)

[167] *Ibid.*

[168] While Adrienne insists that "No body can exist without communion," the experience of the body need not be limited to that of sexual communion. For those who are virginal, for example, the primary experience of bodily communion is that between mother and child. (*Theologie der Geschlechter*, 165)

[169] *Hohelied*, 44.

ly experience any one part of herself (her womb, for example) as given to the man; rather "her whole body belongs to her whole husband."[170]

The same analogy of a woman being awakened to love by a man—more specifically in this case, of a virgin "becoming a woman" through the love of a man—is used by Adrienne to describe the mutuality of love between Christ and the Christian, with the result not only that the Christian becomes thereby the body of Christ, but also that he or she thereby contributes to His terrestrial mission. Precisely in giving us—His "members"—the possibility of becoming one body with Him, He also gives us thereby, Adrienne remarks, the possibility of fulfilling His humanity with Him.[171] Hence, although we are really "nothing" and He is everything, "His Everything would not be complete if we were not in Him."[172] With this, we touch upon the mystery of the reciprocal relation of fullness and fulfilment between Christ and the Church. Of course, it is the Lord who has the priority in this relationship: He is the first to fill up, Adrienne insists. Indeed, He fills up *everything*, not least of all the Church, who is thereby His fullness. As such, *He has a certain need of her* to reveal his fullness and to transmit it, whereby it may also be said that Christ is filled up by the Church. There is, then, "a reciprocal relationship of fullness and fulfilment between the Lord and the Church." To emphasize either side of the relationship to the neglect of the other would be to obtain "a completely empty concept of fullness," for any fullness "that could not deploy itself, could not pour itself out, could not fulfill itself, would not be a real fullness at all." As is typical of Adrienne, here too she points to the Father-Son relation as an archetype: "[E]ven the fullness of the Father, in order to be itself, needs the Son to contain it, and for its part the fullness of the Son flows back to the Father." Similarly the Christ-Church relationship is one of reciprocal filling up, "even though the Lord, insofar as He is the all-transcending head, is the one who gives infinitely and the Church the one who receives infinitely."[173] The divine bridegroom of the Church "is over the bride but draws her to Himself, in order thereby to *fill her up*

---

[170] *Theologie der Geschlechter*, 163.
[171] *Der erste Korintherbrief*, 390.
[172] *The Farewell Discourses*, 128.
[173] *Ephesians*, 73-74.

in Himself: that He might *fill Himself up in her* by pouring out His entire energy into her."[174]

As one body with the Lord, the Christian participates in this mystical marriage of Christ and the Church, in virtue of which it is impossible to distinguish between what the Lord gives and what the Church has received to give back in turn.[175] "In the reciprocal surrender the limit between yours and mine vanish; the *I*, without even noticing, is led into the *Thou*."[176] Adrienne describes hereby the act of human communication as a sort of dynamism between the word that is spoken and the word that is received in order to draw a comparison with the Word of God within His Church.[177] The analogy may also describe, however, the movement between Christ and the Christian in the Church. This specification—*in the Church*—is important, because the Christian's "measure" of open receptivity never matches that of Christ's own gift of self in virtue of which the former is enriched and fulfilled (cf. Jn 1:11-12). It is only in the "breadth" of Mary's own unlimited fiat that the Christian can truly be said to receive the Lord, such that his personal gift of surrender (*Hingabe*) takes the form of enriching receptivity (*Hinnahme*).[178] Hence it is to her, the bride-body of Christ, and thus the first cell of the Church that we now turn by way of conclusion.

VI. Conclusion: Mary–Church, the Body of Christ

The foregoing exposition of the Eucharistic communion between Christ and the Christian in one body is clarified for Adrienne in the lives of the saints. These, she explains, are those who realize—each one individually—the Church's act of surrender to the Lord, whereby She—due to *His* own prior surrender *to her*—

---

[174] *Ibid.*, 75.

[175] *Ibid.*, 231. The Church, argues Adrienne, is "the fullness of Christ" without whom he cannot exist (*Theologie der Geschlechter*, 99).

[176] *Ibid.*, 98.

[177] Similarly, Adrienne argues that apart from the Church, the Lord's words "are robbed of the vitality of their truth; they exist in isolation here and there, as if torn from the root of their life." (*Ephesians*, 240).

[178] Mary's consent to the Incarnation and Cross is "essential" as "an archetype, an example making discipleship possible for the whole Church." (*Three Women and the Lord* [San Francisco: Ignatius Press, 1986], 27). "If the Church were to so communicate in her entirety and in her faithful as the Lord surrenders Himself to her, then she could be wholly recast according to the Lord's intention. (*Das Hoheleid*, 43).

is one body with Him. "Each is a part [of the Church] and each is the whole."[179] As such, these matured Christians are "the practical exposition of the Eucharist," the proof that the Lord "takes us with into His love,"[180] by taking us into His body. Having been nourished by this heavenly bread, they are, with Him, "in body and in soul bread for the fellowman."[181] And, like the bread and wine offered at the altar of sacrifice, which initially are "nothing more than *good things,*" they have been transformed into Christ's body by His action and their 'contribution' of faith.[182]

This mystery of "the whole in each" and "each in the whole" of the Church and her saints is concretized most especially in the person of Mary, Virgin-Mother and Bride of Christ, in whose "train" all the saints find their place beside Christ.[183] "Mary is in the name of all women the Mother of God, and the Church is in the name of all human persons the bride of Christ, whom she has become through Mary."[184] Every form of Christian fecundity—whether spiritual or physical, virginal or spousal—is recognized by Adrienne as "patterned on Mary."[185] Because she offered herself so completely to the Lord in body and in soul, she did not have to choose between marriage and consecrated life, Adrienne argues.[186] Her self-gift "goes beyond the measure of human surrender"[187] to include the Son's self-surrender to the Father, with the result that

---

[179] *Subjektive Mystik*, 266.

[180] *Die Johannesbriefe*, 180.

[181] *Objektive Mystik*, 500; cf. *Birth of the Church*, 121.

[182] These "good things," Adrienne explains, are really willed by the Lord as a gift expressing the Church's faith, which is required of her by the Lord "for this creation to occur. For the Son wants to be created in faith and to give himself to His Church, so that in accepting Him in faith we live in Him and no longer in ourselves." (*The Holy Mass*, 84)

[183] Balthasar explains that Adrienne referred to the saints as "the 'train of the Mother of God', which means, more precisely, that all holiness and all prayer of the saints radiate from the innermost center of Marian-ecclesial consent to the word of God." (*First Glance*, 72)

[184] *Apokalypse*, 387. Adrienne explains that the "attitude of the woman" presented in Ephesians 5 with reference to the Church in her relationship with the Lord is "deduced from the attitude of every Christian in relation to the Lord; and it goes without saying that every Christian is subject to the Lord and lives by the Lord's obedience toward the Father in order to obey Him, the Lord." (*Ephesians*, 225)

[185] *Handmaid of the Lord*, 170.

[186] *Maria in der Erlösung*, 7.

[187] *Handmaid of the Lord*, 162.

her vocation is that of virgin-mother *and* bride.[188] This means not only that Mary is simultaneously the mother of Christ and the spouse of Joseph, but also—and herein lies the genius of Adrienne—that she, the Mother of Christ, becomes His Bride.

Already at the Annunciation, Adrienne recognizes in Mary's unbounded *fiat* a sort of bridal gift of self, whereby she receives the Lord in a manner likened unto that of Eucharistic Communion. Hence the beginning of the Mass "is a kind of embodied expectation and pregnancy of the Church, in union with the Mother." At the offertory, the Christian is invited by Adrienne to offer his "whole soul" as Mary offered hers, and the consecration "corresponds to the actual descent of the Son into the Mother's womb." Hence, when the Lord offers Himself in the Eucharist, His surrender contains hers, "and it is she who teaches the Church to surrender herself according to the Lord's example." She therefore accompanies the Christian in his reception of the Eucharist, making up for his deficiencies, as it were, so that he might worthily receive the Lord within her own spotless *fiat*.[189] In this way she is, as Adrienne expresses it, the "mediatrix of self-surrender".[190] This is so much the case that even the most basic Christian attribute of being a member of Christ's body is, Adrienne explains, a participation in the Marian quality of being the "body of Christ," a quality which is given to her in virtue of her divine maternity: through the "encounter, contact and merging" of Christ's corporality with hers, not excepting her consent.[191]

This Marian mission of nourishing and sustaining the assent of self-surrender in other Christians is also a consequence of the fact that her physical bodily surrender—which is itself the revelation of her more profound spiritual surrender—is a sort of "counter-action" opposed to Adam and Eve's distancing of themselves from the Lord. As such it expresses "a new creation of human unity"[192]: the unity of

---

[188] Both the religious and the married states were, Adrienne teaches, lived by and founded by Mary together with the Lord. (*Ibid.*, 123)

[189] *Ibid.*, 151-154. On Mary's assistance to the Christian in "expanding" his soul to "meet" the demands of the Lord, see also *Ibid.*, 164.

[190] *Ibid.*, 170.

[191] *Maria in der Erlösung*, 59.

[192] *Ibid.*, 18. Adrienne specifies that this is a spiritual unity between God and man which should determine man's own unity. (*Ibid.*)

one who freely accomplishes the perfect self-surrender corresponding to—so as to be receptive of—the Lord's own perfect self-surrender, which precedes and accompanies it.[193] The Virgin receives
corporally within herself the eternal Son precisely because she
receives Him so fully spiritually, Adrienne teaches.[194] "Her pregnancy is a token of how great the surrender of her contemplation
is."[195] On the other hand, her word of consent is also revelatory of
a divine encounter: In it is expressed both her own word, by which
is meant the "determination of her free will," and God's word: the
word of God as faith and the "Word of God in the highest sense:
the Son."[196] As such, her faith not only accomplishes, but also precedes that of the prophets.[197] For this reason too, she is the "outline" and "germ" of the Church,[198] "the *Una Sancta*," which is
founded "with the first Word (…), that He [Christ] spoke on
earth."[199]

---

[193] Consonant with the traditional portrayal of the Church as the New Eve born of
Christ "asleep" on the Cross and of Mary as pre-redeemed by her Son's merits is
Adrienne's presentation of Mary-Church as the fruit of Christ's salvific mission,
in which she has a real share. The "first-born of the Redemption, just as Adam
was the first-born of Creation," Mary corresponds to her Son's plan "by support-
ing Him with love and faith all her life long." (*The Cross: Word and Sacrament*,
34) Her "pre-redemption" (*Vorerlösung*) is in fact, Adrienne teaches, a consequence of her mission as helpmate of the Redeemer: "The idea of 'co-redemption' is 'older' than that of pre-redemption. This latter is a consequence of the
first, a means to the end." (*Maria in der Erlösung*, 9) With her *fiat*, she determines the beginning of Christ's mission upon earth just as He determines her
beginning in eternity. Indeed, because He wills that she accompany Him in His
redemptive mission, her "later-given consent possessed the power of already having worked with the Son in His reception of the Mother." (*Ibid.*, 11)

[194] *Ibid.,* 18. With this, Adrienne echoes the teaching of St. Augustine: "Virgo ergo
Maria non concubuit et concepti, sed credidit et concepti" (Sermo 233, 3,4, "In
diebus Paschalibus, IV" *PL* 38:1114); "Christum prius mente quam ventre con-
cipiens" (Sermo 215, 4: "In redditione symboli," *PL* 38: 1074). Cf. Pope John
Paul II, *Redemptoris Mater* (March 25, 1987), 13 (and note 35).

[195] *Handmaid of the Lord*, 157.

[196] *Maria in der Erlösung*, 11. Similarly, Adrienne explains that "Mary keeps all
of her Son's words in her heart and lets them mature there, as she let the Son himself mature in her. It / he is the same." (*Theologie der Geschlechter*, 99)

[197] See *Maria in der Erlösung*, 29. In the "conversion" of Old Testament faith to
New Testament faith through the Incarnation (and thus also by way of the Virgin's
consent), Adrienne recognizes a pre-figuration of the reception of the Lord in
Holy Communion. (*Objektive Mystik*, 127)

[198] *The Cross, Word and Sacrament*, 34.

[199] *Theologie der Geschlechter*, 99.

In this encounter of Mary's word of surrender to God and God's own Word surrendered to Mary, Adrienne recognizes a heavenly encounter of obedience: The Son's obedience to the Father meets that of Mary-Church in a common surrender to the divine will.[200] The one relationship (Father-Son) is, in fact, fruitful in the other (Son-Mother/Bride), which is to say that there is more than an analogical likeness implied in the speyrian comparison: "Just as the eternal and unique surrender between Father and Son flows out into the temporal and unbounded devotion of the Eucharist, so the unique virginal relation between Mother and Son flows out into the endless bestowal of her spiritual motherhood."[201] Through her participation in the Son's Eucharist—already at the Incarnation, and ultimately at the Cross—she is the universal Mother of mankind. Together, precisely as Mother and Son, they form "the first virgin couple".[202] This means that Christ's redemptive action "retroactively affects the Mother" so as to make of her the mother of all,[203] beginning with John, the "son" born of their virginal love.[204] Mary therefore assumes and accomplishes the mission of Eve to be the "mother of the living" by means of her ready willingness to give of herself to the Lord.[205] On the other hand, John and Mary form a virginal couple born of the Lord's love on the Cross. Together they are the "founders of a new lineage: that of his priests and monastic people."[206] In uniting this "couple," the Lord establishes the Church's structure, but he also establishes Christian marriage,[207] which—according to the original Speyrian insight—is, as we have seen, illuminated by this virginal relationship. Indeed, the Cross forms "every

---

[200] There is, as Adrienne puts it, "an encounter which leads to unity" (*Maria in der Erlösung*, 6).

[201] *The Birth of the Church*, 123-24.

[202] *Farewell Discourses*, 266. In this transformation and expansion of her vocation from the Mother of the Christ to the Mother of Christians, Adrienne notes a corresponding suspension of the limits between the I (of Christ) and the Thou (of Mary-Christ), whereby "the one is fruitful in the other." (*Theologie der Geschlechter*, 100). "In receiving God's seed," Adrienne explains, "she becomes fruit." This means, first of all, that she becomes the Lord's mother, but also that she becomes the Church, the Lord's Bride. (*Ibid.*, 99-100)

[203] *The Birth of the Church*, 123.

[204] See *The Cross, Word and Sacrament*, 34.

[205] *Maria in der Erlösung*, 26.

[206] *The Birth of the Church*, 130. "Male and female virginity arise out of the Cross," Adrienne teaches, for it is there that "the Lord initiates those closest to Him into His innermost mysteries of life." (*Ibid.*, 133). See also *Handmaid of the Lord*, 123-132.

[207] "In joining together and blessing this particular spiritual couple [Mary and

human relationship; in this case it yields the word which brings together Mary and John, Church and mankind, woman and man."[208]

More fundamentally still, the Cross—precisely as the fulfilment of the Lord's self-surrender which began at the Incarnation—is the fulfilment of His terrestrial mission to found the Church in obedience to the Father, a Church "which will survive Him on earth and yet will only be able to live through contact with Him."[209] This contact is assured through the sacraments, especially the Eucharist, whereby the Church lives the mystery of her bridal-maternity, precisely as the body of Christ. As such she "appears in her true nature": not as an independent being, organized in one manner or another in accord with the Lord's will, but as intimately connected with His own nature as God-man and Redeemer so as to live in Him by grace as He lives in the Father by nature. "She is a component part of the Lord, which He Himself brings forth and maintains, in order to present it at every moment to the Father."[210]

As a member of this one body of Christ and the Church, the Christian will recognize his own body as an expression of His "spiritual belonging" to Christ, who takes up the Christian's obedience to Him into His own obedience to the Father. He who was obedient in the body even unto death, does not cease to fulfill this obedience, Adrienne argues, when we, His members, obey together with Him, manifesting thereby the unity of our spirit with His and thus also the power of His grace.[211]

John]—thus relieving them of radical loneliness after His departure—the Lord is here instituting into the visible Church something greater than they. The blessing from the Cross institutes the nuptial blessing." (*The Cross, Word and Sacrament*, 33)

[208] *Ibid.*, 35.

[209] *Ibid.*, 53.

[210] *Colossians*, 35. "If He is one with His Church to the point that He forms one flesh with her, He effects this mystery within the mystery of His being one with the Father and the Holy Spirit." (*Ephesians*, 241) See also *Farewell Discourses*, 364; *Hoheleid*, 50-51; *Gebetserfahrung* (Einsiedeln: Johannesverlag, 1965), 13.

[211] *Der erste Korintherbrief*, 185. "The Christian will order his relationship to the body taking his lead from the experience that the Lord and his Mother had of the body. What the Lord knew in the eternal divine decree of the Incarnation, what Mary learned through her motherhood, he has to learn through Christian stewardship of the body, perhaps best of all by practicing bodily penance: that the body, whatever use it is put to, will always have to be an instrument of the Christian's mission." (*Ephesians,* 37)

THE CONTRIBUTORS

MSGR. ARTHUR B. CALKINS, S.T.D.

Ordained a priest of the Archdiocese of New Orleans, Louisiana in 1970, Msgr. Calkins currently lives in Rome and serves as an official member of the Pontifical Commission "Ecclesia Dei". He is also a corresponding member of the Pontifical International Marian Academy and the Pontifical Roman Theological Academy. He has a Master's Degree in theology from the Catholic University of America, an S.T.L. in Mariology from the International Marian Research Institute in Dayton, Ohio, and an S.T.D. from the Seraphicum in Rome. In addition to contributing many academic articles to books dedicated to Marian Co-redemption and mediation, he has also published many scholarly articles in such journals as *Miles Immaculatae, Homiletic & Pastoral Review, Doctor Communis, Divinitas and Immaculata Mediatrix*. He is the author of *Totus Tuus: John Paul II's Program of Marian Consecration and Entrustment* (New Bedford, MA: Academy of the Immaculate, 1992).

FR. DONALD H. CALLOWAY, M.I.C.

A convert to Catholicism, Fr. Calloway is a member of the Congregation of Marians of the Immaculate Conception. A frequent speaker at Marian conferences around the world, he holds a B.A. in philosophy and theology from the Franciscan University of Steubenville, Ohio, M.Div. and S.T.B. degrees from the Dominican House of Studies in Washington, D.C., and is finishing an S.T.L. in Mariology from the International Marian Research Institute in Dayton, Ohio. The title of his Licentiate thesis is *Purest of all Lilies: The Virgin Mary in the Spirituality of St. Maria Faustina Kowalska.* He has written articles for such journals as *Homiletic & Pastoral Review* and *Ephemerides Mariologicae,* and is the editor of *The Immaculate Conception in the Life of the Church* (Marian Press, 2004). He is currently the House Superior of the Marian House of Studies in Steubenville, Ohio.

FR. BASIL B. COLE, O.P., S.T.D.

A member of the Order of Preachers (Dominicans), Fr. Cole holds a B.S. degree from the University of San Francisco, S.T.L. & S.T.Lect. degrees from Le Saulchoir, Etiolles, France, and an S.T.D. from the Angelicum in Rome. He has held many academic positions, including Instructor in Dogmatic Theology at Pilarica College, Adjunct Professor of Moral Theology at St. Albert's College, and Visiting Professor of Spiritual and Moral Theology at the Angelicum. He has published many academic articles in such journals as *Angelicum, Priest, Thomist, Homiletic & Pastoral Review* and *Faith and Reason.* Among his books are *Music and Morals* (Alba House, 1993), and two books he co-authored with Paul Connor, O.P., *Christian Totality: Theology of Consecrated Life* (St. Pauls, 1997) and *A New Catechism of the Consecrated Life* (Asia Trading Corporation, 1999). He is currently Associate Professor of Dogmatic, Spiritual and Moral Theology at the Dominican House of Studies in Washington, D.C.

DONALD DEMARCO, PH.D.

A corresponding member of the Pontifical Academy for Life and a founding member of the American Bioethics Advisory Commission, Dr. DeMarco is Professor Emeritus of Philosophy at St. Jerome's University in Waterloo, Ontario, Canada. Having earned a science degree from Stonehill College and studied at the Gregorian University in Rome, he also holds an M.A. and Ph.D. in philosophy from St. John's University, New York. He has written many scholarly articles in such journals as *Homiletic & Pastoral Review, Canticle* and *National Catholic Bioethics Quarterly.* Titles from the twenty books he has written include The *Anesthetic Society* (Christendom Press, 1982), *Biotechnology and the Assault on Parenthood* (Ignatius Press, 1991), *The Heart of Virtue* (Ignatius Press, 1996), *New Perspectives on Contraception* (One More Soul, 1999), and his most recent work, co-authored with Benjamin Wiker, *Architects of the Culture of Death* (Ignatius Press, 2004). He is currently Adjunct Professor of Philosophy at Holy Apostles College and Seminary in Cromwell, Connecticut.

GLORIA FALCÃO DODD, S.T.D.

Born in Washington, D.C., Gloria was homeschooled for most of her elementary education, before attending Oakcrest, an Opus Dei high school in Washington, D.C. She holds a B.A. in theology from Christendom College, M.Div. and S.T.L. degrees from the Dominican House of Studies in Washington, D.C., and an S.T.D. from the International Marian Research Institute in Dayton, Ohio. Her *summa cum laude* doctoral dissertation is entitled: *The History and Theology of the Movement for the Dogmatic Definition of the Virgin Mary's Universal Mediation, 1896-1964.* During the XXI International Mariological Congress in Rome, Italy (December 4-8, 2004), Gloria presented a paper titled "Mary, Mother of the Church, in the Movement for the Definition of Mary as Mediatrix". She has been an Adjunct Professor of Theology at the Notre Dame Graduate School of Christendom College in Front Royal, Virginia. Currently, Gloria and her husband Ennis, live in Fort Wayne, Indiana, where she teaches religion at Bishop Dwenger High School.

FR. NICHOLAS L. GREGORIS, S.T.D.

One of the founders of the Diocesan Oratory of St. Philip Neri in Mount Pocono, Pennsylvania (now reconstituted as the

Priestly Society of the Venerable John Henry Newman in the Archdiocese of Omaha), Fr. Gregoris holds a B.A. in classical languages from Seton Hall University, an S.T.B. from the Gregorian University in Rome, and an S.T.L. and S.T.D. from the Marianum in Rome. He has been an Assistant Professor of Theology at the Pontifical College Josephinum in Columbus, Ohio, and has written articles for such publications as *Homiletic & Pastoral Review, The Catholic Answer, National Catholic Register* and *L'Osservatore Romano*. He is the author of *"The Daughter of Eve Unfallen": Mary in the Theology and Spirituality of John Henry Newman* (Newman House Press, 2003). He currently serves as Managing Editor of *The Catholic Response*.

FR. PAUL M. HAFFNER, S.T.D.

A priest of the diocese of Portsmouth (England), Fr. Haffner currently lives in Rome and is Professor of Theology at the Regina Apostolorum University. He holds a B.A. and an M.A. from the University of Oxford, as well as S.T.B., S.T.L, and S.T.D. degrees from the Gregorian University in Rome. He is also an invited lecturer at both the Gregorian and the Lateran University. He has published articles in *Christus, Ecclesia, Sacerdos, Anthropotes, Lateranum, Humanitas* and *Inside the Vatican*. His books include: *A Methodology for Term Papers and Theses* (Gracewing, 1995), *The Mystery of Creation* (Gracewing, 1996), *The Cross and the Rain Forest: A Critique of Radical Green Spirituality*, with R. Whelan and J. Kirwan, (Eerdmans, 1996), *The Sacramental Mystery* (Gracewing, 1999), *The Mystery of Reason* (Gracewing, 2001) and *The Mystery of Mary* (Gracewing, 2004).

KENNETH J. HOWELL, PH.D.

A convert to Catholicism, Dr. Howell was previously Associate Professor of Biblical Languages and Literature at Reformed Theological Seminary in Jackson, Mississippi. He holds an M.Div. from Westminster Theological Seminary in Philadelphia, a Ph.D. in Linguistics from Indiana University, and a Ph.D. (history of science) from Lancaster University, England. He has published numerous articles in such journals as *Logos* and *Studies in History and Philosophy of Science*. He has authored three books: *Mary of Nazareth: Sign and Instrument of Christian Unity* (Queenship, 1998), *God's Two Books: Copernican Cosmology and Biblical Interpretation in Early Modern Science* (UND Press, 2002), and *Meeting Mary: Our Mother in Faith* (Catholic Answers, 2003). Currently Dr. Howell is Director and Fellow of the John Henry Newman Institute of Catholic Thought at the University of Illinois at Champaign-Urbana, and Adjunct Professor of Religious Studies at the University of Illinois.

SR. M. ISABELL NAUMANN, I.S.S.M., S.T.D.

A member of the Secular Institute of the Schoenstatt Sisters of Mary, Sr. Naumann was born in Germany and studied in Germany, Australia and the United States. Having a broad background in scriptural studies and spirituality, she holds an S.T.D. in Mariology from the International Marian Research Institute in Dayton, Ohio where her dissertation, *Cum Maria ad Altare: Toward an Integration of Mariology and Ecclesiology*, dealt with the thought of Fr. Joseph Kentenich. She has written research articles for the Mary Page of the Marian Library (Dayton, Ohio) and the Spanish Mariological journal *Ephemerides Mariologicae*. She is a member of the faculty of the International Marian Research Institute (Dayton, Ohio), a Visiting Professor at the University of San Carlos (Cebu, Philippines), and Lecturer at both the Catholic Theological College (Melbourne, Australia) and Good Shepherd Seminary (Sydney, Australia). She resides in Melbourne, Australia where she currently serves as Lecturer and Deputy Director of the John Paul II Institute for Studies on Marriage and Family.

MICHELE M. SCHUMACHER, S.T.D.

The mother of four children, Dr. Schumacher has served as director and founder of the Office of Family Life and Social Justice for the Diocese of Yakima, Washington, and as an Adjunct Professor of Theology in a master's program offered by the Archdiocese of Portland in conjunction with the Religious Institute for Religious and Pastoral Studies of the University of Dallas. She holds an S.T.L. from the University of Fribourg, Switzerland and an S.T.D. from the John Paul II Institute for Studies on Marriage and Family in Washington, D.C., where her dissertation topic was *Christological and Marian Mediation: The Dramatic Integration of Human Freedom into Divine Communion according to Hans Urs von Balthasar.* She has published many scholarly articles in such journals as *Logos, Internationale Katholische Zeitschrift: Communio* and *Nova et Vetera*. She is also the editor of *Women in Christ: Toward a New Feminism* (Eerdmans, 2004). She is currently an external research collaborator in the Department of Theology at the University of Fribourg, Switzerland.

Books by
Fr. Donald H. Calloway, M.I.C.

The Immaculate Conception in the Life of the Church
(Stockbridge, MA: Marian Press, 2004), 198 pgs

The Virgin Mary and Theology of the Body
(Stockbridge, MA: Marian Press, 2005), 284 pgs

To order, contact:

Marian Helpers Center
Eden Hill
Stockbridge, MA 01262

1-800-462-7426
www.marian.org